109
25.00

ROSELLE PUBLIC LIBRARY

3 3012 00289 4323

P9-BZJ-973

Advance praise for *Conquering the Sky*

"Tise—dogged researcher, mesmerizing storyteller, human encyclopedia on Wilbur and Orville Wright—has dug out the moment-to-moment, nearly secretive, details of seven days in May 1908 when the Wright Brothers changed the world. Anyone who loves airplanes will love vicariously experiencing the very beginnings of powered controlled flight."

—David Hartman, aviation writer, TV documentary producer,
and original host of *Good Morning America*

"Larry Tise takes us back to six weeks in the spring of 1908 when Wilbur and Orville Wright returned to the Outer Banks of North Carolina. It was a critically important period, when the brothers would fly for the first time in over two and a half years, carry the world's first aircraft passenger aloft, test a new set of controls and prepare to demonstrate their machine to a waiting world. Wilbur and Orville, the local residents of the Outer Banks, and the newsmen who seek to break one of the great new stories of the century come to life in these pages."

—Dr. Tom D. Crouch, Senior Curator (Aeronautics), Smithsonian Institution,
and author of *The Bishop's Boys: A Life of Wilbur and Orville Wright*

"*Conquering the Sky* is the most thorough report on the Wright brothers' 1908 experiments at Kitty Hawk that has been written to my knowledge. It will fill an important gap in the Wright brothers' history."

—William Harris, former mayor of Kitty Hawk, retired director of the
Wright Brothers Memorial, and President of the First Flight Society

"Larry Tise has captured the drama of a brief but crucial era in aviation history, when the Wright brothers' flying machines first made history worldwide. Extensively researched and far-reaching, this story provides enduring inspiration."

—Kathleen C. Winters, author of *Anne Morrow Lindbergh: First Lady of the Air*

"In this sprightly new book, Larry Tise separates facts from the myths and deconstructs the many unreliable newspaper accounts about the events at Kitty Hawk. Full of colorful characters and telling details, Tise's book takes readers aloft during the first turbulent years of powered flight."

—Jeffrey J. Crow, Ph.D., State Historian for North Carolina and
Deputy Secretary of Archives and History,
North Carolina Department of Cultural Resources

"When the Wright Brothers returned to Kitty Hawk, North Carolina, almost four and a half years after their first flight, to test their patented and improved aircraft for public demonstration, a dozen or so correspondents dogged them, hoping for a scoop or a photograph. Larry Tise recounts the stream of misinformation and missed opportunities that issued from Kitty Hawk, leaving the public unprepared for the spectacular performances of Orville Wright in the United States and Wilbur Wright in Europe in the ensuing months. The failure of the fifth estate contrasts comically with the triumph of the Wrights in this lively, fascinating history."

—Alex Roland, Professor of History, Duke University

"A perceptive examination of a brief but significant episode in the truly amazing story of the two brothers who pioneered practical powered flight. With unique insight, Larry Tise shows how those seeking news of the Wright brothers were misled with fanciful tales and fishermen's yarns, and how easily the truth was distorted and presented as published fact."

—Philip Jarrett, specialist historian and author on pioneer aviation

Previously Published Works by Larry E. Tise

Proslavery: A History of the Defense of
Slavery in America, 1701–1840 (1987)

The American Counterrevolution:
A Retreat from Liberty, 1783–1800 (1998)

Benjamin Franklin and Women (2000)

Hidden Images: Discovering Details in the Wright Brothers'
Kitty Hawk Photographs, 1900–1911 (2005)

CONQUERING THE SKY

The Secret Flights of the Wright Brothers at Kitty Hawk

Larry E. Tise

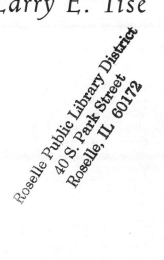

Roselle Public Library District
40 S. Park Street
Roselle, IL 60172

palgrave
macmillan

CONQUERING THE SKY
Copyright © Larry E. Tise, 2009.
All rights reserved.

First published in 2009 by PALGRAVE MACMILLAN® in the United States—a division of
St. Martin's Press LLC, 175 Fifth Avenue, New York, NY 10010.

Where this book is distributed in the UK, Europe and the rest of the world, this is by
Palgrave Macmillan, a division of Macmillan Publishers Limited, registered in England,
company number 785998, of Houndmills, Basingstoke, Hampshire RG21 6XS.

Palgrave Macmillan is the global academic imprint of the above companies and has
companies and representatives throughout the world.

Palgrave® and Macmillan® are registered trademarks in the United States, the United
Kingdom, Europe and other countries.

ISBN 978–0–230–61490–1

Library of Congress Cataloging-in-Publication Data
Tise, Larry E.
    Conquering the sky : the secret flights of the Wright brothers at Kitty Hawk / Larry E.
Tise.
        p.   cm.
    Includes bibliographical references and index.
    ISBN-13: 978-0-230-61490-1 (hardcover)
    ISBN-10: 0-230-61490-6 (hardcover)
        1. Wright, Wilbur, 1867–1912. 2. Wright, Orville, 1871–1948. 3. Aeronautics—
United States—History—20th century. 4. Aeronautics—United States—Biography.
5. Aeronautics—United States—Flights—History—20th century. 6. Wright Flyer
(Airplane)—History. 7. Science news—United States—History—20th century.
8. Trade secrets—United States—History—20th century. 9. Kitty Hawk (N.C.)—
History. I. Title.
TL540.W7T569 2009
629.130092'273—dc22
[B]

                                                                                    2009007227

A catalogue record of the book is available from the British Library.

Design by Letra Libre, Inc.

First edition: October 2009
10 9 8 7 6 5 4 3 2 1
Printed in the United States of America.

The month of May, 1908, will doubtless be known to future generations as the most important period in the development of aerial navigation. There may have been other months when more was accomplished in a rudimentary way, but during the middle week of May civilization learned that mechanical flight was at last a reality and not a mere human aspiration. The world received its first news that this dream of the ages had been realized—that Wilbur and Orville Wright of Dayton, Ohio, had surely mastered the mighty problem, and, with the sea gulls and the buzzards, were soaring about over a desolate strip of beach on the coast of North Carolina.

And, singularly, too, of the world's millions eagerly interested in the matter, there were exactly five persons there as witnesses of these magical performances—five newspaper correspondents, each of whom had regarded the Wright Brothers as little more than theorists, dreamers or fakirs, until they saw the big aeroplane mount into the air, and, clacking like a great sea bird, come circling over their heads. I went down to North Carolina a pronounced skeptic. I had no doubt that the Wrights had been very successful in experimenting with their motor driven machine, but I did not believe they had made conspicuous progress in sustained flight and I did not believe they had made a record of twenty-four miles as [previously] claimed by them.

I believe all of these things now and much more. . . .

Byron R. Newton, Correspondent
New York Herald
Kitty Hawk, North Carolina, May 1908
"Watching the Wright Brothers Fly,"
Aeronautics Magazine *(June 1908)*

CONTENTS

PREFACE

Although Wilbur and Orville Wright learned how to fly by 1902 and discovered how to put a powered controllable airplane in flight by December 1903, the world did not, in fact, discover the Wright brothers until May 1908. And the inventive but elusive brothers were found and exposed to the world for the first time that spring precisely where they had originally learned how to fly—at Kitty Hawk, North Carolina.

While many a book have been written and thousands of yarns have been spun about how the Wright brothers conquered the air at Kitty Hawk on December 17, 1903, almost no stories have been told of how they literally sent the world soaring in 1908, taught a legion of gaping aeronauts how to put a plane in the air and keep it there, and astonished thousands upon thousands of eyewitnesses in both America and in Europe with their amazing feats. When the Wright brothers returned to Kitty Hawk in May 1908 and there unintentionally began to show the world how to fly, they inspired headlines that blazed across hundreds of newspapers around the world and provided grist for almost daily stories of heroic exploits and American grit. They were among the first Americans of the twentieth century—other than rich tycoons and political heads of state—to attract an international press following.

It was partly because they were shy, private, and even secretive men that they became the subjects of the popular international press of the day and of an infant cadre of paparazzi. But it was also because they were known to be pioneering in the realm of mere dreams—of men flying like birds. And, it was widely thought, though not at all proven, that they had advanced beyond all other humans in achieving real flight.

There had been rumors since 1902 that they were flying—and flying quite well. There had been a few photographs published of their gliders—including the sleek machine that they sent into the air a thousand times at Kitty Hawk in the fall of 1902 and again in 1903. Images of this machine had appeared in newspapers, in engineering journals, and in such lofty publications as *Scientific American* in the United States. The same pictures had been replicated in illustrated magazines across Europe. The appearance of these photographs, in fact, had inspired a whole new cadre of flyers and the construction of a new raft of flying machines in France, Italy, and Germany.

But the Wrights had released no picture nor allowed one to be published of any of their powered airplanes, either on the ground or in flight. Although they had taken a photograph of their very first powered flight on December 17, 1903, and this photograph would eventually become one of the most famous documentary photographs in history, they had carefully kept it filed away in their shop in Dayton. And although they had taken many photographs of their powered test flights at Dayton during 1904 and 1905, they withheld all of these from publication as well. Nor would they allow visitors to bring a camera onto their testing grounds or to make any photographs of their camp, their machines, or the wings and wires that controlled their machines.

Because so many historians of flight and biographers of Wilbur and Orville Wright have focused on their activities and experiences prior to 1903, the story of how they prepared for their historic public flights five years later has remained largely unexplored and only partially told. But the way in which the Wright brothers proceeded in the spring of 1908—returning to Kitty Hawk, their own hatching place where they had first aspired to soar—was characteristic of their special personalities and outlooks on the world. They yearned for the sandy surfaces and windy climes at Kitty Hawk to try out a number of new features of their pathbreaking flying machines. They needed to test entirely new guidance systems for their planes. They also had to make sure they could carry the additional weight of a passenger before they went public. All of their flights prior to 1908 had been solo flights—pilot only. And up until 1908 the pilots had guided their crafts from a prone position. Now both pilot and passenger would operate in a more comfortable sitting position—just like the drivers of wagons and horse-less carriages.

At Kitty Hawk they could operate in secret, confidentially, and among old friends. It was at the end of the earth. But it was a safe haven, far from prying eyes. It was a place of retreat, of contemplation, of rigorous exercise and work, of restful sleep to the sound of roaring waves and lapping tides. It was in the face of Big Kill Devil Hill whose lofty heights, windswept surfaces, and looming presence over the ages had produced an air of mystery, a special spine-tingling chill that could not be replicated anywhere else on earth. In the space of a few rejuvenating weeks at Kitty Hawk, Wilbur and Orville would make themselves ready to take on the world.

This is the story of what the Wright brothers experienced in that rarified spring of 1908: How they prepared for what they thought would be a season of se-cret flights at Kitty Hawk. What they actually experienced at the base of Big Kill Devil Hill during a period of several weeks of residence at what was their own soar-ing place. How their activities and presence came to be known across the world. How they were discovered and hounded by a host of big-city reporters and pho-tographers. How the Wrights responded to the presence of a legion of uninvited journalists. How they attempted to avoid any close scrutiny of their flying machine and its flights. How they tried to prevent any photographs from being recorded. And how, despite all of their own efforts and those of a gaggle of experienced re-porters, the news reports that emanated from Kitty Hawk were just about as bizarre and far-fetched as they could possibly be. In spite of the sober seriousness of the Wrights and the hard-driving professionalism of the reporters who came from Nor-folk, Washington, New York, and London to get the story, the newspaper reports of their activities and flights were a virtual comedy of errors.

But underlying the bumbling drama that played out at Kitty Hawk during April and May 1908, there was a far more important story and lesson for the his-tory of the world. During a period of seven days in May 1908, the Wright broth-ers' flying machine and their flights came to be observed vicariously and thus publicly by the world's press. And though the reporters—owing to the special na-ture of the Outer Banks and the odd character of Outer Bankers—were at pains to get their facts straight, they came away from Kitty Hawk after the brothers' last flight on May 14, 1908, convinced that they had just witnessed a turning point in history. They did not witness the ending of that last flight. They perpetually sent forth confused and conflicting stories of what happened during all of those seven days in May. But those reporters one and all knew they had just witnessed the moment when the Wright brothers took an expectant world from the surface of the earth into an age of flight. In the weeks, months, and years thereafter, these reporters explained how they had been present at the precise point in time when it became clear that men indeed could fly like the birds.

This is the untold story of those seven days in May 1908 when the world learned the possibilities of flight and the brothers Wright conquered the sky.

PRINCIPAL CHARACTERS

Drinkwater, Alpheus W. (1875–1962), U.S. Weather Bureau manager and telegraph operator in Manteo, North Carolina, in 1908.

Furnas, Charles W. (1880–1941), mechanic for the Wright brothers, native of Miami County, Ohio.

Gardiner, Gilson (1869–1935), educated as a lawyer, served as a reporter for the Scripps-Howard newspaper chain in 1908 from a station in Washington, D.C.

Hare, James H. (1856–1946), pioneer of photojournalism in the United States, serving in 1908 as a roving special assignment photographer for *Collier's Weekly*.

McGhee, Zachary, Washington, D.C., correspondent for the *Columbia* [South Carolina] *State*.

McGowan, P. H., a veteran reporter, much liked by the Wright brothers, who wrote in the United States for the London *Daily Mail* in 1908.

Midgett, Captain Franklin Harris (1860–1929), resident of Kitty Hawk and skipper of the *Lou Willis* and other shallow-bottomed vessels plying the Albemarle Sound between Kitty Hawk and Elizabeth City.

Newton, Byron (1861–1938), a reporter from the *New York Herald* who covered the 1908 Kitty Hawk flights of the Wright brothers from May 11 to 14.

Ruhl, Arthur, reporter in 1908 with *Collier's Weekly*. As one of the more productive special assignment writers for *Collier's* at the time, he was present for the 1908 Wright flights on May 13 and 14.

Salley, D. Bruce (b. 1872), a freelance reporter from Norfolk who had frequently been a stringer for the *New York Herald*, was writing for the *Norfolk*

Landmark, a rival newspaper to the Norfolk *Virginian-Pilot,* at the time of the 1908 flights.

Ward, Captain Jesse Etheridge (1856–1921), a veteran lifesaver who was serving as captain or Keeper of the Kill Devil Hills Life Saving Station during 1908. He entered the U.S. Life Saving Service in 1880 and served at various stations until moving to Kill Devil Hills in 1899, where he became Keeper in 1901.

Wright, Katharine (1874–1929), ("Sterchens," "Swes," "Swesterchens," "Tochter"), beloved sister of Wilbur and Orville; their closest friend and only confidante back home while they were at Kitty Hawk. She served as the virtual "director" of communications for the brothers in 1903 and 1908. She also handled many business, financial, and procurement functions for them when they were away, especially at Kitty Hawk.

Wright, Milton (1828–1917), father of Wilbur and Orville Wright and bishop in the Church of the United Brethren of Christ.

Wright, Orville (1871–1948) was born in Dayton and left high school before graduation to pursue a career in printing with his brother Wilbur and others.

Wright, Wilbur (1867–1912) was born near Millville, Indiana, and was educated there and in several other places where the Wrights lived.

CHRONOLOGY

1908

April 1, Wednesday   Wilbur notified Kitty Hawk locals of his impending trip to the Outer Banks.

April 4, Saturday   The improved 1905 flyer was shipped from Dayton to Kitty Hawk.

April 6, Monday   Wilbur departed for Kitty Hawk by train at 9:00 A.M.

April 7, Tuesday   Wilbur arrived in Norfolk at noon; he transferred by train to Elizabeth City, where he spent the night at the Southern Hotel.

April 8, Wednesday   Wilbur bought building materials and arranged for Captain Franklin H. Midgett to transport goods and shipping crates to Kill Devil Hills.

April 9, Thursday   Wilbur departed Elizabeth City at noon on Midgett's BM *Van Dusen* and spent the night at Midgett's house in Kitty Hawk.

April 10, Friday   Wilbur arrived at the former camp at Kill Devil Hills and found that the 1903 buildings were in ruins. Captain Jesse Ward, keeper of the Kill Devil Hills Life Saving Station, offered him lodging and meals until a new camp building could be completed.

April 11, Saturday   Wilbur laid out the spot for a new camp building and learned from the lifesavers the fate of the 1903 buildings and their contents.

April 13, Monday   Two local residents (O'Neal and Baum) assisted Wilbur as carpenters on the new building.

April 14, Tuesday   Wilbur walked to Kitty Hawk to check on lumber shipments; he also visited lifesavers at the Kitty Hawk Station and then walked back to camp—a total trek of thirteen miles.

April 15, Wednesday   Charles Furnas, a mechanic for the Wrights from Dayton, arrived in camp.

April 17, Friday   Wilbur sent Furnas to Kitty Hawk to check on the status of a lumber shipment; he found that nothing had arrived yet.

April 18, Saturday   Wilbur walked to Kitty Hawk and offered Captain Midgett a premium of $20 to make a special trip to Elizabeth City to retrieve the last load of lumber.

April 19, Sunday   Captain Midgett delivered the special shipment of lumber and supplies.

April 20–21, Monday–Tuesday   Work on the new building progressed to the erection of rafters and the completion of walls and roof sheathing.

April 22, Wednesday   Orville departed Dayton for Kitty Hawk. Because of high winds, work on the roof of the new building had to be postponed.

April 23–24, Thursday–Friday   Roofing and doors were completed on the new building, and work was begun on the kitchen and on wooden beds.

April 25, Saturday   As Wilbur and Furnas began moving into the new building, Orville and the shipping crates arrived in camp; the three men spent their first night in the new camp building.

April 27, Monday   The assembly of the plane was begun.

April 28–30, Tuesday–Thursday   Work on the assembly of the plane continued—special skids were rigged for take-off and landings; the engine, axles, chains, and gasoline tank were installed, as were the front rudder, seats, and radiator; the take-off track was assembled.

April 30, Thursday   The first newspaper article on the Wrights' presence at Kitty Hawk was published in the *Charlotte Observer*.

May 1, Friday   With winds of 55 to 60 miles per hour, little work on either the building or the plane could be done. A strange article with a Manteo dateline appeared in the *New York Herald*, claiming that the Wrights had flown two miles.

May 2, Saturday   Work began on the control system ("actuating devices"). Another odd article appeared in the Norfolk *Virginian-Pilot*, claiming that the brothers had flown out to sea. Telegraph inquiries were received at both Manteo and the Kill Devil Hills Life Saving Station, seeking information on the Wrights and their flights.

May 3, Sunday   Another fantastic story appeared in the *Virginian-Pilot*, describing the Wrights' daring exploits. D. Bruce Salley, a serious reporter from Norfolk, appeared on the scene to investigate and issued a series of accurate reports, stating that the Wrights had not yet flown. They rested this Sabbath Day, but they were getting frequent telegrams about newspaper headlines.

May 4, Monday   First stationary engine tests were made. A telegram came from the United Kingdom congratulating the Wrights on the great flights reported on this day in the London *Daily Mail*.

May 5, Tuesday   Assembly of the plane was completed, and it was taken out of the shed for the first time for stationary tests on the starting track. No flights were attempted.

May 6, Wednesday   The plane was taken out and placed on the starting track. With Wilbur at the controls, the first flight was attempted—a short hop of 95 feet.

May 8, Friday: Day One of Observed Flights   Flying conditions were almost perfect; nine short flights were completed in the morning and two in the afternoon—it was the first real day of flying. Reporter D. Bruce Salley filed the first accurate story on the brothers' activities; it was published in the *New York Herald*. Completely different, wildly inventive stories—probably written by telegraph operator Alpheus Drinkwater—appeared in the *Virginian-Pilot*, the *New York World*, and the London *Daily Mail*.

May 9, Saturday: Day Two of Observed Flights   Because of high winds and the brothers' sore muscles from hauling the heavy plane, no flights were attempted. News reports on this day proved to be accurate.

May 10, Sunday: Day Three of Observed Flights   Despite ideal flying conditions in the afternoon, the brothers observed the Sabbath by not flying. They took a leisurely stroll on the beach and along the sound—and wrote letters.

May 11, Monday: Day Four of Observed Flights   New reporters arrived. With light winds, the brothers put their starting track on the slope of Big Kill Devil Hill and undertook three flights, at 8:00, 9:00, and 11:00 A.M. The second by Wilbur was the longest of the day: 2 minutes and 31 seconds for a distance of 2,989 meters. Alpheus Drinkwater made his only appearance this day—after all flights ended. Accurate news reports appeared in the *New York Herald* and the London *Daily Mail*.

May 12, Tuesday: Day Five of Observed Flights   Winds gusts of 30 miles per hour all day made flying dangerous. Again sore from Monday's hauling, the brothers spent the day tinkering on their plane. In the pages of the *Herald*, Byron Newton speculated that the brothers would attempt a world record flight the next day. More reporters arrived in Manteo.

May 13, Wednesday: Day Six of Observed Flights   With winds of 14–16 miles per hour in the morning, flying conditions were perfect. Both brothers made good flights, which were observed by all outside reporters—several of whom walked into the Wright camp, angering the brothers. Thinking they would not fly in the presence of the press, all reporters departed for the day. With perfect winds, the Wrights resumed their flights at 6:00 P.M.—each of them making complete circles and returning to the starting points. Learning of these flights from lifesavers or fishermen who returned to Manteo that evening, the journalists amended their already-filed stories, reporting incorrectly that the Wrights had performed extraordinary flights with two people aboard.

May 14, Thursday: Day Seven of Observed Flights   This was the most historic day of the 1908 Kitty Hawk flying season. All reporters were present in seclusion; James Hare was present to take his historic photographs. The Wrights completed three remarkable flights: first, at 8:00 A.M., Wilbur completed the first passenger flight attempted by the Wrights (with Furnas on board)—a short hop of 1,800 feet in 28⅗ seconds. Orville then made a second passenger flight (with Furnas on board) of just over 4 minutes, covering 2.5 miles—a grand lap around the three principal Kill Devil Hills and returning to the starting point. After lunch, Wilbur alone began what the reporters thought would be a record-breaking flight. After making two loops around the smaller Kill Devil Hills over a period of 7½ minutes and a distance 5 miles, the engine suddenly stopped and Wilbur came to a crash landing behind one of the hills. Since the crash occurred out of their view, the reporters returned to Manteo, believing the flight had ended safely and as planned. Later in the day they learned about the crash landing from lifesavers arriving in Manteo. Once again, they were forced to amend their stories based on second-hand information, and the newspaper headlines the following day focused mainly on the unseen crash and not on the historic flights.

May 15, Friday   Both brothers and Furnas spent the day hauling parts of the wrecked machine back to camp. Two reporters—Gilson Gardiner and P. H. McGowan of the London *Daily Mail*—"invaded" the Wright camp to take photos and conduct interviews. The brothers made light of the preceding day's crash.

May 16, Saturday   Cleanup of the wreckage was completed. Rather than attempt repairs for further flights, the brothers decided to break camp and move forward. Meanwhile, in Paris, the French aeronaut Henri Farman challenged the Wrights to a public flying duel with a challenge prize of $5,000 for the winner.

May 17, Sunday   Wilbur departed the camp in secret, heading to Europe by way of Manteo, Norfolk, and New York City. At the Tranquil House in Manteo, he learned the names of the reporters who had been observing their flights and refused to issue any comment on the Farman challenge. Orville remained at Kill Devil Hills with Furnas, cleaning up, packing, and mapping out the flying field.

May 18, Monday   Wilbur departed Manteo on the *Hattie Creef* in the company of the reporter Zach McGhee. At Norfolk he was intercepted by the reporter D. Bruce Salley. He talked freely with both reporters—but refused to comment on future plans or the Farman challenge.

May 19, Tuesday   Upon his arrival in New York City, Wilbur was immediately intercepted by a reporter from the *New York Herald*. Here, too, he basically avoided commenting on the Wrights' plans.

May 20, Wednesday   The *New York Herald* published for the first time a highly doctored version of one of the photographs taken by James Hare on May 14. A secret trip for Wilbur to meet inventor Thomas Edison and then Chinese minister Wu Ting Fang in Orange, New Jersey, had to be canceled because of heavy rains. Instead, Wilbur composed a series of letters giving detailed instructions for Orville to follow in his absence.

May 21, Thursday   Wilbur departed secretly from New York, bound for France on the cruise liner SS *Touraine*.

May 22, Friday   A new round of sensational articles, said to be based on interviews with Wilbur, appeared in the *New York Herald* and the *Virginian-Pilot*. Meanwhile, Orville finally departed from Kill Devil Hills via Manteo and Norfolk and then took an overnight steamer to Washington, D.C., to inspect the flying field at Fort Myer.

May 23, Saturday   Orville arrived in Dayton at noon and was immediately deluged by hundreds of letters on the Kitty Hawk flights and requests from reporters for exclusive interviews.

May 27, Wednesday   Orville issued a press release describing the purpose of the Wrights' activities at Kitty Hawk and the success of their flights.

May 28, Thursday   The *New York Herald* mounted a bold advertising campaign, promising to reveal the Wright brothers' secrets in its next newspaper.

May 29, Friday   The *New York Herald* published drawings filed by the Wrights for their French patent and correctly demonstrated that the Wrights' special secret was a novel control system.

May 30, Saturday   *Collier's Weekly* published a landmark article titled "History at Kill Devil Hill" by eyewitness reporter Arthur Ruhl with a selection of James Hare's photographs taken at Kitty Hawk on May 13–14.

May 31, Sunday   Orville prepared his official story of the events at Kitty Hawk and sent it to a variety of scientific and technical journals, including *Scientific American*.

June 1, Monday   The journal *Aeronautics* published Byron Newton's authoritative article "Watching the Wright Brothers Fly."

June 3, Wednesday   Orville, as persistently instructed by Wilbur, began writing an article for *Century Magazine* to outline the Wrights' unique accomplishments in flight.

June 8, Monday   Orville, hounded by Wilbur to analyze the cause of their engine failure at Kitty Hawk, determined that Wilbur had crimped the fuel line—thus starving the engine of fuel—prior to their last flight. Wilbur, meanwhile, arrived in Le Mans, France, which he chose as the site for his inaugural flights in Europe.

June 13, Saturday   *Scientific American* published Orville's official version of the Kitty Hawk experience with the title "Our Flying Tests at Kitty Hawk."

June 22, Monday   Orville finished writing and illustrating the important *Century Magazine* article.

August 29, Saturday   *Scientific American* published a spectacular full front-page photograph of Wilbur Wright's plane in flight at Les Hunaudiérès Race Track at Le Mans, France.

September 1, Tuesday   *Century Magazine* published Orville's article, "The Wright Brothers' Airplane,"* written entirely by Orville. The article turned out to be the most complete history of the Wright brothers' entry into flight written by either brother.

---

* As a part of this important article, Orville Wright decided to include a copy of the epochal photograph of the Wright brothers' first powered flight at Kitty Hawk on December 17, 1903. This was the first time this carefully guarded historic photograph appeared in print— almost as an afterthought—proving once and for all that the Wrights had actually flown in a powered machine much earlier, in secret, just as they had been claiming for five years when they finally went public in 1908.

TO OLD POINT COMFORT

The Outer Banks of North Carolina, ca. 1900
Kitty Hawk usually provided the Wright brothers steady winds, soft sands, and privacy from peering eyes. But when the brothers returned to Kitty Hawk for secret test flights in May 1908, telegraph reports emanating from Manteo alerted the world to their impending sensational feats.

Wilbur Wright—lank, tall, chisel-faced, and determined—departed Dayton, Ohio, at 9 o'clock sharp on the morning of April 6, 1908. He traveled by train from Dayton to Cincinnati and from there, direct and nonstop all the way to Old Point Comfort, Virginia, located at the mouth of the expansive James River. The route was well known to him—following first along the Ohio River, then eastward across West Virginia to Richmond in old Virginia, and there the track began to meander alongside the ancient River James. He had made the trip every year from 1900 until 1903 and saw familiar territory every mile of the route. By plantation after plantation, from which came the members of Virginia's dynastic early political leadership, the train would make a whistle stop at the colonial capital of Williamsburg before coming to the end of the line at Old Point Comfort, now a part of Hampton, Virginia. Established when the first settlers came to Jamestown in 1607, Point Comfort had eventually become the train stop for the mighty Fortress Monroe, whose walls had overlooked the tiny station since long before the American Civil War. Monroe, ironically engineered by General Robert E. Lee, had been the only military base in the South that had, in defiance of the Confederacy, remained under the control of U.S. authorities throughout the Civil War.

Wilbur, traveling alone, made his 1908 journey through the heartland of the former Confederacy. Although he had been paired almost from birth and certainly by his teenage years with brother Orville—as playmates, as explorers, as printers, as bicycle makers, as tinkerers with kites and gliders and engines—he had chosen to make this particular trip without Orville. Of the almost inseparable pair, Wilbur was the adventurer, the explorer, the pathfinder. Wilbur was the trail blazer, penetrating the wilderness and charting the route; Orville then followed along and built the road. Wilbur was the dreamer. He framed the challenges they faced and established their goals. Orville paved the road for their achievements. Wilbur was the writer and the orator, stating their points; Orville then filed the claims until they won the case. In their quest for patents over the years, Wilbur had developed the mind of a declaimer and a litigator. He was capable of knitting together a steel-trap legal brief. Orville's role was to file the briefs, pursue their day in court, and uphold the resulting adjudications.

They were separated by four years in age. Wilbur was ten days shy of his forty-first birthday as he glided along toward the coast of Virginia. Orville was thirty-six at the time—both of them mere youths from the perspective of most of the movers and shakers in their world. And yet together they had already published a news-paper, formed a successful bicycle-making business, and built and tested a series of aeronautical devices—both gliders and powered aeroplanes. Theirs was already one of the most creative partnerships in the history of invention. They qualified to be known as the inventors of what they called a "flying machine" and already held patents on such a device in the United States, France, and Germany; and they were in the process of applying for patents in many other nations, including Austria, Belgium, Italy, Russia, Spain, and the United Kingdom.

As of the moment when Wilbur departed for Kitty Hawk in 1908 the broth-ers were not much known beyond the confines of their home town of Dayton or outside of an international circle of flying enthusiasts. Even though the world nei-ther knew nor much cared about their accomplishments prior to April 1908, they could easily have foisted upon the world anytime after about October 1905 the world's first device that could not only get into the air but could stay there almost as long as they wanted it to remain in flight. They had practiced religiously and honed their flying skills, and they knew that they could fly virtually any place and at any time they chose. But the time and place had to be right—at least according to their standards.

Between 1900 and 1903 they had developed and tested a series of gliding ma-chines at Kitty Hawk, North Carolina. In December 1903, they had briefly put a powered machine in the air. Then, in 1904 and 1905, they had built bigger and bet-ter versions of their powered flyer. Although flying one of their machines was much like riding a wild bronco, by October 1905 they felt that they had tamed the beast sufficiently to claim that they actually possessed the ability to produce the world's first useful and somewhat reliable airplane. Certain that they could manufacture a flying machine that could meet a number of potential needs in war, business, and sport, they redirected their energies from that time forward from engineering a fly-ing machine to marketing their invention to a selected group of potential buyers.

While the brothers Wright were partners, Wilbur was both by age and na-tive instinct the voice of authority. Whenever they held any kind of powwow, it went almost without saying that Wilbur possessed the majority vote. It was always he who established their plan of action and who, usually without objection, made decisions for the partnership. It was in this role of leadership and position of com-mand that Wilbur began the process of deploying the brothers' energies in the spring of 1908.

This was the fifth time Wilbur had led their business ventures from Dayton to Kitty Hawk. He had blazed this trail in 1900, setting the stage for him and Orville to launch into the realm of flight. And now in 1908 he was just as conscious that he had been called upon again to guide them out of the miasma of flight inac-tivity in which they had been mired for more than two years. Try as they might, the brothers had not been able to sell a single airplane since they stopped flying in 1905. It had become clear that the only way they would ever make a sale was to start flying again and to show reluctant investors in business and government the capabilities of their flying machine.

Just as he was totally confident in 1900 that he could fly better than any man who had ever walked the earth, Wilbur was—eight years later—persuaded that he could show the world how to conquer the sky as had never been contemplated or demonstrated by any other human being. He was absolutely certain that in the five-year interval since those first powered flights in 1903, he and Orville had ad-vanced beyond all other flyers in the world. And he knew that whenever and wher-ever they took to the air again, they would be able to show the world what it was to climb like birds into the sky, and to soar there as long as they wanted. The ques-tion had always been when and where they would do it—never whether they could get there.

That question had seemed to be far in the future when they last flew at Huff-man Prairie in October 1905. Despite the passage of two years since their pio-neering flights at Kitty Hawk in 1903, no one else in the world was yet capable of sustained or even short flights. But during 1906 and 1907—inspired in part by ru-

mors of the Wright brothers' 1904 and 1905 flights—French pilots were beginning to get the knack of at least limited powered flight. Their planes also assumed
the shape of a biplane—based on the presumed configuration of Wright flyers.
Because French aeronauts did their experiments with grandiose publicity and on
public fields in and around Paris during 1906 and 1907, such names as Santos-
Dumont, Farman, Bleriot, and Delagrange came to be synonymous in the public
presses with the imminent emergence of powered flight. But despite the heroic ac-
colades won by these daring young men in France, their flights were mere puddle
jumps compared to what the Wrights had already accomplished and to what they
knew they were capable of performing.

Wilbur Wright had ample opportunity to mull both the recent past and impending prospects as his train clanked along toward Old Point Comfort. He was
clear in his mind that this return to Kitty Hawk was propitious in every respect for
the brothers. There he and Orville would be able to hone their flying skills again.
More than that, they would be using a modified version of their tried and true 1905
flying machine. With that same craft at Huffman Prairie, he and Orville had made
6 flights exceeding 17 minutes—one of them lasting 39 minutes and 23 seconds.
That was comforting.

But if they were going to be able to sell their machines to the governments of
France, Germany, Italy, Russia, Spain, and the United Kingdom (not to mention
the United States)—the great competing military powers of the era—they were
going to have to show that with their machines they could surpass flight times and
distances that even they had not yet attempted. Skeptical military procurement officers in these perennially warring nations knew well how to buy ships and artillery
and firearms. But they did not have a clue when it came to flying machines. After
two years of talk with agents in all of these nations, it became clear that there were
a number of benchmarks their planes would have to achieve prior to any successful sale.

First of all, they needed to show that they could carry two people on their
demonstration machine—presumably a pilot and a reconnaissance officer. That,
Wilbur mused, they had never attempted. Second, the plane needed to fly at a speed
of at least 40 miles per hour. That was possible. And, third, they needed to show

that their plane could stay airborne for a period of at least one hour. That, both brothers knew, would definitely require some trial-and-error testing. But they would also need some good luck.

Wilbur was confident that their trusty 1905 machine, with modifications, could do all of these things. To make sure it could, the brothers had devised a completely new control system. This would allow the pilot to sit up in the machine (rather than flying in the prone position of all their earlier planes). This would also make it possible for the pilot to guide the plane's direction and altitude basically with the forerunner of a control stick. They also installed a larger fuel tank and a much larger radiator to provide adequate gasoline and cooling for much longer flights. All of these new features, however, required testing and practice to eliminate unforeseen operating difficulties.

Wilbur knew that they could have conducted these new tests at Huffman Prairie, their Dayton flying field. But there were some severe disadvantages in using that location. There—owing to the absence of sustained winds—they found it necessary to use a derrick and catapult starting device to get off the ground. After attempting to start from tracks such as they had used at Kitty Hawk in 1903, they turned to the use of a catapult on September 7, 1904. They had no choice but to use such a device on those grounds, while at Kitty Hawk, with greater and steadier winds, such a starting mechanism was not necessary. Also, without the soft sands of Kitty Hawk, they hovered their plane very close to the ground at Huffman, rarely getting more than 30 to 50 feet above the earth's surface. They still had many bumps and scrapes, but no broken bones. To prove their plane capable of use for military purposes they would have to go much higher and remain at altitudes of 150 to 300 feet above ground. The sands at Kitty Hawk, Wilbur hoped, would ease any spill that might occur when they descended from these loftier heights.

But the most fundamental purpose of their return to Kitty Hawk in 1908 was the one that was paramount in Wilbur's thinking as he proceeded southward. They needed to test their new systems, the added weight of a second person, the greater heights, and longer flights in a place where predictable failures and false starts would not matter; where they would only be performing for themselves and not for an audience; and, most important, where none of their secrets of design and flight control could be stolen from them. That meant they wanted no rival aviators around, and certainly no photographers or anyone from the working press.

But the world was already abuzz in the early months of 1908 with excitement about flight and the daring men who were attempting to conquer the sky. As a few French pilots showed their abilities to jump bigger and wider puddles, the world press was filled with an endless stream of stories about virtually anyone attempting to fly. Newspapers abounded with rumors of impending flight. The paparazzi of the day sleuthed every flying field, followed the many self-proclaimed aeronauts, and set up tripod cameras wherever flyers appeared in hopes of recording images of historic ventures into the air.

Wilbur and Orville Wright were prime suspects for the press. There were many rumors about the flights they had supposedly made in 1903, 1904, and 1905. There were already numerous leaks about their negotiations with generals among the military powers. Their quiet boasts in these negotiations about prior flights of up to 39 minutes were well known—but not believed. Indeed, their very secretiveness was like a mighty magnet attracting reporters who wanted to expose their secrets and thereby get what might just be one of the greatest news stories of the opening decade of the twentieth century.

Wilbur knew from the many nibbles—sometimes outright confrontations—he had experienced with the press that reporters had picked up the scent and were hot on the trail of getting the Wright brothers' story. Given the slightest hint, he thought, hungry journalists might close in for the kill. He and Orville could no longer fly without interference at Dayton or almost anywhere else in the eastern half of the United States. Kitty Hawk, he believed from past experience, was still off the beaten path, a place where the press could not simply drop by. It was also a place where they were not likely to have an audience of any size or importance—at least with respect to leaking important details about what they were doing. The place was inhabited by a strange sort of people—talkative indeed—but who mainly chattered among themselves. These locals had been both helpful and hospitable during all of their earlier trips.

Yes, Kitty Hawk would be a safe haven for the most important experiments and practice flights the brothers had undertaken since 1905. But the planned flights would be more than just experiments. These were proving tests to determine if the modifications to their machines would actually work. Since Wilbur anticipated that he and Orville would depart from Kitty Hawk to begin public flights in both Europe and elsewhere in the United States, he used much of his quiet and singular time on the train from Dayton to Old Point Comfort to imagine how the next weeks and months would roll out for him and Orville.

At Kitty Hawk in this spring of 1908, as Wilbur envisioned it, he would produce and direct what would be Act Two in the cosmic drama that would make the Wright brothers forever known across the world as the progenitors of powered flight. As he saw it, their accomplishments in 1903 amounted to the world's first controlled flight of a powered flying machine. In 1904 and 1905 they had perfected their powered flying machine. Now, at Kitty Hawk, they would set the stage for the grand opening of a new act in which he and Orville would demonstrate their unique flying abilities to an expectant world audience. The stages where the drama would ultimately unfold were public flying fields in France, Germany, Italy, and the United States.

But there were many preliminary tasks required backstage at Kitty Hawk and in the wings at Dayton to prepare for an imminent performance that the world would quickly notice and never forget. Perhaps never before had so skilled a director made use of the world's newest technologies to gear up for a historic pageant that would soon play itself out in the world's great capitals—Paris, Berlin, Rome, London, and Washington, D.C.

Wilbur rehearsed his theatrical vision over and again in his mind on his train ride to Old Point Comfort. He imagined it so vividly that the stage directions, the lines, and the action became inscribed in his capacious mind and absorbed into the timbre of his being. While seemingly a shy man, he could already feel the thrill that would come in this new season of flying—as no one ever had—before presidents, generals, senators, captains of industry, dukes and dames, kings and queens, in some of the most visible settings the world could provide.

For some men national capitals were places to visit—to go to in order to gawk at pretentious buildings or to lobby for money or to secure government contracts. But for Wilbur they were the places where the giants among men had previously walked—Jefferson and Jackson, Lincoln and Grant, Voltaire and Napoleon, Goethe and Bismarck, Tocqueville, Hugo, and Jules Verne—larger-than-life figures who shaped history, ideas, and imagination. He had read the words of all of these men and studied their autobiographies as he had long dreamed about the dimensions of human existence. Unlike Orville, who thrived on mechanics, applied mathematics, drafting, and the sciences of materials, Wilbur was a man of ideas and ideals, of dreams and drama. And after so many years of dreaming, of scheming, of playing out hundreds of dramatic scenarios in his mind, the grandest of all theatrical events man could imagine was about to begin.

Ten days later he would pass his forty-first birthday on the Outer Banks of North Carolina with barely a notice. In his diary on April 16 he would write: "This is my birthday but I have little chance to get out to celebrate owing to a driving rain from the N.E. [northeast]." But by then he was already wholly engaged in arranging the props for Act Two. He was absorbed in landing the lumber to complete a building where he and Orville would assemble their precious plane—the one they would use to show they were ready to conquer the sky.

Chapter One

RETURN TO THE
SOARING PLACE

Alpheus Drinkwater Telling the Wright Brothers' Story at the Wright Memorial in the 1950s
Drinkwater (1875–1962), the sole telegraph operator in the area, transmitted from the weather office in
Manteo all of the stories—fact or fiction—on the activities and secret flights of the Wright brothers in
1908.

Wilbur and Orville Wright were without a doubt from the same specific pool of genes. And yet, in many ways, they were distinctively different. Standing side by side, Wilbur, because of his exceedingly thin frame and elongated arms and hands, seemed much taller and more athletic. Orville could have passed as a short and scrambling baseball player, being ideally formed for the position of shortstop. Wilbur's was a more limber and shifty frame, suited perfectly for a shooting guard in basketball. Both had receding hairlines: Wilbur was practically bald by the time he was a young man, while Orville's hair was sandier than brown in color and receded more slowly. Neither of them could be in the sun for any length of time without getting severe burns on their heads. The brothers were thus seen almost constantly under caps of many and varied descriptions. After being out of doors for weeks on end, Wilbur's skin would turn into a deep olive tan. Orville's became redder and ruddier as days passed.

Both men went through the public world with tightly closed lips and a look of somber seriousness. Wilbur was never seen with any semblance of a whisker on his face; Orville, from young adulthood to death, was never seen without a mustachio—bushy, but well-groomed. Wilbur was almost never seen with a smile; Orville often sported a warm, even glowing, smile. Both of them had keen senses of humor, but Wilbur's jokes were of a sharp and cutting nature—expressed mainly in one-line comments or in deft flourishes in his letters. Orville's humor was expressed much more in teasing, joking, and pranks played on family and friends.

Wilbur was sternly respectful of authority—especially that of their father, Bishop Milton Wright. Very little warmth could be detected in their relationship. To Wilbur, the patriarch of their family was always to be addressed as "Father." Orville, however, was able to treat their father almost as a chum. Calling Bishop Wright "Pops," he launched into his letters home as if he were sharing gleeful and playful stories. Both brothers loved to tease their sister, Katharine. Neither ever addressed her, at least in their letters, in any form of her Christian name, nor as "Sister" or "Sis." She was always addressed playfully as "Sterchens," "Swes," or even "Swesterchens," sometimes as "Tochter"—all of which were playful renditions of German words "sister," "little sister," or "daughter." As their father's branch of Methodism originated among German residents in Pennsylvania and the Midwest, German labels and terms abounded in their household. Both of them loved to spin yarns to their sister about the great dangers and challenges they faced in encountering mosquitoes, storms, mice, and strange men on the Outer Banks of North Carolina. They loved to describe how they heroically confronted such trials— initially as virtual Quixotes, but ultimately as savvy operators who were able to solve the most complex of problems and to unravel the most fearsome of riddles.

Partly because their mother had long since passed from the scene (at age 58 in 1889 when Wilbur was 22 and Orville was 17) and because their older brothers, Reuchlin and Lorin, had moved on to marriages, families, and careers, Wilbur and Orville faced their early years of manhood in close combination with their father and only sister. Although their father was kept on a respectful periphery of some things, the foursome operated pretty smoothly as a family and team. Wilbur and Orville never compromised the family quartet by bringing female companions into the mix. They were frequently ribbed by their friends for the absence of either girlfriends or wives. But either their shyness in relating to women or their constant focus on the problem of flight kept them from making the kind of investment that was required to form relationships with women. Both of them seemed to get from each other and from their close-knit family a sufficiency of emotional fulfillment. This intense devotion to family would cause anguish for Orville in the long, lonely years of his life after the death of their father and Katharine's eventual marriage and death. But Wilbur died before he finished his only serious courtship— a lifelong affair with the mistress of flight.

In 1900 when Wilbur and Orville Wright decided to move from a virtual family business of designing and making bicycles to the fabrication of airplanes, they concluded together that they needed a suitable place to test their flying machines. It was Wilbur who reached out from the family's Dayton circle and did the research to find the proper place for tests. It was he who first wrote to the U.S. Weather Bureau and consulted with the Smithsonian Institution in search of a proving ground. It was Wilbur who contacted the French-American engineer Octave Chanute—one of the grand old men of the science and craft of flying—to register a somewhat audacious boast that he, Wilbur Wright, thought he knew more than anyone else who had ever tried to fly and that he would therefore very soon start flying.

It was Wilbur who collected the data and then, in partnership with Orville, decided that the most suitable testing place would be Kitty Hawk, North Carolina, and determined roughly how the initial craft would be designed. It was left to Orville to convert those dreams, hopes, and imaginings into a real flying machine and into shipping crates that could transport the parts of the craft from Dayton to Kitty Hawk and to make sure that the right tools were taken along to assemble and repair the machine on site.

Wilbur—"Jullam" to his brothers and sister—was, after all, four years older than Orville and had from their shared childhood been the natural-born leader, the voice, and the commandant of the pair. Wilbur, born in 1867, was thirty-three when they first went to Kitty Hawk in 1900; Orville, born in 1871, was twenty-nine at the time. Also on that first venture in 1900, Wilbur had forged ahead from Dayton to Kitty Hawk eighteen days early, making sure the pathway had been safely opened for baby brother "Bubbo," as Orville was known within the family, to join him. Wilbur discovered the train routes, got himself from Dayton to Norfolk, Virginia, and from there to Elizabeth City, North Carolina. The last leg of his pilgrim trip was via water—a harrowing boat ride across Albemarle Sound to Kitty Hawk. In superb big-brother fashion, he described the dangerous ordeal he had undergone to the family in Dayton and gave his little brother essential information and advice on how to accomplish the treacherous passage. Once Orville joined him at Kitty Hawk—weeks later—the two brothers were reunited as a pair and ready to conduct their first experiments in flight.[1]

In the subsequent years of testing at Kitty Hawk in 1901, 1902, and 1903, there was no more real scouting or trailblazing—on land, that is—to be done. So the brothers traveled together from Dayton to Kitty Hawk and back again, conspiring, consulting, and frequently arguing with animation and loud voices all along the way. On these trips they worked together on logistics, buying materials, build-

ing sheds at their campsites next to Big Kill Devil Hill near Kitty Hawk, and lugging food, tools, and machine parts across sandy expanses to their sheds. And most
important, they worked like horses draying their ever-larger flying machines up
the steep inclines to the top of the 100-foot-high Big Kill Devil to launch the twelve
hundred or so glider flights they would attempt over that three-year period. And
when they went from relatively light gliders to a 750-pound gasoline-driven powered flyer in 1903, they shared the responsibility of getting the behemoth in place
for flying and alternately serving as its test pilot.

Wilbur's avid pioneering and Orville's adept engineering and mechanical skills
had taken them from the ranks of dozens, probably hundreds, of would-be flyers
in 1900 to the status of accomplished glider engineers and pilots in 1902. From
there they became the first men on earth to control a powered flying machine across
an expanse of level ground at least a few feet above the sandy surface. That was on
December 17, 1903, and it would become the most celebrated day in the history
of flight—at least in the United States. Trying to build upon that historic triumph
in 1904 and 1905 at Huffman Prairie near Dayton, they again united their engineering skills to make additional small hops in a powered flyer, leading up to the
astonishing feat of a controlled flight of 39½ minutes over a course of 24 miles on
October 5, 1905. At that moment they were the only human beings on earth who
could fly an airplane at will and virtually to the limits of human endurance and fuel
supply. Not in France, not in England, not in Germany, nor anywhere else in the
United States could another human being reproduce such an incredible feat.

The only problem was that—despite all of the savvy, experience, and ability
the brothers possessed—hardly anyone on earth believed they had actually accomplished such a deed. While there had been a handful of local witnesses, all of
them were Dayton neighbors and friends. The Wrights had deliberately decided
to conduct their experiments in private, to keep what they were learning to themselves, and to keep other aspiring flyers from absconding with their methods.

They also had a couple of other entrepreneurial ideas in mind. From the time
they were able to exercise full control of their gliders in the fall of 1902—well before their first powered flights—they decided to seek a patent on their discoveries. They wanted to have exclusive control over their inventions. They only had

to observe the financial successes of the Bells, the Edisons, and the Fords as a result of their own patents to realize the importance of controlling one's intellectual knowledge. Thus, from the moment of their first successes with that glider, they began envisioning the piles of money they could derive from selling exclusively protected flying machines to eager investors in all corners of the globe. By October 1902 they were convinced that they had not only learned to fly; they were also sure they could produce a flying machine for sport, exploration, or warfare that could be sold potentially for thousands, if not hundreds of thousands, of dollars.

It was specifically to protect their investment and their proprietary knowledge—as they conceived it—that they stopped flying entirely on October 16, 1905. From that day—when Wilbur took a last grand triumphal circuit around their flying field at Huffman Prairie—until the day he left Dayton for Kitty Hawk two and a half years later, neither he nor Orville flew or attempted to fly a single time. For a pair of adventurous male human beings in their mid-thirties who got their principal endorphin and testosterone thrills in life from flying, this self-imposed abstinence would have been painful if it had not held out the promise that they would one day come to be compared with the likes of Christopher Columbus, Robert Fulton, and Thomas Edison in the pages of human history. It was the possibility of transforming their powers of invention into a successful financial empire that drove them forward from 1905 to 1908. In this pursuit they had plenty of famous contemporary models in the likes of Andrew Carnegie, John D. Rockefeller, and, yes, Alexander Graham Bell—all of whom had amassed both fame and fortune by that time.

They had begun protecting their proprietary knowledge as soon as they thought they had something to protect. Amid the euphoria of being able to produce and replicate controlled glides in September and October 1902 at Kitty Hawk, their honored mentor and friend Octave Chanute advised that they should immediately seek a patent on their flying machine. As soon as they returned to Dayton from Kitty Hawk at the end of that October, they began the process of drafting an application for a U.S. patent. They formally submitted the document five months later on March 23, 1903. The revealing aspects of the nature and timing of their application were twofold: first, they filed the application a full eight months prior to their first attempt to put a powered flyer in the air; and, second, their application was not for a wing, a rudder, a tail, a stabilizer, or the configuration of a flying apparatus—it was rather for the whole ball of wax—nothing less than the entire "flying machine." Wilbur and Orville Wright were nothing if not audacious, and they were vitally animated by ambition.

They did many other things as well to protect their proprietary knowledge and information. They swore their colleagues and friends in Dayton to total secrecy. They also got a gentlemanly pledge of privilege from another group of aspiring flyers who had been with them to Kitty Hawk. No one in whom they confided was to reveal that they had begun to transform themselves in December 1902 from glider engineers and pilots into the creators of a full-fledged powered flying machine. Outside of Dayton, only Octave Chanute and George Spratt, both of whom had been with them at Kitty Hawk during tests in 1901 and 1902, were entrusted with the secret. While it was not easy for Chanute to keep such a special piece of knowledge—he parlayed almost daily with people throughout America and Europe interested in flight—he knew that he must keep this particular professional confidence. For Spratt, himself an aspiring aeronaut, it was much easier. While he was bent on flying with every fiber of his being, he lived largely in isolation as a farmer and part-time family doctor in Coatesville, Pennsylvania. A melancholy loner, Spratt had mostly limited his discussions of flying to just three human beings: Chanute, Wilbur, and Orville. And also, judging from his letters to them, he only shared the volatile ups and downs of his constantly shifting emotions with these same three trusted friends.

They also decided by December of 1902 that their Kitty Hawk experiment station would no longer be an open salon on flight for other would-be flyers. In prior years Chanute had routinely recruited and sent one or more of his numerous aspiring flyers either to be test pilots for his own machines or to serve as intern assistants to the Wrights. In 1901 Chanute had sent Edward Huffaker, previously a model airplane designer at the Smithsonian Institution and resident of Chuckey City, Tennessee, to be with the Wrights during their glider experiments. Huffaker was there to test Chanute's latest idea for a glider. But he was also there to assist the Wrights and to take detailed notes on all of their experiments for the use of

Chanute. Huffaker turned out to be a thorn in the brothers' sides and ever after a butt of many of their jokes.

In 1902 Chanute had sent along to Kitty Hawk Augustus M. Herring, another designer and pilot with Smithsonian experience, to test two more of his designs. Herring, Chanute, and Spratt were present in October 1902 when the Wrights' new glider proved to be the most airworthy craft ever designed by human beings. Chanute's machines sat crumpled in wind, dust, and rain as the Wrights' glider literally soared from every side of Kill Devil Hills. Through the lenses of the Wrights' camera, Herring could be observed in stances of fury and disgust that the Wrights were off flying while he was still firmly glued to the earth.

Despite Chanute's solemn vow of secrecy to the Wrights, he could hardly keep himself from revealing all while on his annual European tour during the winter and spring of 1903. Across Italy and France he met numerous aspiring flyers and gave lectures to aeronautic and engineering clubs wherever he traveled. As he spoke in his native tongue to French colleagues and friends at the Aero-Club de France in Paris on April 2, 1903, barely a week after the Wrights had filed their patent application, he spoke adoringly of the great flying successes of the Wrights—flights that he had personally witnessed at Kitty Hawk. He showed photographs of the Wright flyers hovering above Kill Devil Hills. And he hinted quietly and revealingly about some of the secrets of the Wright brothers' recent accomplishments. His contacts and audiences were filled with men of all ages who had talked wistfully about flying for dozens of years. By and large, however, none of them had ever been one meter off the ground except perhaps in a hot air balloon. Chanute's witness to the successes of the Wrights instantly tantalized and fired these same men with new ambitions to get on with their own dreams of conquering the air.

Chanute also—forever wishing to present himself as the world's greatest living guru on flight—could not restrain himself from leaving the impression wherever he spoke that all of these young Americans—Huffaker, Herring, Spratt, and, the Wrights—were among his many students and protégés scattered across the United States. Nor could he restrain himself from hinting that he could arrange for the opportunity to witness the next rounds of flight tests being conducted by his many contacts—including the forthcoming Wright flights scheduled for the fall of 1903. He virtually promised Captain Ferdinand Ferber, of the French army, that he could go to Kitty Hawk in 1903. He also confidently informed British flying enthusiast Patrick Y. Alexander that he could be at Kitty Hawk at the same time. The secretive Wrights, aghast at Chanute's genial invitations, gently slammed the door on a visit by Ferber—and any other French agent or flyer for that matter—while they eventually relented in favor of Alexander's visit to Kitty Hawk. They had met the British financier, liked him, and thought they could trust him. But, in the end, Alexander became occupied in the fall of 1903 with other business in America and literally missed the opportunity of a lifetime, to observe history being made.

Leading up to the powered flight tests of December 1903, Wilbur and Orville Wright confidently believed that success would be theirs. They never doubted it for a moment, not even when they experienced successive failures of the lightweight but brittle aluminum they had used for the casing of their propeller shafts. Confident of their technical prowess by 1903, their only concerns were that the weather might become too cold for their gloveless fingers to manipulate engine parts and that it would not be possible to squeeze in a powered flight before Christmas. Their bold confidence was, of course, rewarded on December 17 when they accomplished four short and bumpy, yet totally successful, flights.

Although they did not know it at the time of their first powered flights, they also carried back to Dayton in their bag of exposed glass plate negatives a dramatically clear image of the initial moments of their first flight. Although the flight was only 120 feet in distance and consumed only 12 seconds, the resulting photograph proved for all time that their powered machine did indeed rise off level ground with a pilot aboard at 10:35 A.M. on December 17, 1903. Not only did they have a crystal-clear picture, they also had five witnesses—all local Joes from the Outer Banks of North Carolina—to the world's first powered flight under the control of a human pilot. From that moment forward the lives of these five men would be forever blessed— or perhaps cursed—because they were the sole living witnesses of this extraordinary piece of human history. They would become renowned celebrities in the isolated villages and hamlets of North Carolina's barrier islands. If the Wright brothers were able to swagger across the world as the first men to actually fly a powered airplane, these locals would be able to brag forever about their presence at the historic moment—at least across the 50 to 100 miles that surrounded Kitty Hawk and Kill Devil Hills.

The Wright brothers were firm both in their resolution not to permit outside observers—other than Chanute and Spratt (although both left before the powered tests)—to come to Kitty Hawk in 1903 and in their confidence that they would be flying before Christmas Day. But they were not quite as clear in their own minds as to how they should handle publicity, namely the newspaper press, with regard to their inaugural powered flights that December. They definitely wanted no outside cameras around to photograph either their glider or their newly minted powered flyer, on the ground or in flight. Likewise, they wanted no written descriptions of how their planes operated. But, like almost all aspiring inventors with a newfangled mechanism that they wanted to sell, they definitely *did* want publicity. And they wanted a lot of it.

They were thus willing and eager to talk with reporters about what they were going to do at Kitty Hawk, and they were more than ready to share with reporters the nature and extent of their successes after the fact. But they did not want any photographers or reporters present when they were in the process of attempting to perform their daring deeds to report on whether or not they succeeded. That was one of the reasons why they had gone to the remote region of the Outer Banks of North Carolina in the first place: to be so far away from interloping journalists or photographers that they would be able to invent and conduct tests in peace and secrecy.

The Wrights' schizophrenic desires, on the one hand for solitude to protect what they wanted to keep secret and, on the other hand, for publicity to make their success known, were muddled by another factor they never fully took into account. The overlooked wild card element was that the principal witnesses of their attempts to fly from 1900 through 1903 were not other aeronauts, but rather a band of swarthy, mustachioed lifesavers and Outer Banks fishermen. These folk were more proficient in catching fish and telling yarns than in any of life's other pursuits. These were no freshwater or surf fishermen with rubber boots and fancy fly rods.

They were fishermen who were as salty, profane, and swaggering as any men on earth. They grew up on fishing boats plying ocean waters amid blowing gales and writhing seas. Not only did they know the sea and the air above that transformed ocean waters from placid lakes into raging torrents; they could also spin tale after tale of their near-death experiences with wind and water in graphic, gripping, and spine-tingling detail. And they could roll out lurid images of the sea creatures they encountered and sometimes caught.

It was, after all, because these fishermen could dare to face the angry ocean in the midst of the worst storms that they were also employed as lifesavers. The string of lifesaving stations, which populated the North Carolina coast at seven- or eight-mile intervals from the 1880s until the modern Coast Guard came into existence in the 1920s, was filled with such men. It was their profession to race into the teeth of a storm to rescue humans and to salvage precious cargoes from ships that foundered in the shallow and treacherous waters off the coast of North Carolina. That is why the area was known from the time of the earliest explorers on as the Graveyard of the Atlantic. And while the people they saved moved on gratefully to other destinations, it remained for the lifesavers who never left the Outer Banks to recount and embellish over and over again the dangers they faced in those harrowing moments and the obvious heroism they humbly and deftly demonstrated in each instance.

While Kitty Hawk and Kill Devil Hills were utterly remote from the civilized world in most conventional terms in the first decade of the twentieth century, these lonely lifesavers were remarkably connected with the outer world in other ways. Because of their daily and nightly patrols along sandy shore lines, they actually had face-to-face linkages with lifesavers from adjacent stations many times a day. Since they were required to prove that they had completed their patrols by exchanging medallions at the midway point between stations, news and rumors could be passed orally from lifesaver to lifesaver in dramatic detail across a hundred miles in the space of a single day, almost surely embellished in every retelling. In the days of telegraphic communication, before telephones had appeared in businesses and homes around America, these lifesaving stations were, moreover, on the cutting edge of modern technology. They were linked through a closed circuit of telephone and telegraph lines that provided another means of transmitting information across America almost instantaneously from any point in the system.

This telegraphic and closed-circuit telephone web was designed to be an emergency communication system among lifesaving facilities. But it was also used by lifesavers, their families, and other locals who had a need to get a message delivered anywhere in the United States or even across the Atlantic. This ever-present capability, both at the nearby lifesaving stations and at the Kitty Hawk weather bureau, had enabled Wilbur and Orville to communicate daily and hourly with such people as Chanute, Spratt, and Herring on logistics for getting to and from their Kitty Hawk camp. It made it possible for the brothers to keep in daily contact with their family in 1903 as their powered flights were anticipated and for them to inform their father, Bishop Wright, and their sister, Katharine, that they had indeed accomplished man's first powered flights just hours after they happened on December 17, 1903.

The Wright brothers valued this ability to keep in touch with those who they wanted to know about their doings at Kitty Hawk. But by the same token, they were constantly frustrated by the leakage of information they did not want to go abroad. Even so, they were bemused when some of these stories appeared in the press—especially surrounding their first powered flights in 1903. Many of the stories were so wildly imaginative that the brothers believed they could only have been fabricated in the minds of impulsive reporters who sold their stories by the inch of type published and by the sheer sensationalism of the story. While they sometimes observed the lifesavers talking to reporters, they shrugged off the misinformation handed out within their hearing by the surfmen. Believing that no sane reporter would ever believe the yarns of these simple Outer Bankers, they never quite appreciated the inner need and penchant of the lifesavers to bolster their self-importance by spinning even simple stories to the outer reaches of credulity.

In their dealings with Outer Bankers, the Wright brothers loved playing the role of city slickers in the wilds of America. Whereas they were just average guys in the context of a bustling, industrializing Dayton in their starched white shirts, ties, and pin-striped pants, on the Outer Banks they stood out as strange creatures.

They poked fun in their letters home about the poverty and backwardness of the Outer Bankers, but they were also themselves frugal penny-pinchers who avoided lavishness and were proud of their ability to do for themselves and to get by on very little. While they looked different and spoke with different accents, they still felt a measure of commonality with the Outer Bankers they came to love and appreciate. Despite their differentness, they felt right at home with these untutored common folk.

One thing they especially valued in lessons learned from the Outer Bankers was their ability to live with the sand, the mosquitoes, and the changing weather that characterized the Kitty Hawk area. The soft sand was a welcome surface to cushion some of their sudden glider landings. But it was a nuisance when it came to walking, cooking, and sleeping. While they came to live with the omnipresence of sand in shoes, beds, and teapots, they never could come totally to grips with the problem of clambering to the top of Big Kill Devil lugging a glider that was constantly trying to go where the wind would take it. Not only were they scaling a hill, they were also pushing against sand that constantly gave way so that two tiring steps upward were required to make one step of progress forward. But the lifesavers had marvelous wagons with wide wheels and giant spokes that enabled them to roll heavy boats across the sands. Such "trucks" as these were easily adapted by the Wright brothers to assist in hauling their much heavier powered flyers across the sandy surfaces.

Wilbur and Orville had learned much about the people and the rugged environment of the Outer Banks during their four years of test flights that culminated in the powered flights of '03. But they had also learned much about themselves. First of all, they learned that landlubbers from the mostly flat Midwest region of the United States could adapt to the unpredictable weather of the sounds and barrier islands of North Carolina. Both of them were frightened to the core by the tiny and almost helpless skiffs that were used to cross the shallow sounds from Elizabeth City to Kitty Hawk. What they interpreted as near-death experiences in crossing these waters was in actuality an almost daily and routine experience for the boatmen who plied these vastly wide and open pools of water little more than four to six feet in depth, but hundreds of square miles in width and breadth. What they saw as slovenliness on the part of the captains of these boats in not sticking to strict schedules for carrying people and cargo across Albemarle Sound was actually good native savvy in knowing when it made no sense to attempt a crossing because of adverse weather conditions. In time, the brothers came to live with the capriciousness of both weather and men as life was required to be pursued on the Outer Banks.

They also learned something about the inner core of their own beings. They found, with experience, that they could wait out almost any natural or man-made hazard. If conditions were not right—the wind too strong or weak, the threat of rain or storms too troubling, or the assault of mosquitoes or wild pigs too uncomfortable or menacing—they learned to bide their time and pursue other useful activities. They learned to bite their lips in disappointment when one of their local hired hands—such as their first ground crewman, Dan Tate—did not show up for work until hours after they expected him—if at all. The Wrights were men of independence, control, and self-sufficiency; but they learned in North Carolina to live with the locals who were just as frustratingly and cussedly independent as they themselves were.

In addition to learning to do commerce with a tribe of people oriented to ocean waters, there were also certain religious and spiritual overtones to the Wrights' encounters with North Carolina. Although they grew up in a home with a father who lived and breathed the practice of religion every day of his life, Wilbur and Orville, except in certain particulars, did not seem to be very religious at all. There is no record that they ever attended a religious service of any type during their many accumulated months in North Carolina—although they were frequently invited to do so. There are no references to prayer in any of their deliberations or in any of their yearnings to be lifted heavenward on flying machines. The words sin, love, evil, salvation, worship, God, Jesus, and Satan almost never appear in any of their letters or diaries—except in humorous connotations.

But despite the absence of any terms of religious devotion in their conversations or writings, they observed Sunday as a day of rest at Kitty Hawk—saved for reading, for visiting, and for the writing of letters. No matter how urgent their need to complete some mechanical task, to repair a building, or to work on their camp, they would not do anything that had the outward appearance of physical labor on Sunday. Nor did they ever take advantage of any spectacular conditions for flying to attempt a flight on what they viewed as their duty or desire to keep the Sabbath as a holy day of rest. Rather, they took Sunday as a time to visit and spend time with the lifesavers, locals, and friends at Kill Devil Hills or at Kitty Hawk, sitting on the front porch and talking.

But observance of the Sabbath hardly scratches the surface of their religious engagement with the Outer Banks of North Carolina, and with Kill Devil Hills in particular. From their first visit in 1900 until their last trip for flying purposes in 1911, both Wilbur and Orville experienced Kitty Hawk as a place of solemn re-treat, a locale for contemplation with their inner beings, and as a haunt where they could commune with nature. Throughout their active flying days until Wilbur's death in 1912, they referred to Kitty Hawk as a place of pilgrimage where they could get away from the hubbub of business, of daily routines, and of the tawdry parts of life involving human rancor and lawsuits. They disliked the rival-ries, dishonesty, and competition that grew out of their special discoveries about flight, and they hated the endless string of lawsuits that pulled them down from the lives of research, invention, and analysis that they loved best. Kitty Hawk be-came for them in symbol and in reality an escape from all of the sordidness of the world of business and commerce.

That they saw Kill Devil Hills and Big Kill Devil, which loomed over their camp, as sacred territory is revealed in their reverent and loving respect for the site. On every trip they took to the place, they would first climb to the top of Big Kill Devil to determine its elevation, triangulate the slope of the hill on the north side, which they used for gliding, and observe the expanse of God's earth that could be seen from the tallest point on the coast of North Carolina. They needed the meas-urements to make calculations of distance and descent for their glider flights. But they also used the moment—frequently on Sunday—to contemplate what they were about, what they were trying to accomplish, and how they fit into the rich and vibrant natural order they could see all about them on the Outer Banks. Their photographs of Kill Devil Hills—without human forms in the pictures—reveal their recorded appreciation of this place of reverence and discovery.

In addition to being a retreat, Kitty Hawk was a place where God's nature was evident in abundance with every glimpse of the environment, every gander into the sky, and with every step they took from tent or shed to fetch water, go for groceries, or venture a flight. The air was filled with birds of all sizes, shapes, and colors; the ocean and the sounds were brimming with fish; the sands were replete with turtles, crabs, and every form of fly, flea, or other insect known to man. If they were not careful, the roaming pigs that populated the Outer Banks would eat anything they left outside or unprotected, and an army of mice would take care of any edibles inside. So abundant were the mice that both brothers rhapsodized frequently about their encounters with the tiny beasts.

But then there was Big Kill Devil Hill, located in a wilderness. It was a place for contemplation and conquest, a mountain of triumph and defeat, an ever-present symbol of travail, of sacrifice, of challenge, of giving and of taking away. It could be treacherous and windswept, enshrouded with thunder and lightning, or uplifting and life-giving. The Hill was a constant presence where they huddled in the wilderness and where they could seek to understand the will of God, the foibles of man, and the laws of nature. It is clear that Big Kill Devil became for Wilbur and Orville more than just a place to practice flying. It was the place where they became men, discovered truth, and suffered the consequences and travail of the truths they discovered.

Chief among these consequences was the discovery of a gem of great value, so rare and precious that it held within its glow the potential seeds of self-destruction. It was on Big Kill Devil Hill that the Wright brothers uncovered the secret of flight. And like all great discoveries in the course of human history, how the brothers handled their newfound treasure would determine whether they would enjoy its benefits or inherit a treacherous whirlwind. In this case, from the moment they came face-to-face with the god of flight, the question became whether they would use their knowledge to conquer the world or be consumed by the secrets they possessed.

It was the theory and firm conviction of the Wrights that their solution to what they called "the problem of flight" was entirely simple—so simple, straightforward, and direct, in fact, that any keen observer of their flights, their machines, or of photographs of their planes would quickly be able to figure out their secret. Thus, as soon as they had fabricated and flown what they believed to be the world's first "practical" flying machine during tests on Huffman Prairie near Dayton, Ohio, in October 1905, they abruptly and deliberately stopped flying so as not to risk potential exposure. They were, they believed, so far ahead of the rest of the inventing world that they need not fly again until they were ready to reveal their special secret in the most financially advantageous circumstances they could achieve.

But between October 1905 and April 1908, when they finally decided to resume flying, the world of flight underwent a revolutionary transformation. The circumstances began to change in 1906 and increased in pace during 1907. Inspired in part by rumors that the Wrights had flown at will in 1904 and 1905 and that their flyer had taken the shape of a biplane, French pilots were beginning to get the knack of at least limited powered flight.

Alberto Santos-Dumont, a Brazilian transplanted to France; Henri Farman, a Briton also living in France; and Louis Bleriot and Léon Delagrange, full-fledged Frenchmen, were beginning to make names for themselves as they achieved short flights at fields near Paris before throngs of witnesses. The theatrical and melodramatic Santos-Dumont had covered a distance of 220 meters at Bagatelle in the Bois de Boulogne, near the heart of Paris, on November 12, 1906. As far as most of the world was concerned, then and far into the future, this short leap skyward qualified him to be recognized as the true pioneer of powered flight among humankind. For this achievement, Santos-Dumont would forever be honored and revered both in France and in Brazil as the world's first real aeronaut of powered planes. Only in the United States would the secretive 1903 flights of the Wright brothers be recognized as the true origins of powered flight. When Santos-Dumont astounded audiences at Paris in 1906, the earlier flights of the Wrights were only rumored and as yet unconfirmed in France and Europe—or even in the United States, for that matter. The Wrights' silver bullet historical photograph proving their first flight on December 17, 1903, had not yet been published. Nor had the Wrights allowed any photographs other than their own to be taken of their further tests at Huffman Prairie in 1904 or 1905. The world was filled with men who made large claims about great achievements in flight. Thus far, the Wrights were just two among a host of boastful men whose flights had not been observed, photographed, or reported by news reporters. In the world of flying—filled as it had been for many years with wild and unsubstantiated claims—knowledgeable folk in both Europe and America had long since adopted the aphorism of "seeing is believing" as their only reliable credo. The Wrights, from this point of view, had not been seen and thus, as nice and clean-cut as they might seem, could not be believed.

In 1907 the waiting gaggle of would-be flyers got into the act with tremendously celebrated but short flights, mainly at Issy-les-Moulineaux, near Paris. But they were public flights and could be seen by crowds of observers and reporters and, best of all, they could be photographed. Bleriot made short hops of up to 500 meters there in November 1907. Delagrange had done so as well. On November 9 Farman topped the others with a flight of 1 minute and 14 seconds over a course of 1,030 meters. In late 1907 Farman, in particular, was capturing great attention as he attempted to win the famed Deutsch-Archdeacon Prize for the first French pilot who could make a sustained powered flight. Before Farman, a number of fliers could leapfrog across a field in a series of hops, but he was the first to cross a field in a straight line with no intervening bounces.

While no one had yet seen any Wright brothers' flights, the rumors arriving in Europe of their great flights in America had drawn forth a number of such prizes to encourage French pilots to make sure that their nation would continue to be recognized as the homeland of flight. The French were not the only ones caught up in the frenzy of public flights. Even Orville Wright himself got the itch to see one of these glorified efforts. On November 18, 1907 Orville attended one of Farman's many attempts to win the Deutsch-Archdeacon Prize at Issy-les-Moulineaux. Like thousands of others who attended Farman's bold and widely publicized flying spectacles, Orville was there eagerly watching to see if Farman might just blast into the air and discover the secrets of flight he and Wilbur had already experienced in 1903, 1904, and 1905. Fortunately for the covert plans of the Wright brothers, Farman's performance that day was just another series of hops and not a true launch into the high-stakes realm of powered human flight.[2]

The newfangled machines sported by the French aeronauts, most of them inspired by pictures of Wright gliders, were much like newly hatched birds—

awkward, spindly, unsure, and resulting in many thuds into the earth. They were, to the Wrights, reminiscent of the seasons of their early tests with gliders at Kitty Hawk between 1900 and 1903 and with powered machines both at Kitty Hawk and Dayton from 1903 to 1905. Young hatchlings required a lot of trials and many failures, they knew. But the French pilots, they could readily see, were on the verge of suddenly soaring into the air.

The mere sight and the disturbing number of aspiring aeronauts around Europe in 1907 sent a shiver down the spines of the Wrights and set them to thinking more soberly about their quickly eroding position in the process of launching the world into flight. While they had discovered how to fly before anyone else, would they be able to get credit for having done so? That was crucial. But nearly as important was the question of whether they would be able to recover expenses for their years of testing and efforts and enjoy some greatly desired financial gains.

As a result of another of brother Wilbur's trailblazing schemes, Orville had ended up in Paris, where he could conveniently observe Farman's plane and his rudimentary attempts at flight. Just as he had led the way to Kitty Hawk in 1900, Wilbur became persuaded in early 1907 that he should venture across the Atlantic to France where he alone would be able to sell a Wright flyer to the French government. No one, he believed, was better qualified than the original inventor to make the case for the Wright flying machine. He left the United States in May 1907 confident that he would be able to pitch American ingenuity to France.

Like many other Americans who had wanted to sell their inventions to the French government, from Benjamin Franklin to Robert Fulton to Dr. Richard Gatling and beyond, Wilbur soon shared the experience of his forerunners by spinning his wheels for months on end against a never-ending stream of petty French bureaucrats. Finally, in July, he thought he had cleared a pathway for a sale to the French government. He telegraphed Orville to join him in Paris as soon as possible to seal the deal. Orville rushed to Europe to help close the negotiations. But instead of concluding a contract with the French government on the definite sale of a Wright flyer, the two brothers spent the next five months meeting frustrating dead ends not only in France, but also in Germany and in the United Kingdom.

Unable to conclude a deal themselves with any of the European governments, they decided in early December 1907 to hire a French-American business syndicate that would represent them in selling their machines to European governments. Although the Wrights considered themselves to be shrewd negotiators and businessmen, they finally had to concede that the governments of Europe—just like private observers in the world of flight—adhered to the credo of needing to see before they could believe. No public official would commit to buying something that had not been demonstrated publicly. The company that would handle their sales was Charles R. Flint and Company, an international munitions dealer, with offices in New York, London, Berlin, Paris, and Saint Petersburg. The Flint enterprise had more experience than any other company in taking American-made tools of war to the military powers of the world.

In attempting to sell their flyer, the Wright brothers experienced either feast or famine. No sooner had they concluded their deal with Flint and Company to represent them in Europe than the U.S. government, not wishing to be left behind, came courting them for its own airplane. But these army officials also wanted to see a plane actually flying as a part of the purchase arrangement. In that the U.S. government had never contracted for the construction of a powered, propelled flying machine before, the U.S. Army Signal Corps—the contracting entity for the first airplane—conferred several times with the Wrights both as it designed a request for bids and as it moved in the direction of evaluating proposals for its first flyer. The Wright brothers were all too happy to comply by providing specifications for a plane they knew they could deliver. Using information supplied by the Wrights, the U.S. Army advertised for proposals to build the airplane described by the Wrights in early 1908.

Much to the surprise of the Signal Corps and also of the Wrights, the U.S. Army received three purportedly viable bids to deliver the airplane specified in the published bid documents. The Wright proposal was the most expensive of the three at $25,000. Of the other two bids, one was submitted by a competent mechanical engineer for only $1,000. The man acknowledged that he would not recover his costs at such a low figure. The second competitive bid was for $20,000 and came from one of the Wrights' most despicable rivals—Augustus M. Herring.

While he had a long association with the Smithsonian and other builders of flying machines, he had never produced one that worked. He had, however, been present at the 1902 Wright camp at Kitty Hawk and the brothers feared that he might have taken along some of their most important ideas on the control of flight.

Rather than putting itself in the embarrassing position of going with the highest bidder, the Army—which was inclined to believe that only the Wrights could ultimately deliver the required plane—accepted all three proposals. But it did so on the shrewd condition that only those builders who were able to deliver a satisfactory craft on a timely basis and who could demonstrate their capabilities in publicly observed trial flights would be paid.

So, finally, the question of when and where the Wrights would demonstrate their flying prowess—publicly—had been answered through their endless months of negotiations in France and the United States. They would be put to the test most likely in June 1908 in both France and America, but certainly by August 1908.

Where they would fly in France was not yet known. Since they would be doing their demonstrations under the aegis of a business syndicate, the exact place would have to be selected and specified by the syndicate. The flight location in the United States, however, was already determined. As specified in the request for bids, these flights would be at Fort Myer, an old U.S. Army post just inside northern Virginia and almost within gazing distance of the U.S. Capitol in Washington, D.C. The progress of battle during the U.S. Civil War had been closely observed by Union government officials from Fort Myer. The onset of the era of flight would also be seen at the historic fortification.

There was another somewhat disturbing surety facing the Wrights as they headed toward Kitty Hawk in the spring of 1908. Owing to the sudden confluence of separate contracts to produce planes and to perform measured test flights in both France and the United States at virtually the same time, it would be necessary for the brothers to go their separate ways during the summer of 1908. In order to fulfill the provisions of the two distinct and very different contractual obligations, one brother would have to do the demonstration flying in the United States and the other in France. Never had they flown separately—so complementary were their roles in inventing and proving flight that the concept of flying separately had never even crossed their minds. But now—unless a contractual mountain could be moved in either France or the United States—it was going to be necessary for them to fly separately and simultaneously in both places.

In this era when Americans were still immersed in the wise teachings of George Washington that they should always avoid entangling alliances with Europe and the Europeans, Wilbur had already determined that in his role as trailblazer he would deal with the wily agents of the Old World. He relished the challenge of demonstrating American ingenuity across the Atlantic. Just as he had played out other scenarios for Act Two in his mind, he could easily see himself flying over and above a bewildered bevy of French aeronauts. He could see himself shrewdly shaking hands with viscounts, kaisers, and kings as Wright airplanes were accepted into the service of European armies. Yes, it would be better, he thought, for brother Orville to operate on the known terrain of America.

But those were matters for another day in the not-too-distant future. There were much more immediate issues on Wilbur's mind as his train arrived at Old Point Comfort. Since the fact of their American and French contracts had already appeared in the press, everyone who cared to know was aware that the Wrights would have to prepare for the upcoming public flight demonstrations somewhere. They could no longer fly without notice at Dayton or almost anywhere else in the eastern half of the United States. But Kitty Hawk was still off the beaten path, Wilbur and Orville thought, a place where the press could not simply drop by. At Kitty Hawk they were not likely to have an audience of any great size or importance. Leaks to reporters were thus unlikely. In this matter, they counted the ever-present lifesavers as almost mute friends, a simple folk who would not understand what they were seeking to accomplish. This was a presumption that they would very soon learn to regret.

Chapter Two

OF SWAGGERERS
AND SCRIBES

Lifesavers at the Kitty Hawk Life Saving Station, Kitty Hawk, NC, 1900
The swarthy and colorful surf men at the Kitty Hawk and the Kill Devil Hills Life Saving Stations served
the Wright brothers from 1900 to 1908 as construction assistants and ground crews; but also as proud
conduits of both information and tall tales about audacious flights being performed by the brothers.

Wilbur Wright—assured, confident, and excited about his impending return to flying rather than negotiating, tinkering with engines rather than writing up sales proposals, breathing the fresh air of the flying field instead of the dank smoke of business offices—almost shivered with anticipation as he swung down from the train at Old Point Comfort on April 6, 1908, to spend the night overlooking the vast body of water where the James River almost imperceptibly becomes the Chesapeake Bay. On the morning of April 7 he headed to the nearby dock to ferry over to Norfolk. Arriving there at noon, he had plenty of time to look at ships and ferries and all manner of steam- and gasoline-driven craft that plied the watery expanses lying between Hampton, Newport News, Chesapeake, and Norfolk. Norfolk was also a good place to walk and look for books, magazines, and other reading materials that might be welcome diversions at Kitty Hawk. In a more leisurely manner than usual, he boarded another train in Norfolk at 6:00 P.M., which took him across the Virginia border into northeastern North Carolina and to his final train stop at Elizabeth City.

Wilbur and Orville had been to Elizabeth City many times. It was the virtual headquarters town for trains, boats, and ground vehicles to merge for business and commerce in that corner of North Carolina. It had been the destination for coastal arrivals in North Carolina from the seventeenth century forward and the departure point for the Wrights on every trip they ever made to Kitty Hawk. It was the market depot where they went for lumber, food, and supplies to be shipped over to their camp at Kill Devil Hills. It was also a place of frustration where they spent many hours waiting for the right boat to take them across the Albemarle Sound to the Outer Banks.

And it was a place that the Wrights had come to know very well. Here Wilbur was able to inventory the people and places he and Orville had known in prior years. In reporting his findings to Orville back in Dayton in 1908 he was able to play the big-brother advisory role he knew and liked best. Their favorite innkeeper,

M. L. Sawyer, had committed suicide, so Orville, he wrote, should stay at the new Southern Hotel and not the old Arlington. Wilbur encountered John T. Daniels at the Elizabeth City depot. He was the lifesaver who had taken the historic photograph of their first powered flight in 1903. Daniels reported that their old sheds at Kitty Hawk had long since been ransacked and destroyed. Captain Franklin H. Midgett, who plied the waters between Elizabeth City and Kitty Hawk, was just as cantankerous and half-reliable as he had been in 1902 and 1903. Wilbur was not sure whether Midgett's old boat, the *Lou Willis*, would be able to carry all of the lumber they would need for a new shed and also the huge crate in which the 1905 flyer—engine, wings, and all—would be shipped by train to Elizabeth City. And, oh yes, Orville should be careful to catch the correct train between Norfolk and Elizabeth City. Otherwise he would be wasting his time. And, by the way, the desired train was 50 cents cheaper than the other.[1]

Wilbur was like a caged lion in Elizabeth City until the morning of April 9 when he finally got on Midgett's larger craft, the BM *Van Dusen*, for the passage to Kitty Hawk. Also loaded on the boat was a shipment of lumber Wilbur had purchased at Kramer Brothers, hardware from Sharber & White, and a 55-gallon barrel of gasoline from Grandy's—all in Elizabeth City—that would be needed for the plane. By the time Midgett got the heavily laden vessel over to Kitty Hawk, it was too late for Wilbur to head on down the four-mile trek from Kitty Hawk Bay to Kill Devil Hills. So he stayed overnight with Captain Midgett and his family.

After spending the night at Midgett's house, Wilbur proceeded to the old camp at Kill Devil Hills, which he found in ruins, as reported by John Daniels. With no place to hang his hat at the camp, he arranged with the lifesavers at the Kill Devil Hills Life Saving Station to take up quarters there until a new shed could be built. Captain Jesse Ward—the genial, jovial, and fatherly commandant at the station—was happy to make a place for Wilbur and to make him one of the guys for a few days. Besides, Wilbur knew most of the men from the old days and told Orville that they would be in good hands for ready assistance with their much larger and bulkier plane. Gone were Daniels and Adam Etheridge—both of whom had helped them on the morning of December 17, 1903—but in Captain Ward,

Willie St. Clair Dough (another observer of the first flight), Robert Wescott, and Uncle Bennie O'Neal they would be working with familiar faces.

From the Kill Devil Hills Station, Wilbur watched fretfully, impatiently, and finally angrily for the next ten days as he waited for the lumber, materials, and other supplies to be delivered from Kitty Hawk and for another shipment of lumber to arrive from Elizabeth City. On April 16 Wilbur vented his pent-up frustration in a letter to his father back in Dayton:

> This is my eleventh day from home and only one day's work has been done on the new building. Two days were spent getting to Elizabeth City. Two were lost at Eliz City waiting for the boat. One was spent on the sound en route to Kitty Hawk. Friday and Saturday were spent selecting a location, landing and hauling lumber to it. Monday was spent putting in foundation and sills. Tuesday, Wednesday, and today, Thursday, have been spent in waiting for more lumber to arrive, and storms to pass. We hope to get down to work tomorrow.[2]

From his perspective, the entire population of the Outer Banks was on a slow pace that kept him from getting on with the flying he was dying to do. By essentially bribing Captain Midgett to make extra trips to Elizabeth City and personally supervising the shipment of lumber across the sandy road from Kitty Hawk to Kill Devil Hills, he finally had the materials he needed to put up a new shed. By hiring a couple of locals to do some of the carpentry and working with them in cutting every board and driving virtually every nail, by April 24 Wilbur had completed a building that could be used as the Wright brothers' combination dormitory, kitchen, hangar, and workshop.[3]

Even while Wilbur fussed with the procurement of materials and the construction of a new camp, he continued to monitor the whereabouts and activities of his brother Orville. From his temporary quarters at the lifesaving station he continued to produce and direct what would be Act Two in the cosmic drama that would make the Wright brothers not only the progenitors of the world's first powered controlled flight, but also the human actors who would demonstrate flight for an expectant world audience. The stages for this act had been chosen, it was true—

Fort Myer and somewhere in France—but there were many preliminary tasks required, here in Kitty Hawk and at Dayton, to prepare for the world debut of one of the greatest pageants the world would ever see.

Wilbur just needed to make sure that the preparatory tests and flights were conducted without distraction or hindrance. And these had to be accomplished in a hurry because both France and Washington were calling, and there was little time to prepare. So Wilbur looked across the sandy flats next to Big Kill Devil Hill from his vantage point at the lifesaving station, itching to get underway, but forever wary lest any uninvited guests should appear to interrupt their progress.

On April 15 Wilbur spied what appeared to be a stranger loitering around the flying camp. It turned out to be the Wrights' mechanic, Charles Furnas, whose arrival was much earlier than Wilbur expected or wanted. There was little for him to do and no place for him to sleep. Rather than have Orville there as well with no flying to be done nor a place to lay his head, Wilbur telegraphed his brother not to come for another week, at least. Captain Ward noted in the Kill Devil Hills log for the eighteenth, "Mr Wilber Wright of Dayton Ohio has bin staying at the Station nights this week." On the twentieth he noticed that their barrel of gasoline was leaking—almost half gone. It had been recklessly thrown from Midgett's boat and punctured. Sitting in the sun, the precious fuel to propel powered flight was quickly evaporating.[4]

According to the original plan, Wilbur and Orville shipped their 1905 plane from Dayton on April 4. After Wilbur departed, Orville sent the rest of their equipment on the tenth. On Wilbur's revised schedule, Orville was to depart Dayton on the twenty-first. By that time Wilbur hoped to have the plane already in camp with the new shed done and to be in the process of assembling the machine for flights upon Orville's arrival. But as it turned out, it took Orville three days to get from Dayton to Elizabeth City, and he arrived there the same day as all of their freight shipments. He thus supervised the transportation of the plane, tools, and himself across the Albemarle Sound to Kitty Hawk on the twenty-fifth. Fortunately, it happened that the new shed was ready that same day, and the Dayton crew of Wilbur, Orville, and Charlie Furnas moved into the camp—the place where the era of worldwide flight would momentarily be launched.

Although their new quarters, filled with boxes of equipment, were still quite cluttered and cramped, Wilbur and Orville began to receive a string of visitors on April 26, 1908, the day after they moved in. Captain Ward and Bob Wescott came calling from the lifesaving station and George Baum rode his horse down from Kitty Hawk. Already Captain Midgett and his sons Spencer and Truxton had delivered lumber, gasoline, and hardware on horse-drawn carts. Augustus Harris and Oliver O'Neal, nearby Outer Bankers, had been helping with the carpentry over the past week, and their old friend Bill Tate, the former postmaster of Kitty Hawk, had helped them get things organized. Wilbur, of course, had already encountered John T. Daniels in Elizabeth City. He also had visited some of their old friends in Kitty Hawk and sat chewing the fat—but only on the Sabbath—on several front porches there. While there, he also stopped by the Kitty Hawk Life Saving Station to say hello to the lifesavers before heading back down the sandy pathway to Kill Devil Hills.

Wilbur had spent almost two weeks rubbing shoulders and eating grub with the men at Kill Devil Hills. It had been a veritable two-week homecoming for the Wright brothers with a host of Outer Bankers who not only admired them, but also were endlessly curious about what they would be doing in Kitty Hawk this time. The Wright brothers had already achieved a measure of world fame, but their international renown was nothing compared with their celebrity in and around the Outer Banks of North Carolina.

Since early April, the local band of Outer Bankers had been accustomed to Wilbur's presence. They had also met Charlie Furnas for the first time. And, finally, they were able to greet the very friendly and agreeable Orville upon his return. But they were interested in a lot more than any new engineering marvels the Wrights might be planning to introduce at Kitty Hawk. Their principal goal was to gain enough basic information about the Wrights' current activities to able to swagger around the Outer Banks and practice their homegrown form of braggadocio.

Whether at the lifesaving stations, among fishing boats moored at Collington Island, in Kitty Hawk Bay, and at Manteo harbor, or in the hardware and tackle shops where they crossed paths with other locals, these men yearned to have news to spread and stories to tell. In such places they could serve as authorities on what the Wright brothers were doing this time, describe the enormous shipments of freight coming over from Elizabeth City, and give eyewitness accounts of the Wrights' grand plans. Having inside information about such large and interesting activities as those of the visiting Wrights was one of the choicest morsels of swagger anyone on the Outer Banks could ever have. Nothing could be of greater interest—except, of course, a torrential nor'easter or the wreck of a passenger ship anywhere between Cape Hatteras to the south and Cape Henry above the Virginia border to the north.

In fact, the Outer Banks of North Carolina were already abuzz with a good dose of Wright brothers mania by the time Orville arrived. It had been kindled barely three weeks earlier when Wilbur Wright sent a letter out of the blue to Bill Tate saying that he and Orville were headed to the coast. Then came Wilbur, the building materials for a new camp, Furnas, and finally Orville. The huge boxes and crates of tools, hardware, and airplane parts appeared with Orville. While the Wright brothers might not exactly have been household names around America and the world, their names were definitely on the lips of Outer Bankers in April 1908.

Besides, almost any topic other than fishing, storms, humid nights, and mosquitoes was welcome news to break the humdrum of coastal life. The locals who previously had been privileged to see the Wright brothers up close were already in a grand position to transmit Wright stories—true, embellished, or entirely fabricated—from minds that had been imagining for years what it must be like to fly. These people saw flight among gulls, terns, and eagles every day. And they were adept at sailing across shallow sounds and taking their rigs into the sea. But not until the Wrights came along had they seen grown men trying to act like birds.

The lifesavers had been instrumental in sending forth exaggerated stories about the Wright brothers' exploits—somewhat haphazardly—in 1903. But in 1908 they were much more prepared to serve as the mediators of Wright news stories. Captain Jesse L. Ward, Keeper of the Kill Devil Hills Station in 1908, gladly welcomed Wilbur as a celebrated temporary lodger at the station when he arrived there on Friday, April 10. Captain Ward had been at the Kill Devil Hills Station since 1899 and had been the Keeper since 1901. He had thus observed every Wright maneuver at Big Kill Devil from the brothers' first venture there in 1900. As one of the first locals to acquire a gas launch, he had also ferried the brothers when needed to and from Manteo.[5]

Also at the Kill Devil Hills Station in 1908 were three other veterans who were well known to the brothers and who had been on hand and of assistance to them on the two occasions in December 1903 when they had previously attempted their first powered flights. These were Willie St. Clair Dough—one of the five observers of the first powered flight—Benjamin W. (Uncle Benny) O'Neal, and Robert L. Wescott. The other regular members of the 1908 Kill Devil lifesaving crew were William Weatherington Midgett, Willis Tillet, and William Otis Twiford. Of the seven regulars at Kill Devil Hills in 1908 two had family homes in Manteo or on Roanoke Island (Dough and Wescott). Others had their own gas launches and made regular runs to Manteo (O'Neal and Midgett)—often to fetch materials needed by the Wrights.

Since Wilbur took all of his meals at the station, Ward and his regular crew had plenty of time to query the elder brother about past exploits and present plans. With the arrival of Charlie Furnas on April 15, the lifesavers had more and perhaps better fresh meat to prey upon. They shared much more in common with the young mechanic than they did with either of the reserved brothers. Both Wilbur and Furnas kept on eating and sleeping at the station for another ten days—plenty of time for camaraderie to develop from the experience of shared encampment. Indeed, on April 13 one of the lifesavers, Wescott, consulted with Wilbur on the design of his homemade perpetual motion machine. According to Wilbur, "he did not explain its nature except that it had to do with the boiler or generator of the gas or medium rather than the engine." It seemed to Wilbur to be "an ordinary steam engine." But Wescott argued that "it will practically eliminate the necessity of fuel or at least reduce the quantity to insignificant proportions."[6]

And when the Wrights and Furnas moved into the nearly complete camp building upon Orville's arrival on April 25, the daily connections between the lifesaving station and the aerial camp continued. Wescott delivered Wilbur's heavy trunk to the new camp on April 24. On April 26 Ward and Wescott made a lengthy visit to the newly completed camp. On April 30 the brothers asked Midgett to make a trip to Manteo to fetch a can of cylinder oil. When the brothers needed help getting their heavy flying machine on its starting track or to bring it back from distant landing spots, Dough, O'Neal, and Tillett were on hand to help with the lifting and hauling. They did not bother to take time off from lifesaving duty to provide this assistance. Lifting an airplane, after all, was not all that different from maneuvering a lifesaving boat. Also, when there were no assigned tasks for the lifesavers, given the proximity of the Wright camp to the station, they were almost always available, eager and waiting for any invitation to assist.[7] Every moment of interchange with the brothers—listening to their banter and observing their operations—provided grist for both the imagination and the tongues of the lifesavers.

Wilbur, Orville, and Charlie Furnas worked from April 27–29 to reassemble the 1905 powered flyer, stitching and sewing the fabric surfaces for wing, elevator, and tail surfaces, and oiling up engine parts. But Kitty Hawkers and lifesavers were already four weeks into spreading rumors on the subject of what was about to happen at Kill Devil Hills. Not only were they talking among themselves, but their rumors also were percolating and spreading abroad to city and state news centers in North Carolina and Virginia. Someone among the Outer Bankers, in fact, sent a letter to the state capital in Raleigh alerting Carolinians to the Wright brothers' plans. Received from Manteo on April 29 at the Raleigh office of the *Charlotte Observer*, the letter brought "news of a very interesting experiment in progress on the sea beach at Nags Head." The next day the Charlotte newspaper published the first article on the Wrights' new activities in North Carolina and surmised:

> Very naturally there are plenty of people who desire to watch these experiments in order to see what the secrets of the design are, and very naturally the Wrights want a place far from the crowds. Some years ago when a flight was made from Nags Head news of it got out and telegrams poured in. The people in that section naturally take much interest in the new machine and in the experiments generally and they are aiding the Wrights in every way possible.[8]

As of April 30, therefore, the presence of the brothers on the Outer Banks was already well known, and their hopes for anonymity and solitude in those parts had already been compromised.

And yet what happened over the next three days is almost inexplicable unless one understands that the Wright brothers, far from being in the isolated wilderness they desired, were actually operating in a highly porous environment. It is instructive to compare and contrast what the Wrights were doing on those days with what was published abroad about their activities. On April 30 Wilbur recorded in his diary that he and Orville "spent the day on track, front rudder framing & seat fittings & radiators." No flight tests were conducted. On May 1 they did almost exactly the same. In fact, no flight tests were possible because the wind reached speeds of 55 or 60 miles per hour, creating a severe wind chill. Wrote Wilbur: "The strong draft through the building went through our blankets also and nearly froze us." While the winds died down on May 2, the work routine was much the same. They "spent the day on actuating devices, &c. As this is all new work it takes much time. Charley worked most of the day on track and finished up a dozen rails each about 14 ft. long."[9]

But on those same days newspapers from Norfolk and northward were filled with banner headlines that the Wrights were flying at will up and down the coast and were also making flights far out over the Atlantic. The *New York Herald* of May 1 said they flew two miles distant on April 30.[10] The Norfolk *Virginian-Pilot* of May 2, in a story filed the day before, claimed that the brothers had flown ten miles out to sea on April 27–29. That particular news report went much further in its extravagant details. Their flights were a total of twenty miles in length; their plane was capable of carrying a dozen passengers; and the craft was able to circle under complete control and land wherever the pilot desired or where the brother who remained on earth signaled for a landing. Indeed, "the life-savers at Nag's Head watched the peculiar shaped thing sail away in the distance until it resembled only a black speck on the horizon, like some bird that inhabits the seashore in search of food for itself and [its] young."[11]

The news reports not only erred in reporting that flights had occurred, but also in characterizing any flights that ever had or would occur at Kitty Hawk for many years into the future. The extravagance was such that the reports could not have been written by any observer of actual flights, but could only have been written by someone with a vivid imagination. The stories were so absurd that the Wrights, when they read them, could only laugh at the wild exaggerations. And given the brothers' complete distrust of the press, the articles reinforced their attitude that working reporters were not to be trusted to report anything about flight either fairly or accurately.

But if one reads the news reports circulated prior to the Wrights' actual flights, these brief sagas have certain characteristics that could only have been conceived by captains of fishing boats—not by either flyers or observers of flight. Setting aside for the moment the fact that the language of flight as of May 1908 was still in the process of being invented and that observers of flight at the time were struggling to find the terms to describe what they saw, the fabricated first stories of Wright flights emanating from Kitty Hawk could only have come from individuals familiar with the sea—most plausibly, a special set of fishermen who also happened to be lifesavers.

The first story to be sent abroad had a dateline of May 1, 1908, and was posted at Manteo, North Carolina. Published in the *Virginian-Pilot* at Norfolk the following day, the story bristled with vague allusions to astonishing flights by the Wrights. But it was very hard to find any facts in the story. The titles and subtitle appearing with the article made great claims:

WRIGHT BROTHERS SAIL OVER LAND AND SEA WITH AEROPLANE
Daring Aeronauts from Ohio Master the Air and Brave Dangers of the Deep to Show World Their Invention
FLIGHT SUCCESSFUL IN EVERY PARTICULAR

In the text of the article the pilots are given the names of John and Wilbur Wright. It is said that they flew ten miles out to sea. In addition, the plane covered twenty miles over land; it took off and flew under perfect control, sailing above the trees in the area. Both of the brothers jumped on the plane and brought it to a hovering position at the outset of the flight and just before landing. The plane's flight resembled that of a giant bird of prey: "It sailed around the spot from which it made its flight like some carrion bird, locating the exact spot of the thing on which it would prey, and then slowly but surely dropped down." Also, this was said to be only the first plane under construction in the Wright brothers' shed. A second plane, which was already in the process of being assembled, was designed to carry a dozen passengers.[12]

In addition to these imprecise descriptions of the flight, the author went on to use some of the terminology he knew well to describe the plane and its pilots. The pilots steered "their aerial navigator back to terra firma as easily as a harbor captain steers the ordinary little tug boat." Over land the plane flew at "a height not more than six feet from the earth and sailed along as peacefully as a tug boat in sheltered harbor." On the day the plane headed out to sea it had been slightly modified for the purpose: "There was something in its center that resembled the bridge of a ship, on which the captain usually stands and signals the engine room when coming into port. Into this bridge, both of the daring men jumped and started on the trip to sea." The author of the fantastic article definitely knew his nautical terms. But he seemed to be at a loss for words or concepts pertaining to airplanes or even airships.

The author's distinctive point of view is revealed in several passages. First of all he or she saw things locally: "Newspapers up North have been waiting almost with breathless anxiety for some tidings of the results of their experiments." But the source of information about the Wright brothers' doings was even more particular as the writer revealed that his information came directly from the Wright camp: "Up to last night not a word had gone out from the camp of the experimenters, which is as closely guarded as the cell of a condemned murderer." The informant, moreover, even told his story from the point of view of the ever-vigilant lifesavers. When the Wright plane headed out to sea, he wrote: "From the shore the lifesavers at Nag's Head watched the peculiar shaped thing sail away in the distance until it resembled only a black speck on the horizon." But just in case the erstwhile flyers might experience difficulties in the "angry waters below them, the brave men who guard the coast prepared to launch their life boats and pull in the direction of the thing in the air." But any thoughts of a rescue operation were set aside when the plane, "magnified through the glass of the captain of the life-saving station, was seen to turn and make for the shore."[13]

What was the source of this jumble of fiction and fantasy? There was no newspaper in Manteo at the time. The closest papers were across the Albemarle Sound in Elizabeth City. There were no reporters living in the area and no stringers floating about submitting articles for publication in national newspapers. At that point, there was no journalist on assignment in the field investigating what was happening in the Wright camp. Yet, someone had to have access to and understand the mustachioed and swaggering lifesavers who went forth from Kill Devil Hills. This someone was in a position to hear the lifesavers as they fabricated tall tales about what they thought the Wrights were about to do, just as they bragged about their own fishing expeditions or their frightening, gallant rescues at sea.

The Kill Devil Hills Life Saving Station with its suddenly self-important men was the seedbed for the rumors that got spread abroad and that got converted into sensational stories. At the same time the Wrights and Furnas moved into their camp on April 25, Captain Jesse Ward learned that the big bosses of the Life Saving Service were about to descend upon the Kill Devil Hills Station for a periodic inspection. The inspection was scheduled for April 27. Thus on Sunday, April 26, Captain Ward and surfman Wescott sauntered over to the Wright camp ostensibly for a Sabbath Day visit—the kind where you put your feet up and, in Carolina parlance, chew the fat. It was, in fact, an intelligence-gathering enterprise so that Ward and his men could explain to the inspectors the following day how they were not only ready to save lives, but that they also were, in fact, at the moment engaged in furthering the causes of science, engineering, and humanity. No other lifesavers on earth could claim that they were being called upon to provide such a unique service to mankind.[14]

Fully staunched with the latest intelligence from the Wright camp, Captain Ward and his men were quite ready for their inspection on the twenty-seventh. At 2 P.M. Lieutenant C. S. Craig and Superintendent R. H. Morgan arrived at the station. According to Captain Ward's report for the day, the inspection proceeded as follows: "Inspected the Station and all material. Drilled the Crew in use of all material and Left the station at 4 PM for Nags Head Station." Although the visit was brief and the Wrights at the time were in their camp repairing "a number of [airplane] ribs broken & strained in shipping and hauling" and beginning to sew together parts of the plane, the inspector's call was long enough for the lifesavers at Kill Devil Hills to transform their own perceptions and claims of importance into third-hand information. When the inspectors left for Nags Head they were primed to transform third-hand information into fourth-hand ideas, and so on through the oral communication channels of the system of lifesaving stations. When Wilbur made an innocent visit to the station that evening to pick up "our brazing torch & a burner for [our] oven," the stories of the Wright brothers' imminent feats had already been spread abroad into the lifesaving world.[15]

In that the first extravagant articles that emanated from the Outer Banks on the activities of the Wright brothers referred to the observations and experiences of the lifesavers at Nags Head and not at Kill Devil Hills, the system of third and fourth handing of information through the lifesaving stations seems to have been at play. As the Life Saving Service inspectors moved southward, each lifesaver was turned into a sieve for the broadcast of what the Wrights intended to be confidential information when they interacted with the men at Kill Devil Hills. What was actually happening at Kill Devil Hills was thus reported as "news of a very interesting experiment in progress on the sea beach at Nags Head." And instead of referring to the experiences of the men at Kill Devil Hills, the first news stories claimed that "the life-savers at Nag's Head watched the peculiar shaped thing sail away in the distance until it resembled only a black speck on the horizon."[16]

The swaggering stories continued for another several days prior to the arrival of an outside reportorial voice on the scene. The *Virginian-Pilot* at Norfolk, which had published the original article, continued for a time to run the wonderfully creative stories—coming from the lifesavers, without a doubt. In a story posted on May 2 and published on the third, the *Pilot* reported that:

> The remarkable sea trip of the two inventors is looked upon as the most phenomenal feat ever accomplished by aeronauts in any part of the world. It is said that the French government has offered the Wright brothers $250,000 for their

invention, but the inventors being Americans, prefer to sell their invention to their own country, and are holding out for more money.

In addition to these rumors, the paper also speculated on what type of power was being used by the Wrights in their new plane. Although it was presumed that the plane was propelled by a gasoline engine, "just what power is used is known only to themselves."[17]

The sensational articles in the *New York Herald* and the *Virginian-Pilot* of May 1 and 2, almost certainly emanating from information supplied by big-talking life-savers from one or more or of the area stations, coincided with another news item that appeared across the Atlantic, in France, that bore directly on what the Wright brothers might be doing at Kitty Hawk. On May 1, when the sensational stories about the Wright brothers began arriving from Manteo, the semiofficial French aviation magazine *L'Aerophile* published a set of drawings of the Wright flying machine that the brothers had filed in their application for a French patent on November 18, 1907—the same day Orville watched Henri Farman's attempted flights at Issy-les-Moulineaux near Paris. The government of France moved quickly to issue three exclusive patents to the Wrights for the flying machine, and the official patent document was dated January 27, 1908. It would be another three months before the normally adept and comprehensive *L'Aerophile* picked up the information and published its article.[18]

It was, indeed, the simultaneous appearance of the *L'Aerophile* article and the outlandish news reports from North Carolina on May 1 and 2 that ignited a sensational new chapter in the history of flight both in Europe and in the United States. The *New York Herald*, which in 1908 considered itself to be the newspaper of record in Europe and in the United States on matters pertaining to flight, immediately picked up the *L'Aerophile* article at the *Herald*'s Paris offices and moved into action. That same day, the *Herald* sent a telegram to the weather bureau in Manteo, North Carolina, seeking information on what the Wrights were doing at nearby Kitty Hawk. This inquiry resulted in a brief article in the *Herald* bearing the date of May 1, which was listed as a "Special Dispatch to the Herald." On the same day the *Herald* also initiated contact with the *Virginian-Pilot*, setting a domino effect into action. Since the *Pilot* was the newspaper of record for the Outer Banks of North Carolina at the time, and since it proudly claimed to have published the first account of the Wrights' historic flight of December 17, 1903, it was only logical that its editor and reporters should already be familiar with the Wright brothers' activities in the area.

It is probable that the inquiries of the *New York Herald* innocently unleashed the instant tale-telling campaign among the lifesavers and fishermen around Manteo and Kill Devil Hills. At least this seems apparent from a notation in the Wright brothers' diary of May 2, where Wilbur Wright wrote:

> The N.Y. *Herald* has telegraphed the Weather Bureau operator at Manteo for information regarding us. Mr. Dosher also telephoned the K.[ill] D.[evil] Station today for information. He evidently had been asked by some paper to get news.[19]

This was the same Joseph J. Dosher who had been the weather station operator at Kitty Hawk when the Wright brothers accomplished their historic flight in 1903. It was he who had supplied the essential information that year used by the *Virginian-Pilot* to write its exclusive article covering the Wrights' first powered flight. Although he had moved away from the area when the Kitty Hawk Weather Station had been closed in 1904 (according to Wilbur "300 miles north of here"), he still had many contacts among the residents of Kitty Hawk and the lifesavers at Kill Devil Hills. He was also known personally and trusted enormously by Wilbur and Orville Wright.

When the U.S. Weather Bureau closed the Kitty Hawk Weather Station in 1904, the office was transferred to Manteo and the operations of the station there were taken over by one Alpheus W. Drinkwater, who was in the process of becoming a colorful and legendary local figure. One is driven to conclude that both the *Herald* telegram to Manteo and the Dosher call to the Kill Devil Hills Life Saving Station ended up in the hands of this same Drinkwater. Although he later denied sending out information on the Wrights to the *New York Herald* or to anyone else at this time, a certain cat-and-mouse deceitfulness was one of the major ingredients of his special persona.

And he savored every moment of it. Indeed, the fingerprints of Drinkwater's yarn-spinning hands are visible all over the curious and ill-founded stories that bore the Manteo dateline before, during, and after the arrival of fully capable and competent members of the working press. He was perversely attracted to the stories of the Wright brothers on the Outer Banks of North Carolina and later thrived on claiming a lifelong association with the Wrights.

Drinkwater was, in fact, a curious and troublesome figure in the history of the dissemination of information about the Wright brothers' activities in North Carolina. While he was known to the brothers because of his position as the weather station manager and telegraph operator in Manteo, he never directly befriended them and was later obliquely ridiculed by Orville Wright for his claims of friendship. For many years he led local folk to believe that he had been the source of information on the Wrights' first powered flight in 1903 and that he enjoyed a special relationship with the Wrights. Since he outlived all of the other locals who knew the Wright brothers and who had been their local contacts, Drinkwater was able to enjoy a largely self-fabricated measure of local veneration that he did not necessarily deserve.

Whatever his merits or special pleasures, Drinkwater ran the only semipublic telegraph office in the Outer Banks area in 1908 from the U.S. Weather Station in Manteo. And he definitely knew how to siphon off the stories told by the lifesavers from Kill Devil Hills and Nags Head. Collecting the details of these stories was easy, since some of the lifesavers and members of their families ferried almost daily to Manteo for supplies, mail, and information. Plus, many of the lifesavers were descended from families in and around Manteo and on Roanoke Island. Drinkwater could easily gather up second- and third-hand information from these families and friends. Since the lifesavers came home on their off-duty days, it was easy for Drinkwater to soak up any morsels of the stories they told. So long as he was the principal source of information about the Wrights, he could unfold the stories of the brothers' travails any way he wished, with no one to check either the authenticity or accuracy of his tales.

But Drinkwater, at this crucial moment on May 1, 1908, had another ally who could provide him with a variety of savory morsels that could be used to spice his creative tales. His comrade-in-arms was almost assuredly none other than Captain Jesse Ward. Captain Ward made a sudden and inexplicable disappearance from the Kill Devil Hills Station at 2 A.M. on the morning of May 1—an unheard of hour for anyone to take leave from a lifesaving station. His departure was so out of the ordinary that it bears further analysis.[20]

It was quite normal for one or another lifesaver at the Kill Devil Hills Station to have a day off during the week. Indeed, the daily logs of the Kill Devil Hills Station show that one of the lifesavers was on leave virtually every day of the week. Normally the lifesaver's day off would begin around 11 A.M. or at 12 noon. The precise time coincided with the return of the surfman who was on leave the prior day. Occasionally, due to illness, funerals, or court duty, a lifesaver might be gone for a number of days. But no matter which day or the number of days of leave authorized, it was the duty of the station's keeper to appoint a substitute.[21]

According to the May 1, 1908, Kill Devil Hills Station log—and in a relative slap-dash hand—where Captain Ward was required to list the "Member of Crew Absent (Including Keeper)" he wrote "Keeper." In the column for the "Exact Period of Absence," he wrote "Left at 2 am." In the column for "Cause of Absence," he indicated "Liberty." And in the last column where he was required to list "Name of Substitute," he left a blank. Very unusual. In the report for May 2—written in a different hand—the "Exact Period of Absence" was listed as "3 Days" and "Liberty" was changed to "Leave." W. T. Tillett was on that day listed as his substitute. The same information was listed on the logs for May 3 and 4. The log for May 5—finally again in Ward's hand—stated, "Keeper returned to duty at 8 pm."[22]

Neither Ward nor the other lifesavers had to account for their whereabouts (at least in the official records) when they were at "liberty" or on "leave." However, given all of the celebrated international events about to happen at the very back door of the Kill Devil Hills Lifesaving Station, it is unthinkable that Ward would have decided to take an impromptu vacation to rest up or to go fishing. Given the fact that in later years he liked to proclaim that the Wright brothers would not have been able to fly without the day-to-day assistance of the lifesavers, it is more likely that he suddenly went on leave so that he could instead get even more deeply engrossed in the making of flight history. The only good explanation for his 2 A.M. departure from his keeper's post is that he wanted to be free to waft to and fro from Kill Devil Hills to Manteo so that he could ferry the latest information from Big Kill Devil to the county seat and to meet and greet any celebrity reporters who might arrive on the scene to get the true story on the Wright brothers. And, of course, in the meantime, to consult with Alpheus Drinkwater on sending out the latest Wright brothers news from the only available telegraph office in the vicinity.

Then, too, Captain Ward must have been chagrined to learn that the first stories about the Wright brothers' activities suggested that they were being observed by lifesavers at Nags Head, not at Kill Devil Hills. He was surely also upset that stories about flights already made could be going abroad when he had been able to see firsthand out the back window of his station that the Wright brothers were still fumbling with engines and wings and were not at all ready to fly. And since he and his friend Alpheus Drinkwater had received simultaneous requests at each of their stations, perhaps the two of them could combine their energies and create a local Wright brothers news bureau.

Drinkwater had been shoveling out one sensational story after another to whoever would accept his telegraph messages until he was challenged by experienced news professionals far away from North Carolina. Ward's presence in Manteo beginning on May 1 surely helped Drinkwater respond to a demand for more precise information from the Outer Banks and to speculate more accurately on what kinds of flights were about to take place and when they might happen. Indeed, on May 3 the *New York Herald* was already trying to cover its tracks with a brief article that sought to correct, or at least downplay, the misinformation it had previously published, which had been supplied by Drinkwater:

> The first real test of the Wright brothers' aeroplane, to be made at Nags Head, N.C., by its inventors for the government, is expected early next week, according to the information received here to-night from the isolated spot where the flying machine is being made ready. It is positively denied today that any remarkable flights had been made with the machine such as were described in a report sent out yesterday.[23]

This cautionary note was followed in an article filed on the same date but published on May 4 by the London *Daily Mail*—another newspaper that prided itself on reporting major activities and advances in the realm of flight at the time.[24] From that point on, although Drinkwater's tell-tale voice could be detected in many further efforts to escalate the activities and achievements of the Wrights, the world's press establishment at the time realized that they must go to greater lengths to get the facts about what was really happening in May 1908 at Kitty Hawk.

Flight, the possibilities of flight, and the potential consequences of flight had left an indelible mark on the minds of adventurers, governments, military planners, and the press throughout the world by the spring of 1908. The subject, the risks, and the potentialities were too earthshattering, too important to be left in the hands of an imaginative telegraph operator—especially one who was getting his kicks out of embellishing the stories of fishermen and lifesavers being sent to far-off city slickers who, from an Outer Banker's point of view, probably knew no better anyway.

If Alpheus Drinkwater's early embellishments to the tales of the lifesavers served no other purpose, they alerted the world's press to the location of the Wright brothers' new flight experiments, and to the possibility that news reporters—if they could get there in time—might have an opportunity to actually see a Wright brothers airplane in flight. The world press knew and had often reported that the Wrights had signed contracts to produce planes that would soon have to be publicly tested in both Europe and America. If newspapermen and magazine writers were able to move quickly, it might just be possible for them to get a preview of the show that would be forthcoming later in the year. Given the frenetic competition among publishers to sell newspapers on every street corner and among editors to produce banner headlines on breaking news stories, getting the first crack at the Wright brothers' story commanded the attention of the editors in chief of every major news outlet. They immediately dispatched their most aggressive, audacious, and sure-footed reporters to the Outer Banks, warning them to mind the clock to meet every deadline for a news morsel that their paper would be the first to print.

Despite the remoteness of Kitty Hawk and Kill Devil Hills and all of the diffi-culties of getting there, over the next five to seven days reporters and photogra-phers from some of the world's most competitive publications descended on the place. Among those who made the trip and ended up filing important stories about the Wright brothers' 1908 flights at Kitty Hawk were some of the most excellent practitioners of contemporary journalism. The *New York Herald*, one of the most ruthlessly competitive papers of the day, sent Byron Newton, one of the true au-thorities on aerial matters at that moment. Gilson Gardiner of the *Chicago Journal* and William Hoster of the *New York American* wrote graphic and compelling de-scriptions of any event they happened to witness. P. H. McGowan from the Lon-don *Daily Mail* had been covering would-be aeronauts for nearly two decades in both Europe and the United States. *Collier's Weekly*, rapidly establishing itself as America's first weekly magazine of photojournalism, put two reporters on this very high-profile story—Arthur Ruhl, a master storyteller, and James H. Hare, an ex-pert photojournalist.[25]

These luminaries of the press ran into other eager reporters from regional and local newspapers who would give their own renditions of what the Wright broth-ers were doing at Kitty Hawk. Some of these wrote stories that would be published abroad, giving them credit in a byline. Others saw the reports over which they la-bored eventually published in faraway places denominating them as "special cor-respondents" or with no attribution whatsoever. Such outlets included the Associated Press, the *Charlotte Observer*, the *New York World*, and other newspapers across North Carolina and elsewhere.

With such journalistic firepower represented in the cast of globetrotting re-porters who descended on North Carolina, it was almost certain that the Wright brothers would no longer be able to avoid the observation and critical coverage of the world's press. While the brothers had flown under the cloak of secrecy in prior years at Kitty Hawk and in the quiet confines of their hometown Dayton, the truth of their flying prowess would now be observed and reported once and for all.

Although there were among those who were assigned to cover events at Kitty Hawk a number of well-seasoned reporters—veterans of wars in Europe, Japan, Russia, and South Africa—going to Kitty Hawk was not the same as frequenting one of the popular resorts of the day on Long Island, at the Jersey Shore, or even the nearby Carolina resort at Nags Head. Getting to Kitty Hawk required the same creativity and dexterity on the part of the journalists that had been required of the Wright brothers in their own trips between 1900 and 1908. But by then, the center of activity in that part of North Carolina was slowly shifting from Elizabeth City and even Kitty Hawk to Manteo on Roanoke Island.

With a written history going back to the days of Walter Raleigh and the first English settlement in America and oral traditions earlier than that, Manteo had become the governmental seat of Dare County—a far-flung Carolina county that included most of the northern Outer Banks. Sporting a spiffy new brick court-house completed in 1904, the only telegraph operation in the area, and daily steamboat arrivals from Elizabeth City, Nags Head, New Bern, and often Norfolk, Manteo was also becoming something of a business and tourist center. It was a jumping-off point for sport hunters and fishermen coming from northeastern cities and for tourists heading out to the Outer Banks from the Carolina mainland.[26]

To support all of this bustling activity at the turn of the century, Manteo enjoyed the emergence of a number of quite gracious hotels—among them the Carolinian, the Roanoke, and the Tranquil House. The most popular by far—at least for folk who looked for quality hotel accommodation—was the Tranquil House. Located adjacent to the waterfront where one could hear the voices of arriving visitors and fishermen alike and could easily walk to a great variety of shops for razors, laundry, or boxed candies, the Tranquil House was both a popular hotel and a gathering place for folk with a cultural or informational bent. If you needed information, the Evanses, who ran the hotel, were one of the most connected families on the Outer Banks. With a wide front porch well stocked with rocking chairs to facilitate both people-watching and conversation and an inside drawing room for coffee, smoking, and spitting, the Tranquil had become the hostelry of choice by that time. Its rooms were clean and comfortable. Its food was said to be good. And if you happened to need a picnic basket for a day-long outing, that could be handled as well.

Virtually all of the reporters from cities big and small—New York, London, and Chicago, and Norfolk and Charlotte—ended up at the Tranquil. The Wright brothers also used the hotel whenever they needed to stay over in Manteo, and they recommended it to others who were visiting their camps at Kill Devil Hills. Being on good terms with the owners of the Tranquil, the brothers were also given free access to the hotel register so that they could do a little investigative reporting of their own to find out who was in the area and might be on a mission to check out their activities.

While the scribes were gathering, Wilbur and Orville went on with their preparations for flight—albeit with the awareness that there was a growing buzz around the world concerning their activities. On May 1, when the press invasion began, they suffered through a storm with winds of 55 to 60 miles an hour. It was so cold, in fact, that Wilbur thought they would surely freeze. So they spent the day inside their shed with their gas heater at full tilt working on the "front rudder & actuating devices, and fitted radiators" while also figuring out how to make a lamp out of a gas burner. They did much the same on May 2 when Wilbur commented in his diary, "As this is all new work it takes much time."[27]

Sunday, May 3, was, of course, a day of rest. The Wrights had guests over and visited the Kill Devil Hills Station. Their sister, Katharine, kept them posted on what was happening in the press via a telegram with the information, Wilbur noted, that "the newspapers had published a report of a flight by us." Without noting further the increasing press awareness, Wilbur perhaps unconsciously registered his opinion of all newspapers when he put in his diary that day: "We got some newspapers to stuff our beds to keep the wind out." On Monday, May 4, a workday, they prepared for their first engine tests and actually ran the engine for intervals of three to fifteen minutes. But Wilbur also recorded that they received "a telegram from Mr. Alexander" that day, congratulating them on their first flights. Although at the moment they were cut off from access to daily newspapers, Wilbur smartly noted the importance of this message from Patrick Alexander—the British aviation promoter who had inadvertently missed their historic flights in 1903: "This would indicate that the [erroneous] report has been cabled abroad." Thus, although the reports on their flights up to that time were total fabrications, the world was definitely taking note of their presence at Kitty Hawk.[28]

On Tuesday, May 5, the Wrights, in the midst of a drizzling rain, took their machine out of the shed and tested the operational capabilities of their new control system. At about noon, as they were doing these ground tests, the realities of their new relationship with the world press suddenly hit home. Wilbur reported the arrival of the first of the platoon of reporters—D. Bruce Salley, a freelance writer from Norfolk who wrote primarily for the *Norfolk Landmark* and the *Virginian-Pilot*, but also took on assignments for other publications as well. According to Wilbur, "he had been instructed by one of the New York papers to investigate the reports sent out several days ago of some sensational flights, one of which was said to have extended out over the ocean a distance of ten miles." Salley had checked into the Tranquil House the night before and had arranged for a nephew of one of the life-savers at Kill Devil Hills ("another Captain Midgett") to take him over to the Wright camp the next morning.[29]

Perhaps because Salley was practically a local boy, being from Norfolk, and because the Wrights had become quite familiar with the *Virginian-Pilot* over the years, they spoke quite openly and even revealingly with the young man. They acknowledged to Salley that the fallacious newspaper article describing sensational and entirely fictitious flights had caused them to be flooded with letters of congratulation from around the world, as well as a torrent of telegrams from newspapers wanting more information. They even told Salley that they had gotten a telegram from Katharine about the wrongheaded news stories.[30]

Based on this part of their conversation, Salley filed a brief story that same day from Manteo, in which he spoke of the onslaught of media attention approaching the brothers from around the world and also mentioned Katharine's telegram. Salley concluded this chatty article with a rather gratuitous comment of his own: "These two men are considered the most famous aeronauts in the world. They have come nearer to solving the mysteries of aerial navigation than any aeronaut or set of aeronauts in this or any other country." Certainly such a generous comment might have made the Wrights, if they had seen it immediately, more willing than ever to talk with Salley. But it appears that the Wrights, instead, spoke openly with Salley only in the hopes that he would take their comments and the information they provided and leave them in peace, hopefully not to return.

Whether the Wrights told Salley that they would be flying the next day is not clear. Even though Wednesday, May 6, was a drizzly and rainy day, the Wrights brought out their completed plane to continue trying out their new control systems and to see if they might be able to make an initial test flight. By the afternoon the weather conditions improved so much that they decided to move forward with their first attempted flight. In accordance with the wind direction, they positioned their starting track to head northwest into the wind. When the wind shifted to north-north-east, they shifted the track accordingly. With all systems go, Wilbur took off and headed into the prevailing wind at that moment for a short flight of about 1,000 feet over a span of 22 seconds.[31]

This was shorter than their fourth flight at Kitty Hawk on December 17, 1903, yet Wilbur considered it totally successful. The plane flew at a speed of about 45 miles per hour through the air and "was very much up and down as the operator (W.W.) was thinking more of the side control than of the fore-and-aft control." The landing was not pretty—sand flew everywhere as the plane crashed into the grainy turf. But Wilbur suffered no injury, and damage to the plane was minimal. Scrupulous to record every detail of their work, these few words cover the extent of the day's activities as duly filed by Wilbur Wright in his diary.

Before the day was over, Bruce Salley—working that day as a freelance stringer for a host of newspapers—wrote and filed his story on the flight. Making use of Alpheus Drinkwater's telegraph machine in Manteo, he issued several versions of his exclusive report to any news outlet that would buy it. His various drafts and revisions of the story for different newspapers remained part of the official files of the Manteo Weather Station from that day on, and are still among the historical records of the U.S. Weather Bureau today at its national information facility in Asheville, North Carolina. The fullest version of Salley's story appeared the next day, May 7, in the *Virginian-Pilot*. Shorter versions of the story were accepted by and published in the *New York Herald*, the London *Daily Mail*, and a variety of other newspapers, including the Dayton and Cincinnati newspapers in Ohio read by the Wright family members.[32]

Salley's descriptions of the day's events, however, differed greatly from the turgid, minimal, but nevertheless satisfying account given by Wilbur Wright.

According to Salley, the flight was admittedly a test to try out the Wrights' new control system and was not expected to be of either a long distance or extended duration. But the similarities ended there:

> Although only a test flight, it was successful in every respect, the machine under the perfect control of its two makers, traveling for a distance of 3,000 feet. Apparently it could have been flown a thousand times as far as easily as not. It was made to alight with ease and in perfect safety. . . .
>
> The machine was started easily from a railway about three hundred feet long. It glided rapidly along this, and when it had reached a velocity of about twenty-five miles an hour it left the track, bearing both Wilbur and Orville Wright. . . .
>
> After several preliminary tests, made in the next two or three days, an endurance test of the machine will be made, and on this test an effort will be probably made to fly the machine to Cape Henry, a distance of about seventy-five miles, and return. . . .[33]

While one might quibble with discrepancies in the reported distance of the flight, the length of the starting track, or the velocity, there are several aspects of Salley's story that he most certainly could not have written had he been an actual eyewitness.

No witness could possibly have reported that both brothers were at the controls during this preliminary and nearly aborted test flight, nor that the plane "was made to alight with ease and in perfect safety." And the notation that the initial test would be followed with "an effort . . . to fly the machine to Cape Henry . . . and return" could not have come from either the Wrights or any credible witness. These headline-making assertions and asides had no basis in fact and could only have come from the exaggerated stories of swaggering lifesavers arriving in Manteo at the end of the day on May 6—or, more likely, from the perpetually active and fertile mind of Alpheus Drinkwater. No eyewitness to the flight could have made such colossal errors of fact.

Although Captain Jesse Ward had gone back on duty at the Kill Devil Hills Station the day before, new emissaries in the form of other lifesavers went forth from the station in the direction of Manteo's news center virtually every afternoon. When Ward returned to his post on the evening of May 5, William W. Midgett began making daily water treks from the Kill Devil Hills to Manteo "to attend Court." He went to Manteo on May 5, 6, and 7, bearing information from the Wright camp. In addition to Midgett, there was a steady stream of other members of the crew who got off around noon each day and who were at liberty to carry information and stories to Manteo for use by anyone who wanted to listen. Willis Tillett was off for twenty-four hours beginning at noon on the fifth; W. O. Twiford on the sixth; and Robert Wescott on the eighth. Captain Ward had seen to it that any further information on the Wrights at least got the Kill Devil Hills part right. These members of the crew were almost duty bound to serve as well as messengers from the scene of flight.[34]

Sure enough, the most astonishing parts of Salley's story were the parts that made the headlines in the newspapers where he sold his story. The *New York Herald* described Salley's piece—again without a byline—as a "Special Despatch to the Herald." The London *Daily Mail* claimed that its story came "From Our Special Correspondent." The *Herald* headlines focused on the promised next flight: "WRIGHT BOYS PLAN 150 MILE FLIGHT—Will Test Endurance of New Aeroplane on Long Trip to Cape Henry." The *Daily Mail* headlines, by contrast, concentrated more on the nature of the plane flown: "WRIGHT BROTHERS' AEROPLANE. SUCCESSFUL FLIGHT. MACHINE DESCRIBED." But both articles contained the same precise wording of Salley's much larger article published in the *Virginian-Pilot*.

One especially odd aspect of the article in the *Daily Mail* was an opening statement written in the first person: "At Kill-Devil Hill, close to this town, to-day, I was privileged to witness the first successful test flight of the new aeroplane invented by the famous Wright Brothers [*sic*], of Dayton, Ohio." This statement was from Salley's transmittal note and was not intended to be a part of the story itself, since in any case no author was identified with the published story.

Such a story based on uncorroborated rumors seems strange for a journalist of Salley's abilities—he would later become a full-fledged card-carrying reporter for the *New York Herald*. And it does not comport with the rest of Salley's informative article, which was based entirely on the thorough interview he had conducted with the Wrights just the day before. Indeed, in the balance of his story he gave the history of the Wright brothers and flight in general in quite accurate detail. He described the plane they were flying in all of its particulars, including their new control mechanism. Moreover, he included extensive quotes that had clearly come directly from the mouths of Wilbur and Orville Wright.

In fact, the quotes he got from the brothers that day reveal some of the innocence, naïveté, and simple hopefulness the Wright brothers still felt just days before they stepped onto the precipice of international celebrity and into the cutthroat world of big business and armaments procurement. While the brothers would later argue that the airplane—as a tool of reconnaissance—could be used to end wars, they here argued that the most promising use of the airplane was as an instrument of war making and bomb dropping. Salley also got Wilbur into one of his frequent calculating modes, which set the tone of the story as he brooded on the relative fuel efficiency between airplanes and trains, the relative roles of airplanes and trains in a future transportation system, and the usefulness of the airplane as a mail carrying system. In a sense, Salley captured the calmest and clearest thinking the brothers would be able to do for many months or even years to come—for Wilbur, probably never again in his short lifetime, since he would die just four turbulent years later at the age of forty-five.

So why would Salley—on a mission to get the true story on the Wright brothers—mar his excellent journalistic efforts with patently false information? There can be only one explanation. The Wright brothers—when they granted a long interview with Salley on May 5 and poured out so much personal information, extensive data on their plane, and their fondest perspectives on the future of flight—almost assuredly on the same occasion revealed to Salley their totally schizophrenic attitudes about the press. Determined as they were to conduct their flight tests in privacy, they surely told Salley that he was not welcome to watch their flights.

Thus Salley, who was at Kitty Hawk to get his story, and having now obtained critical access to the Wrights as well as a revealing interview, was placed in a difficult position. He was torn between wanting to respect their wishes while needing to file a juicy story that, so far at least, was his and his alone to send forth into the world. For Salley, this was the chance of a lifetime. Sitting on the porch of the Tranquil House, he could look across Croatan Sound and see the Kill Devil Hills. He could imagine what the Wrights must be doing. But for what actually happened that day, he was forced to rely upon the stories of the swaggering lifesavers as his only source of firsthand information for eyewitness details about any flights that took place. And on this, of course, he—and the world, as a consequence—were led badly astray.

On the day that Salley's sensational and wrong-headed news article appeared in the *Virginian-Pilot*, the *New York Herald*, and many other newspapers to which Salley sold his story, the Wright brothers were oblivious to the furor that was beginning to build in the world beyond Kitty Hawk. Although it was a Thursday and normally a day of work for the Wrights, there had been rain overnight and also during the morning. As Wilbur wrote, "we did not take the machine out of the shed till afternoon and then only to practice the wing twisting in a wind of about 11 meters"—33 miles per hour or more—too much for the possibility of flight.[35]

But Wilbur also portended what was going to happen on the next day with a cryptic, but revealing, note in his diary: "Orville proposed to make a record flight tomorrow, having gained much experience on his patent hobbyhorse today." This was Wilbur's way of poking fun at little brother Orville, who had obviously spent much of his day sitting at the controls of the plane while it remained in the shed, pulling levers and imagining what it would be like to fly this newly configured machine when his chance would come on the following day.

Everything up to that point—all of the years of work, the tinkering and fabricating, the testing, the revising of designs, the cogitating—had been preliminaries to the day when the brothers would go public with their invention. They had climbed Big Kill Devil Hill more than a thousand times with test flying machines, they had flown a few hops in a powered machine there in 1903, and they had flown mainly short distances hundreds of times at Huffman Prairie near Dayton in 1904 and 1905. But all of that was a precursor to the day when they would show the world how well the Wright brothers—and only they—could fly. Their public demonstrations were scheduled for August 1908—some in France and some in the United States. Little did the brothers know when they went to bed on the night of May 7, 1908, however, that their every word and every move would henceforth be followed and ruthlessly reported in the world's press. It would be the last night of restful and near anonymous sleep they would ever have.

Chapter Three

MIXED MESSAGES
FROM MANTEO

Preparation for Flight, May 1908
Wilbur (tracking away) and Orville (adjusting the engine) prepare their redesigned and rebuilt 1905 flyer
for their historic flights at Kitty Hawk in 1908. As always, three Kill Devil Hills lifesavers in their warm
weather white uniforms are at the ready, both to work and to watch.

It was on May 8, 1908, that the Wright brothers' lives changed fundamentally from having relatively quiet careers of private innocence to exposure to years of public, worldly challenges, triumphs, failures, and temptations. On that day, they crossed the threshold from private beings to public figures and went from being boys from Dayton to men of the world practically overnight. One minute they were inventors on the make; the next, they were the possessors of unique achievements and valuable intellectual property wanted all over the world. One minute, they were interesting human figures; the next, they had become international celebrities.

Before May 8, 1908, hardly anyone would have cared what the Wright brothers wore to work. They looked a bit quirky in their daily attire of neatly ironed shirts, pin-striped pants, and hand-knotted ties, which they wore even when working on dirty gasoline engines. But after May 8 what they wore and how they wore it suddenly became newsworthy. Their hats, coats, and shoes became items worthy of comment in news columns. Where they went, where they stayed, what they ate, who they met, how they traveled, their manner of speaking—all of these suddenly became subjects of intense interest throughout the world. Before that day they could travel anonymously, attracting little or no attention. Soon after that day, the brothers' daily whereabouts and their activities became headlines splashed across the pages of major newspapers throughout the United States and Europe. Never again would they be able to hide from public scrutiny. Whether they liked it or not, they had moved from the realm of mere citizens who could be as quirky as they wanted into that of public figures who had to explain virtually all of their actions. Their freedom and anonymity were forever gone, and almost as if they had been elected to public office, they won celebrity—at a price.

Wilbur and Orville Wright and their mechanic Charles Furnas could not have begun the day on Friday, May 8, with greater innocence or happier anticipation. Wilbur noted in his diary the varying wind conditions at intervals throughout the day: "S.W. 5 a.m. 5 m. Forenoon 5–8 m. Afternoon 8–9 m." Perfect weather for flying. Wilbur's notes indicated the exuberance they felt: "We rose at 5 o'clock and as there seemed favorable chance of flying conditions we hastened to get breakfast and run the machine out. We were ready for the first flight about seven o'clock." With the assistance of three lifesavers from the Kill Devil Hills Station, the six men thus present were able to launch a total of eleven flights during the course of that day.[1]

At the end of each flight, the heavy plane had to be wrestled and ferried across sandy expanses back to the starting track: "We ran the machine back by its own power, but the downward pressure on the front framing, which we carried, was very exhausting." Although all of the flights were short—the longest being 2,230 feet and 59½ seconds (virtually the same as their longest flight on December 17, 1903!)—the Wrights were able to become familiar with the new control system, which was their principal immediate goal. Not only was the day thus perfect for flying, the flying done was very satisfying and considered by the Wrights to be totally successful.[2]

But among the happy events of the day for the advancement of flight, there were two incidents that brought the Wrights up short. Both events portended the massive change that was about to occur in their lives. The first happened in the afternoon after the next-to-last flight for the day—a flight by Orville of about 945 feet in 31 seconds. Wilbur noted: "Mr. Salley, the newspaperman, came over soon after this flight and interrupted experiments." Flustered by the sudden reemergence of the reporter they thought should have been back in Norfolk by then, the brothers refused to talk or to continue their tests until Salley left. When he finally departed, the flights resumed and Wilbur then had the longest flight of the day. Clearly irritated with Salley, the Wrights had reiterated their policy that they would not fly in the presence of reporters and had therefore banished the reporter from the field.[3]

The second unanticipated incident was equally a harbinger, though it did not feel as threatening as having a reporter on the flying field. Sometime during the day, one of the lifesavers from the Kill Devil Hills Station handed the brothers the transcripts of two telegrams received at the lifesaving station and addressed to them by name. Both telegrams came from the London offices of the *Daily Mail*. The transcript of the first message was similar to ones they had received from other newspapers: "London Daily Mail anxious to no [know] if you will telegraph us full description of your flight."[4]

The second message was considerably less mundane:

Wright Brothers
Kill Devil Hills, N. C.

Please accept congratulations on your successful flight.

Will you enter contest for ten thousand[d] pounds offered by Daily Mail for successful flight between London and Manchester.

Please reply

Editor Daily Mail, London

Presumably the "successful flight" referenced in both messages was the test flight of May 6 mentioned in the story from Salley already published by the *Daily Mail*. Since the Wright brothers were not interested in supplying information on their flights, they politely declined—but they were obviously flattered by the proposition of the flight contest to be performed in England. According to the transcript of their response to these two telegrams, they wrote: "Can not make definite statement now. Please mail us particulars of offer."[5]

At the end of the day on May 8, Wilbur and Orville Wright knew they had had a day of successful flights. They were satisfied that they had chased the quizzical Salley off of their flying field and that they had again declined to supply information to another inquiring newspaper. They were probably amused that they had received an invitation to enter the flight contest. But they could not entirely ignore a new level of scrutiny and inquiry that was beginning to surround them.

May 9, the second day in the transformation of the Wright brothers' lives, began unusually quietly for them. The day was clear, but the wind was too strong for flight tests. They still could have gotten the machine out to manipulate and adjust the controls, but the real reason they rested was that "as we were all [so] sore we did not get the machine out." Pushing and cajoling their plane across the sandy surfaces at Kill Devil Hills—even with the handy trucks they had developed for the purpose—was a long and tiring task. They needed a day for their muscles to recover.

But while they mended their bodies and listened to the whistling wind, their names were emblazoned across virtually every daily newspaper in America and dozens of papers in Europe. The headlines people read in far distant places were totally and utterly confusing, because two completely dissimilar stories were emanating from Manteo, North Carolina. One of them came from the pen of the same Bruce Salley who had been tracking the Wrights for the last five days. Although he did not see their first flight on May 6, he did observe most if not all of their flights two days later. His stories, which he filed as a correspondent with both the *New York Herald* and the London *Daily Mail*, reflected the fact that he was doing his homework—there were no more unfounded and uncorroborated stories such as the one he unwittingly wrote on the May 6 flight.

The version of Salley's article that appeared in the *Herald*—despite creative headlines—was presented as a special dispatch to the newspaper and was written almost as if it were an interview between Salley and the editor of the *Herald*. In the article Salley was described not as the newspaper's reporter on the scene, but as "a spectator." The story opened very somberly and without exaggeration:

> The aeroplane of the Wright Brothers was flown almost at will over the sand dunes at Kill Devil Hill to-day as the inventors continued their experiments with the machine, according to D. Bruce Salley, a spectator. He says ten or more flights were made, but as they were all for experimental purposes and not for distance they were all short, the longest of them being a mile and a half.
>
> "The new design of steering gear which the inventors are now using is not yet adjusted to the entire satisfaction of the aeronauts," says Mr. Salley. "It was to experiment with this and to make observations in the rise of the machine and its contact with the ground that the ascensions to-day were made. But short and frequent as they were the machine was always under perfect control, the ascent

being made at the will of the navigator, who would be first one of the brothers and then the other. Not once was the machine other than under absolute control. . . . At no time to-day did the machine fly more than twenty feet from the ground. . . .[6]

Despite the fact that the Wrights had chased Salley off their testing field, even they could not have quibbled with his calm and objective reporting.

The rest of Salley's report took the same balanced approach. He described the weather accurately and gave credit to the lifesavers from Kill Devil Hills for providing essential help to the brothers. According to Salley, "these [lifesavers] and one or two others, with the Wrights themselves, were the sole observers of the experiments to-day." He also corroborated his method of gathering information for the story: "The Wrights positively refuse to talk about themselves or their machine, and all that can be learned is by observation." Ultimately, Salley's conclusion about the significance of the day's flights was well reasoned: "There can be no longer any doubt about the ability of the machine to fly, and fly well."[7]

The London *Daily Mail* also made use of Salley's dispatch, without mentioning him by name, for the bulk of its coverage on the flights of May 8. However, the headlines and the lead sentences of the *Daily Mail*'s article bore no resemblance to Salley's cautious, objective tone. The key element in the headline could not have derived from his balanced writing: "FLIGHT 'ALMOST BEYOND THE RANGE OF VISION.'" Nor could the lead sentence have come from Salley: "They rose with their aeroplane high in the air, and were at 2:45 P.M. still circling almost beyond the range of vision."[8] Salley had plainly written for the *Herald* that the Wrights never got more than twenty feet off the ground.

So what was the source of this contradictory perspective on the flights of May 8? The *Daily Mail* did not simply fabricate the juicy headline. A totally different story had, in fact, been sent from Manteo on the same day that bore no resemblance to either what the Wrights said they were doing or what Salley had faithfully reported. This third version contained the same fictitious claims and creative elements as the tall tales that had been circulating from Manteo even before the Wrights had unpacked their plane. Bearing the dateline of May 8 from

Manteo, the latter article appeared in full in the *Virginian-Pilot* and in banner headlined versions in dozens of other papers around America the following day. A few of the juicy headlines attached to this version of the story reveal its picturesque nature:

3000 FEET HIGH WRIGHTS SAIL OVER OCEAN 20 MILES
TRY TO FLY TO THE CAPES DURING TODAY
THOUSANDS DAILY WITNESS FLIGHTS OF AERONAUTS.
TO BUILD LARGER AEROPLANE.

Such headlines were sure to catch the attention of editors and readers everywhere who were following the emergence of powered flight with bated breath, much as later generations would follow the international space race to put a man on the moon.[9]

The text of the story reinforced in imaginative sketches the sensational implications of the headlines:

They soared to a height of about 3,000 feet, sailed their ship smoothly and gracefully through the air, caused it to duck like a huge gull at their will, ascended and descended with the greatest ease until it appeared that the aeroplane was a living, breathing object.

The Wrights sailed up and down [the coast] and then out ten miles to sea. The ship went so far out that it appeared as a mere speck upon the horizon. Then it came with great speed toward land, sailed up in the air again and then slowly descended and settled on the sandy hill. . . .

That the Wrights are determined to guard their invention is evidenced by the well-organized guard and they have thrown a cordon around the aeroplane that will protect it from prying eyes or from people who may have evil designs. . . .

Since the Wrights have been down on the Carolina coast the villagers have flocked to the scene to witness the experiments. A majority of the spectators has been made up of the fisher folk and the members of the life-saving crew have also been interested spectators. . . .

From what could be learned it is the intention of the inventors to build a

much larger aeroplane that will accommodate about ten persons and then they

will make an attempt at an endurance test. . . .[10]

In addition to the obvious errors and exaggerations contained in these lines, the author of this story claimed that the Wright brothers' base camp was at Nags Head on the Outer Banks, some four miles south of Kill Devil Hills.

While it is difficult to pinpoint the authorship of this piece, it sounds suspiciously like a typical story straight from the mouths of swaggering lifesavers—perhaps again in an elongated story summarized by Alpheus Drinkwater. Descriptions of the Wright plane as operating like a swooping gull, looking like a speck on the horizon, and soaring to 3,000 feet are the types of fabrications generated by observant, but storytelling, lifesavers. References to the brothers cordoning off their plane from prying eyes, to fisher folk and lifesavers as the main observers, to the likelihood that the Wrights were going to whip out a new plane that would carry ten passengers are classic examples of those same surfside characters puffing up their chests and giving authoritative answers to things they actually knew almost nothing about. Whoever was the actual source of this creative spin on the Wright brothers' activities, it made for very poor objective news coverage—but it gave readers an engaging set of images to daydream on.[11]

The problem with this story, of course, was that its graphic headlines were precisely the type of items that newspapers wanted to print. The extent to which it caused consternation was noted both by the Wrights' sister, Katharine, and their father back in Dayton. Their father, an inveterate diarist, wrote in his journal on May 9: "Last evening's 'Herald,' today's 'Journal,' the 'Cin. Commercial,' the 'Cin. Enquirer,' and Dayton 'News' had alleged dispatches concerning the Wright brothers' flights, the 'Enquirer' reporting they had flown 3000 feet high, 30 miles long, and 8 miles out to sea!"[12] The following day, Orville, also concerned about the misleading headlines, wrote home, "The newspapers down in this neighborhood are printing all kinds of stories about our experiments. They have us flying to all points within 50 or sixty miles. A reporter from Norfolk has been here twice. We have not seen anything he has written."[13] But such sensational stories also added greater importance and urgency to the task of those responsible and experienced reporters who were already arriving at the Tranquil House in Manteo and who were on the verge of determining the accuracy of stories circulating across the news media everywhere about Wright flights that exceeded anything the world had ever known.

As was their wont—and since it was a Sunday—the Wright brothers and Charles Furnas took the day off on May 10. Besides, the winds would have been too strong for flying in the morning (northwest 28–33 miles per hour). Instead, they spent the day resting and walking around the area. Wilbur noted, "We took a walk up north about two miles and came back along the sound. Our camp is just about ¾ mile from the sound." They also wrote letters on Sunday. That evening Orville penned a very chatty and information-filled letter to Katharine. Among the things he commented on was the Sunday weather: "This evening would be fine for practice. There is only about 8 miles of wind. Last Sunday also was very quiet. Most of the time the wind blows from 15 to 25 miles."[14] Although they made their Sundays days of enforced rest, these fertile minds were not in relaxed mode. Both brothers played out in mental gymnastics the new kinds of flights they would initiate when the sun rose on that Monday morning.

The quietude of Sunday yielded to a Monday of activity the likes of which the Wright brothers had not known in their ten years of pursuing the problem of flight. On this day it became apparent that they were no longer alone in the world and that their every move was under the scrutiny of prying reporters. In addition to Salley, who arrived on May 4 and never actually departed from Manteo, two additional skilled and hard-driving reporters arrived in time to view the set of three flights completed by the Wrights on this date. The newcomers were Byron Newton, the distinguished writer from the *New York Herald* whose specialty was the subject of flight, and the perceptive William Hoster from the *New York American*.

The weather was ideal for flying. Both Wilbur and Orville took to the skies, and both attempted to maneuver through turns. And both of them had flights of longer than two minutes and covered distances upward of two miles. On the third flight, this one by Orville, there was a slight accident when he sought to make his turn: "In landing he touched one wing, swung round, and landed sidewise, his body breaking the aluminum steering wheels, but nothing else was injured." All three of these flights were accomplished by soon after 11:00 in the morning. But Wilbur noted in his diary, "The work of bringing the machine back over those long distances was very exhausting and we were very tired."[15]

While the brothers did not attempt to fly in the afternoon, Wilbur made a note of the activity that was beginning to take place in the woods a few hundred yards from where they were practicing their flights: "It is said that Salley, the newspaperman, spent the day in the woods over by Haman's old place." He was actually there with the two other reporters, Newton and Hoster, surveying the situation and determining the best way of covering the Wrights' activities. In the afternoon, the Wright brothers had a surprise visit from the other person, besides Salley, who was sending out stories about their flights. Not placing any particular emphasis on his appearance, Wilbur wrote matter-of-factly, "Drinkwater, the Weather Bureau operator at Manteo, came over with a Mr. Grant, said to be a Norfolk attaché of the Weather Bureau, nominally to make repairs on the telegraph line, but when they found we were not out in the afternoon they departed."[16]

Although Drinkwater made this single recorded appearance—not as a reporter, but under the guise of his job as Manteo Weather Station manager—to see the Wrights in the air, he did not see a flight that afternoon. For the rest of his life Drinkwater would make himself into a local living legend claiming that he had been an associate of the Wright brothers and had played a unique role in reporting their earliest flights, but this is the only reference by the Wright brothers of any encounter with the man either in their diaries or correspondence. Although the brothers had extensive correspondence with a number of Carolinians, no letters to or from Drinkwater have survived in their extensive and virtually complete files.

Nevertheless, before the day was over, both Salley and Newton—but apparently not Drinkwater—had filed stories on the flights of that morning. Salley sent a telegram to the London *Daily Mail*—for which he was still the on-site correspondent—with a brief and very accurate summary of the flights: "A telegram from Manteo, North Carolina, states that the Wright brothers this morning continued their aeroplane experiments on the lonely beach near Kill-Devil Hill. The atmospheric conditions were most favourable." Even though Hoster was evidently on-site to cover the flights that day, it seems that he did not get a story in print covering the events of this day.[17]

Salley and the newly arrived Newton probably worked together on the illuminating article that appeared the next day in the *New York Herald*. Newton exhibited an eye for detail and rich color in his story that had not appeared in any previous articles. He calculated the distances the Wright brothers flew by referencing the nearby regularly spaced utility poles of the government-operated telephone system. He recorded precisely the time and duration of flights as well as their pilots, configuration, directions flown, and the estimated elevation of each flight.[18]

In the process, Newton provided some details on the day's activities that were not even noted in the Wrights' own records. For example, he gave a very precise description of Wilbur's flight that day: "Its course was directed north, almost parallel with the beach, for a mile and three-eighths, then it was turned west, passing around a sand hill for five-sixteenths of a mile, after which it circled southeast, back toward the starting point, for three-fourths of a mile." He also gave a vivid description of the sound and appearance of the plane: "Imagine a noisy reaper flying through the air with a rising and falling motion similar to that of a bird and a fair picture of the Wright brothers' flying machine in action is obtained." Furthermore, Newton helped readers understand the physical ordeals required of the Wrights in getting ready for these flights and their creative solutions for moving their heavy plane across the sands: "After the machine lights it has to be rolled back to the rail before it can be started again. To do this it is placed on a pair of wheels, and, with its engine in action, it almost forces itself along." He, too, confirmed the privacy and secret tendencies of the Wrights: "Wright brothers guard their machine with the utmost care. They will not operate in the sight of a stranger if they know it."[19]

With the arrival of some experienced members of the working press—and some who had covered attempts at flight elsewhere in the world—there was at least a promise that the world might get a fair and accurate assessment of what were meant to be entirely secret flights at Kitty Hawk during this incredible brief stretch of seven days. The gathering of such journalists meant that during the remaining few days the Wrights would continue to deploy their plane at Kitty Hawk, their accomplishments had a chance of being reported. Potentially, at least, facts would replace and correct the well-intentioned but fictional accounts previously inspired by Drinkwater and the local lifesavers.

The maneuverings of the heavy plane on May 11—even with the constant assistance of the Kill Devil Hill lifesavers—had been so exhausting that the Wright brothers needed another day off on Tuesday the twelfth. Besides, the winds were from the southwest and were a bit too high, at 20 to 30 miles per hour. Wilbur wrote: "The wind was high all day, and as we were very sore after the long hauls of yesterday we did not get the machine out."[20]

But even as they rested, the gathering of even more fiercely curious scribes in Manteo continued. On May 12, three of the most important journalists in the world of flight arrived at Tranquil House in Manteo. These were Arthur Ruhl, who wrote for *Collier's Weekly*, James Henry Hare, also on assignment for *Collier's*; and P. H. McGowan, reporter for the London *Daily Mail*. Ruhl and McGowan had been covering the world of flight for at least a decade. Hare was one of the most venerated news photographers of his day, having won worldwide renown for his intrepid photographic records of the Spanish-American War in Cuba in 1898 and of the Russo-Japanese War of 1905.[21]

But just as important as the reporters were the ambitious publishers of these two leading news outlets. *Collier's Weekly* (much later to become the popular *Look Magazine*) was in the process of being expanded into the leading illustrated news weekly of the time by Robert J. Collier, the adventurous and ambitious heir to the magazine. Not only was he trying to build America's greatest news magazine, but Collier was also one of the period's most daring dabblers in the art of motorized sport. A hard-drinking publisher and sportsman, his goals were to publish the first illustrated news article on the Wright brothers with a photograph of their plane in flight and to become the first owner-pilot of a Wright powered airplane.

The owner and publisher of the *Daily Mail*, with offices in Manchester and London, Alfred Charles W. Harmsworth, was, if anything, even more ambitious on a national and global scale. Better known to history as Lord Northcliffe, Harmsworth's driving goals were to make money and to ensure that the United Kingdom had the most advanced military hardware, army, and navy in the world.

At a time when England was, in his view, falling badly behind France and Germany in military capability, Lord Northcliffe—along with his principal political ally, Winston Churchill—advocated for the United Kingdom to take the lead in developing the airplane as a tool of war and for the defense of the British Isles. From his perspective, the British Empire needed not only the greatest navy in the world; it also should have the most powerful air force. Ruhl, Hare, and McGowan were thus in North Carolina not only to report world news, but also to advance the grand personal and political agendas of their famous and often controversial employers.

Since the Wright brothers did not fly on May 12, Byron Newton of the *Herald* was able to spend some time giving perspective to what was happening in North Carolina. Instead of facing a deadline for a news story, Newton spent that day writing an article meant to help the world understand what was truly at stake with the Wright experiments. He was quite aware that the Wrights claimed to have flown up to twenty-four miles in a single flight at Dayton back in 1905. But as that had been a private flight, their claims could be given little more merit than many others who had bragged about heroic flights without proof or witnesses. He was also aware that the French pilot Léon Delagrange had, just a month before, on April 11, 1908, flown 2½ miles over the span of 6 minutes and 30 seconds at Issy in France. That flight surpassed anything ever seen in public.[22]

He thus wrote, after some reflection on May 12: "Since more complete details were obtained to-day of the flights made yesterday by the Wright brothers' aeroplane, there has been no doubt that they now exceeded all the world's records." He believed further that their "flight of more than two miles, running three corners and having the machine all the time under good control . . . when officially verified, will surpass the record of Leon Delagrange of France." Therefore, readers of the *Herald* and all people of the world could believe that the Wrights were in the process of making world history at Kitty Hawk. Newton, based on what he himself had seen, believed that "within another week . . . they will perform aerial feats that may mark the beginning of a new epoch in aerial navigation."

But as he sat at the Tranquil House in Manteo writing his story late on the evening of the twelfth, Newton had only one major worry. As he observed the busy registration desk at the Tranquil House, he added a somewhat ominous note in his story to the *Herald* that day:

> Correspondents from all sections of the country, including the London newspapers, are arriving here, and there is a probability that the presence of the newspaper men may bring all operations to a sudden close. The Wrights absolutely refuse to make a flight or even to open the doors of their aerodrome so long as they suspect a newspaper correspondent, or even a stranger, is within sight of the ground.

"Only the lifesaving men at Kill Devil Hill are permitted to be present," he continued. And, unfortunately, "the Wrights have announced that if outsiders persist in visiting their testing grounds they will stop short and seek some other place for their experiments."[23]

Newton also noted in his article on the twelfth that "to-day the Wrights have had the doors of their aerodrome at Kill Devil Hill closed all day. They have been repairing the machine and working on the new motor which does not yet operate to their liking."

With all of the repairs made and their sore muscles somewhat recovered, the Wrights began on May 13 with a new round of flights. The flying conditions were perfect with brisk winds of 14 to 16 miles per hour. Wilbur made the first flight—two-thirds of a mile in the direction of what they called "Haman's old place," an abandoned house on the sound side of their flying field. The flight was short but perfect. It was only marred when out from the shadows of the Hayman (local spelling) house emerged a person who pretended to be a local, but who turned out to be one J. C. Burkhart of Ithaca, New York. The Wrights, believing him to be a reporter—in fact, he was an engineering student from Cornell University—chased him from the field, saying that they would do nothing more if he remained on the site. In his summary for the day, Wilbur noted, they proceeded with repairs to their engine and "the reporter meanwhile disappeared."[24]

Once they got the engine running again, they trudged back to the starting ramp over more than 1,000 meters of unforgiving sand, bearing the machine on their carefully devised dollies or "trucks." Later in the morning, Orville got off the ground on his second attempt and flew almost two miles. He passed between two of the Kill Devil Hills known as Little and West Hill, made a well-controlled turn, and was on his way back when the engine overheated and he was forced to land well short of their camp. Wilbur, Orville, Charles Furnas, and the ever-present life-savers walked the flyer back to camp, only to find a new stranger—this time a real reporter—waiting for them. Wilbur wrote, "We returned to camp and found Mr. Ruhl of the *Collier's Weekly* waiting for us." Once again, the Wrights in uncere-monious terms explained to Ruhl that he must leave or they would not continue their experiments.[25]

By the time of this incident the woods near the old Hayman's House were, un-known to Wilbur and Orville, rife with reporters. As a new arrival, Ruhl just hap-pened to be the only one that morning who had dared to venture into their camp. The hiding crowd in the woods included, of course, Salley, the persistent freelancer; Newton from the *Herald;* Hoster from the *American;* McGowan from the *Daily Mail;* and Hare, the photographer, also from *Collier's Weekly.* Gilson Gardiner from Washington, D.C.—the only reporter not staying at the Tranquil—was also pres-ent for the first time this day, preparing reports for a number of newspapers in-cluding the *New York World,* the *Chicago Journal,* and the *St. Louis Dispatch.* The student J. C. Burkhart, also chased from the field, had joined the reporters, who were attempting to hide in the shadows of the scrub pine trees that grew on the sound side of the island.

In a letter written at the end of the day, Orville Wright described the ludi-crous scene of reporters lurking in the woods. But in the process, he also revealed just how little the Wrights understood of the scene that was unfolding between them and the press. He wrote,

The newspaper men are having a great time now. The *New York American* man came today disguised as a hunter, with whole hunting outfit [actually this was Burkhart the student, not Hoster the reporter]. A reporter from Norfolk named Salley has been over to camp twice, but has been hanging about the woods and behind the hills every day for a week. A reporter from Norfolk [actually Hare, the photographer from *Collier's Weekly*] was over on the hills yesterday. Every time we moved in his direction he moved away. He had a camera, but I don't think he got any picture—at least none at close enough range to show anything. The *New York Herald* has a man here. He has managed to keep himself out of our sights, but he has talked to the men over at the station.[26]

Not fully understanding that they had suddenly become one of the hottest topics in the world press, the Wrights continued for a time to treat the situation as a local cat-and-mouse game in which they thought they were winning the tussle.

At about noon the wind conditions changed somewhat dramatically, so the Wrights decided not to try any further flights. The reporters, thinking that the Wrights were making good on their promise of no further flights in the presence of newspaper writers, soon concluded that the show was over and headed back to Manteo to file their stories on the flights they had witnessed that morning.

But they were wrong on both accounts. It really *was* the weather, and the Wrights were not finished for the day. In fact, Orville described what happened that afternoon in the case of one local family:

Today a man and his wife and ten or fifteen children came over from Collington Island to see us fly. They arrived about one o'clock after we had made one flight and remained all afternoon. They were so interested, and had walked such a long way lugging some of the smaller children, that we would have liked to fly while they were here, but the wind had risen to 20 to 25 miles [per hour], which we thought a little too strong to attempt circles at present.[27]

But the weather conditions changed again at about 6:00 that night, and perfect winds for flight (15 miles per hour) returned. According to Orville, "We made our first complete circles in it." During the evening's flights, in fact, both Wilbur and Orville were able to make very satisfying circles that in both instances brought the plane back to the starting point. According to Wilbur, "I made the circuit of the West Hill and returned to the starting point . . . Orville then made another complete circle and landed at starting point." With no trudging involved that evening, they were able to complete two magnificent flights and get the machine put to bed in the space of just an hour and a half.[28]

The reporters, back in Manteo and wrongly guessing that the Wrights had decided not to fly to avoid observation, were facing end-of-day deadlines and had to file their stories about the day's events. Completely oblivious to the evening's flights, they scribbled their reports and handed them that afternoon to Drinkwater to be transmitted via his telegraph. Newton of the *Herald*, Hoster of the *American*, and McGowan of the *Daily Mail* all waxed eloquently and somewhat creatively as they wrote their stories. According to Newton:

With the ease and swiftness of a huge eagle the Wright brothers' aeroplane made a flight of three miles at ten o'clock this morning, circling about the great sand hills, at times skimming along over the surf, dipping down, rising, turning corners, and landing within a few yards of the starting point. . . . In fact the machine was brought to the ground only because the operators discovered something slightly wrong with the mechanism and it was stated by one of their assistants that the machine could have gone on for twenty miles at the same rate except for the desire of the operator to correct every slightest defect the instant it is discovered.[29]

Hoster's story, by contrast, was a bit more dramatic:

In that memorable scene on the beach at Kill Devil Hill this morning, the Wright brothers, Orville and Wilbur, passed all competitors in aerial navigation, and took a dominating lead in the efforts to solve the problem of the air. Three miles in two minutes and fifty seconds is the marvellous [sic] record which they achieved in their new aeroplane.[30]

McGowan's story was graphic in describing the first flight of the morning:

The propellers whirled like giant fans, but without any rattling. The machine flew, dipping and rising alternately, until it reached the turn of Nag's Head Hill, when Orville Wright turned from south-west to north-west, but instead of proceeding descended gently but rapidly. The flight began at 8:35 A.M. and lasted seventy-five seconds.[31]

All three reporters quite obviously felt that they had been witnesses to one of the most important events in the history of flight that day. They were gearing their rhetoric not only for the moment, but also for the ages.

But in each case these experienced reporters ultimately could not hide just how limited their vantage point was in observing the Wright flights. Being restricted to the woods at the old Hayman's House, they quietly and dangerously departed from their roles as solid-evidence reporters and moved over into the realm of postulation and wishful thinking. According to Newton, "The three mile voyage was accomplished in a little more than three minutes and the aeroplane carried both inventors."[32] McGowan concurred in his special storytelling style:

> This flight was carefully prepared. Both the Wrights were seated in the machine, which came beautifully toward Prospect Hill, skimming the earth at a height varying from twenty to fifty feet. It rounded Nag's Head Hill, a quarter of a mile from me, like a hawk, and went northward, scaring a drove of cattle into the sea. It lifted its head to climb a gentle slope, crossed the hill, came southward on the east side, and stopped like a partridge returning to its nest when half a mile from the barn.[33]

Hoster echoed the observation: "The run included three beautiful turns, and for the entire three miles the brothers sat upright in their machine, guiding it along its course."[34]

However, all three reporters—sent by their papers to record history in progress—somehow got the story of that day's flights both technically and factually wrong. They led their readers and thereby the world to believe that both of the Wright brothers on May 13, 1908, had mounted their plane for a historic flight with two pilots in control. Not only did they miss the most important flights of the

day—those in the evening—they also got the story wrong on the two flights they
did see.

The reporters did explain in their reports the circumstances in which they
had to operate, but they proclaimed them to be adequate to get the story. According to Newton, the Wrights "did not know that they were being observed by any
except the life saving men who were assisting them." Describing the vantage point
he and other reporters had that day, he wrote, "To-day's flights were observed by
a group of men congregated in the woods within a mile of their starting point, and
by another group of disinterested men, who watched them through powerful
glasses from a nearby point." McGowan, meanwhile, thought his perch to see the
flights was almost perfect: "I reached Prospect Hill, overlooking Kill-Devil Hill,
just in time to see the doors of the barn opened and the machine drawn out with
the help of four coastguards." Hoster described seeing the events unfold from much
the same perspective: "At 7:30 the double gates of the mystic workshop were
thrown open, and mounted on wheels, but propelled by its own power, the aero
plane was rolled out to the single track, 200 feet long, parallelling [sic] the beach,
from which it is given its start."[35]

The observant reporters witnessed, or claimed to witness, a variety of details
during the course of the first two flights that day. According to Newton, focusing
on the new operating system of the Wright plane:

> At all times the operator could be plainly seen, bending and turning as he ma-
> nipulated the levers. With a twist of one lever one great wing of the machine
> would tilt up, and away it would shoot to the left or the right. The twist of an-
> other lever, and it would dart downward or upward, the movement being more
> easily accomplished than the manipulation of an automobile under moderate
> speed.

McGowan instead focused on the configuration of the plane for passengers: "No
attempt was made to conceal the machine. . . . The principal recent innovation
consists of two chairs for the operators, only one of whom formerly was able to
ride, and that by lying flat to manipulate the rudders." Hoster was interested in

the reaction of the domestic animals placidly roaming nearby: "A herd of cattle which had been contentedly browsing on the side of the hill caught the sound of the whirring machinery, glanced up as the ship passed over them, and in a mad dash stampeded across the dunes to the cover of a swamp two miles away."[36]

In addition to their visual recounting of the events of May 13, the reporters' accounts contained other elements that are not easily explained, given their remote observation spot. Among the most confusing parts of their stories are a few renditions of direct interviews with the brothers. Both McGowan and Hoster described such conversations. McGowan wrote that after the second flight of the morning, "I crossed the field to the barn and congratulated the Wrights on their splendid performance. They modestly refused felicitations, declaring that they were merely trying the steering gear and the improved 30-h.p. motor." Then he included a direct quotation from Wilbur Wright:

Our experiments show that the motor is not yet perfect. It stopped in both flights to-day. A motor of such power and small weight is extremely delicate and requires further study. For one thing, it is difficult to keep the sand out. The motor's stoppage compelled us to descend. Besides, we need further proficiency in the management of the steering gear.

"Thus Mr. Wilbur Wright spoke of to-day's work," McGowan wrote.[37]

Hoster, meanwhile, claimed that he had a " brief talk this evening" with Orville Wright, who told the reporter:

We do not care to discuss the tests made to-day. We are not yet ready to give out any statements or make any claims. I can say generally that we are satisfied with the progress that we are making, but have not yet fully mastered control of the new rudder to our machine and we are having considerable difficulty with the engine. These, however, are only matters of detail.[38]

In addition to these purported direct quotations, McGowan reported (perhaps for the benefit of his employer) that he had discussed with the brothers the challenge of the Manchester to London flight that had been telegraphed to the Wrights by the editor of his newspaper. Their response: "They alluded appreciatively to *The Daily Mail* £10,000 prize, but evaded questions as to when they hope to try for it."[39]

While Byron Newton did not claim to have interviewed either Wilbur or Orville Wright previously, the May 14 issue of his paper included something never before seen in any other newspaper—an illustration of the purported flight that day with two persons on board.

Although not represented as a photograph of the flight, the caption included with the picture indicated what it was supposed to be: "The Wright Brothers Aeroplane in Flight (Scenery and Surroundings Drawn by Eye Witnesses)." It also bore a copyright notice by "The New York Herald Co. (All rights reserved)." The illustration itself is a clear depiction of the Wright plane, crudely drawn, in flight. The majestically smooth rolling dunes of the Kill Devil Hills, however, were shown as jagged crags with a snarling ocean surf in the background. There had been other purported drawings of Wright planes in flight—especially after their 1903 powered flights—and this creative and fictitious illustration fitted neatly into that genre.[40]

In attempting to assess the muddled and somewhat confusing character of this first full day of the meeting (albeit unwittingly) of the Wright brothers and the world press, it is clear that the Wrights sought to maintain their preferred clear line of separation from the news-gathering reporters. While experimenting with their flying machines, they desperately wished to be left alone. It seems unlikely that they made the comments related by McGowan and Hoster directly to the reporters, given how sensitive they were to unwanted exchanges with the press. Since they mention every other encounter with the press—no matter how minor—in their diary or letters during this sojourn in North Carolina, it is hard to avoid the conclusion that these conversations were invented. While it is true that Orville misidentified two of the press representatives in his letter back home, he did not fail to mention the nature of the interaction he and Wilbur had with them.

But even if these were lapses in the record-keeping of the normally quite meticulous and thorough brothers—especially in matters of the press—there remains the colossal error on the part of all the reporters that the Wright brothers had flown on May 13 with two persons aboard and that those two persons were Wilbur and Orville Wright. When the reporters described in their articles that they had excellent vantage points, could see the doors of the Wrights' shed come open, and were viewing the flights through enhanced glasses, how could they have made such an egregious mistake in what they had seen? They were, of course, under tremendous pressure to get the story from Kitty Hawk, to get it first, and to report it with all possible dramatic effect. And they were vitally conscious of not wanting to be scooped by one of their colleagues—especially since there was such a raft of competing reporters on the scene.

The only possible explanation—unless one wants to impugn these exemplary reporters with unethical sins of commission—is that they once again fell into the alluring trap of relying on the ever-present lifesavers as dependable sources of information. The reporters left Kill Devil Hills en masse on the afternoon of May 13 under the impression that the Wrights were done for the day. By early evening, they had already handed over their handwritten stories to Drinkwater, who immediately began clicking them out telegraphically to the ends of the earth. Satisfied with a hard day's work that included a heat-soaked and bug-infested visit to Kill Devil Hills, the reporters—even at that time on ample expense accounts—were most likely sitting on the porch at the Tranquil House sipping their mint juleps when their news day suddenly got turned upside down. A gas launch arrived at Shallowbag Bay, piloted by a breathless lifesaver (William O. Twiford had gone on liberty from the Kill Devil Hills station at 11:00 that morning) filled to his captain's cap with exciting news. "The Wright brothers have just been flying again," he surely said. "They are flying circles, complete circles," this self-appointed zephyr blew across the wharf at Manteo.[41]

Since all of the reporters present knew that the Wrights had modified their plane to accommodate two persons—a pilot and a passenger—they surely demanded to know of the messenger whether there had been two people on these flights. Understanding how badly the reporters wanted to get a "yes" to this question, it was too tempting for the importuned lifesaver not to grant their wish. Of course there were two, the man admitted, knowing that he had fibbed, but for a good cause. He knew in his heart that the brothers were going to fly with two people. That was one of the reasons why they came to Kitty Hawk. If they did not fly together today, they would surely do it tomorrow. Why not, he thought, make those consarned, bow-tied reporters happy by just nodding in agreement with your fingers crossed behind your back?

Hoping against hope that the man was right, the juleped-up reporters—at least Newton, Hoster, and McGowan, those with the most to gain in getting a true scoop—raced over to Alpheus Drinkwater's telegraph office to revise or amend the stories being sent or already telegraphed to their newspapers. Drinkwater, with a solid chunk of self-importance, made them line up one by one. He took pleasure in making these captive city slickers follow the rules of his office. He would deal with them one at a time. They busily scribbled revisions to their articles—not enough to eliminate the inconsistencies that would remain in their lengthy pieces, but enough to give their editors some leeway in making last-minute amendments and drawing up appropriate headlines. Before they went to sleep that night, they had done their best, and their editors and headline writers would take care of the rest.[42]

When their stories thus appeared in New York and London the next morning, all three of them had been amended by their editors to reflect the anticipated two-person flights and to state that the Wrights were flying in grand circles with the greatest of ease—without mentioning that there had been two additional flights in the evening. But only the *New York Herald* had the time and resources to manufacture an illustration to go along with the sensational headlines that accompanied Newton's article:

WRIGHT BROTHERS MAKE A THREE MILE AERIAL FLIGHT, THEIR
GIANT AEROPLANE UNDER ABSOLUTE CONTROL

Airship, Carrying Both Inventors, Easily Accomplishes Devious Journey Through Space.
Circles, Dips, Rises and Returns Swiftly to Starting Point Like a Huge Bird.
Group of Observers Concealed a Mile Away Are Witnesses of Epoch Making Voyage.[43]

The fact that these reporters found themselves practically forced into following practices that were contrary to expected standards of their craft illustrated the strange environment in which they were operating at the Wright brothers' flying field. Not only did the subjects of their stories not want most types of publicity; the scene of the flights was on an inhospitable strip of sandy and marshy land almost an hour away from Manteo by boat. Their only way of getting to Kill Devil Hills was by private boat, operated by moonlighting lifesavers or random fishermen. And in the absence of being on scene themselves, they had to depend entirely upon the words and stories of these men who rarely had to distinguish between the realms of fact and story—except when the fish they caught had to be weighed!

Chapter Four

THE SEVENTH
DAY IN MAY

*First Published Photo of the Secret
Flights on May 14, 1908*
*World-renowned photojournalist James
Hare, on assignment from Collier's
Weekly to produce the first known
photograph of a Wright airplane in
flight, captured this distant secret image
on May 14, 1908, providing the first
public proof that the brothers had indeed
solved the problem of flight.*

The historic events of 1908 at Kill Devil Hills on the Outer Banks of North Carolina finally culminated on Thursday, May 14—the seventh and last day the Wrights were under the scrutiny of the world's press at Kitty Hawk. This is the day that should most properly be celebrated as the moment when all in the swoop of a single day, the world stopped speculating about the possibilities of flight and watched in awe as it was demonstrated to anyone who could read that men could fly in powered machines with grace and under control.

As on the preceding day, the gathered reporters rose very early from their slumbers at the Tranquil and got ready for a day of observation and investigative reporting across the shallow sound at Kill Devil Hills. As was their habit, they got dressed as if they were going to the office in New York, Washington, or London. Although the hotel always provided a hearty and sumptuous breakfast, they had little time since they knew that their quarry, the brothers Wright, were early risers and would be out ready to fly by 7:00 or 8:00 A.M. at the latest. But they didn't need to worry about food—the Tranquil generously provided a picnic of ample baskets filled with treats that would more than carry them through the day. Thus energized by their morning coffee and ready to heave ho in one of the small local gas launches headed for the Outer Banks, they were off on what would be one of the most memorable outings of their reportorial careers.

The day was clear. The winds were brisk and from the west. It was a fine day for flying and clear enough for perfect observation and photography. Before the day's work commenced at about 8:00 A.M., the reporters were in place in the woods a half-mile from the camp where Wilbur, Orville, and Charles Furnas prepared to fly. As always, the eager lifesavers were there in their summer white uniforms, ready to gawk and help out when needed, never missing a beat in the ever-interesting Wright show.

Wilbur, in his diary that day, and Orville, in a letter to their father written the following day, described the activities of the morning of May 14. Wilbur's brief version was as follows:

We began before eight o'clock with a flight with two men aboard (W. W. & C. F.). A good start was made but the course was soon directed more to the right than it should have been, and in order to keep on the safe side I had Chas. shut off the engine, as we were pointing right at the West Hill. The distance by anemometer was just 600 meters in 28⅗ seconds. Easy landing.

As the brothers were taking turns in these test flights, Wilbur next described Orville's experiences:

Orville and Chas. tried a flight together and after one false start sailed away nicely. They passed around the West Hill, came north alongside the Little Hill by the sound, and back by way of starting point. When about halfway round the West Hill on the second lap, the heating of the engine bearing compelled them to land. I made a measurement of the wind shortly before they passed the building and found its velocity about 18 miles an hour. They say that at one time on the wind-ward part of the course they met a gust that held them practically motionless for a few moments. . . .

The wind gradually shifted to the west and made starting more and more dif-ficult. I made three attempts, with Chas. aboard, to get started but struck wing tips before reaching the end of the track. These false starts consumed most of the morning.[1]

In his letter, Orville summarized the events of the morning in a much briefer, yet more revealing manner:

Yesterday morning we tried carrying two men for the first time. Will made a flight of about 500 ft with Charles Furnas on board, but was unable to steer the machine around the hill. A little later I took him a complete circle, cov-ering a distance of 4120 meters (according to anemometer) in 3 minutes and 40 seconds. Will then made three attempts to get off, but he seemed a little rattled, for every time he made some mistake in operating the handles and failed to get off.[2]

Although the reporters were nestled in their spy corner in the woods and were in the process of recording the morning's events, neither Wilbur nor Orville made a specific reference to the presence or emergence of the reporters on that morning.

Nevertheless, the platoon of journalists got their story—a story they could hardly believe. They had seen for themselves, directly and personally, this time without doubt and not through the stories of any lifesavers that the Wright brothers were launching flights successfully with two people on board. Although they got their city shoes filled with sand, their legs and arms covered with chiggers, their shirts and dress jackets soaked with perspiration, and they were, physically at least, miserable, they got their story. James Hare, the renowned photographer, also got a real photograph of the Wright plane with two people on board. Nobody except the Wrights themselves had ever succeeded in taking a picture of a Wright plane in flight. Certainly no one had ever taken a picture of a Wright plane with two people on board—because the Wrights had never attempted such a feat until that very morning.

The creative display of news stories that emanated from Manteo on May 14 was overwhelming. Never before in the history of attempts at flight had the world press and newsworthy flights of this scale happened to merge on the same day. The reporters—for once happily in competition—churned out their stories with pencils and notepads and lined up at Alpheus Drinkwater's telegraph office to send them out. Some of the other writers present—who were not on deadline—sat on the porch of the Tranquil organizing their notes and contemplating how they could best describe this historic day.

Byron Newton of the *New York Herald* captured the essence of the most successful of the two-person flights—that by Orville Wright with Charles Furnas as passenger:

> In that flight they made an almost perfect circle about one of the sand mountains, covering about two miles in two minutes and thirty-eight seconds. They came down within a few yards of the starting point, and seemed to do it all with as much ease as a skilful chauffeur would stop an automobile in front of the HERALD building.

As for the day itself, Newton described it as "a perfect day, with clear sky and brilliant sunlight, on which every object and every movement along the whole beach could be plainly seen." He also described the electricity that was in the air for the gathered journalists:

> In the group of newspaper men were several veterans, who have been accustomed to witnessing the most important events in the world, but they stood speechless with amazement to-day as they watched the graceful machine gliding through the air and realized that they were privileged at last to see the consummation of man's dreams since civilization began, actual navigation of the air without the aid of gas [i.e., lighter than air balloons or airships].

Thus, without acknowledging the error he had made on the previous day of reporting a Wright flight of two persons, he simply described the first flight of two people he had *really seen* on the fourteenth as a thing of great wonder.[3]

McGowan of the London *Daily Mail*, having also already reported a two-man flight the day before, tried to muddle through a mishmash of information without clarifying exactly when and how the two-person flights had actually occurred. As for that morning, he wrote:

> Shortly after I reached the scene this morning Mr. Orville Wright, accompanied by Furnas, repeated the feat of noon yesterday, making a two-mile flight in 2 min. 40 sec. around a circular sand hill, the directions being west, north-west, and south, and the machine passing over the starting point and proceeding half a mile further.

But in the following summary of two days of flights, he just said that there had been two flights with two passengers without specifying when they had happened: "Two two-man flights exceeding two miles and lasting 2 min. 40 sec."[4]

William Hoster of the *New York American*—the third reporter who had been seduced into reporting a two-person flight the day before—also avoided correcting himself as he described the triumphal flight that morning of Orville Wright and Charles Furnas:

A preliminary run of half a mile was made successfully, and then, with Orville Wright at the lever and Furness[*sic*], the mechanic, beside the inventors, the machine rose from its station outside the storehouse and shooting off toward the north, was so skillfully guided that it made a complete circle back to the starting point in two minutes and forty seconds.

He confirmed that the day was perfect and that all of the activities were observed by only the group of assembled reporters and a half-dozen lifesavers.[5]

Since the reporters had already incorrectly published the news that there were two-person flights on May 13, the historical significance of the Orville Wright and Furnas flight was also obscured. In their incorrect stories of the previous day, they had already asked the question of whether a two-person flight at Kitty Hawk by the Wright brothers at this time would be a world first. Their conclusion on the thirteenth was that, while it might be a first for the Wrights, it was not technically the first duo flight in the world. Between and among this group of reporters was a vast knowledge of flights in their contemporary world, and they concurred that credit for the first two-person flight in the world should instead rest with two French pilots: according to Hoster of the *American*, "When a few months ago De Lagrange and Farman rode side by side on their aeroplane for a distance of 200 feet the world marvelled [*sic*]."[6]

As a matter of fact, the topic of the Wrights' first successful two-person flights was almost entirely submerged owing to what happened later, on the afternoon of May 14. That event was to become the focus of all news stories filed on that date and for many days thereafter. Wilbur Wright described his dramatic afternoon flight in this manner:

After dinner I tried alone with the track shifted more to the west and got off nicely. Skirting the north edge of the West Hill, I passed around the Little Hill by the sound and proceeded down the beach till I had passed the umbrella tree, then turned east and passed over the sand ridge about two hundred feet from its end. Then, turning southward, I passed over the dry ponds and, passing camp, proceeded around the West Hill and the Little Hill by the sound and was continuing the course followed on the first round when the machine suddenly darted into the ground when going with the wind at a velocity of about 85 kilometers an hour. The front framing and upper surface were wrecked. The front rudder & tail & machinery and the wing sections were almost intact. The lower center section was only slightly injured. I was thrown violently forward and landed against the top surface but remained inside the body of the machine. I received a slight cut across the bridge of my nose, several bruises on my left hand, right forearm, and both shoulders. . . . I was practically uninjured.[7]

Orville's description of the event gave a little more detail:

After dinner he [Wilbur] started alone. After making one circle and about half of another, and when running exactly with the wind at a speed in the neighbor-hood of 52 to 54 miles an hour, he suddenly turned the front rudder down by mistake and plunged into the ground. I was watching with the field glass. The ma-chine turned on end—the front end—with the tail in the air. There was a big splash of sand—such a cloud that I couldn't see from where I was exactly what had happened, but I thought the machine had rolled a complete summersault. We were somewhat excited at camp for a few seconds. It was probably thirty seconds before Will appeared. As we found out afterward he was not badly hurt—only a few bruises. Instead of coming out where we could see him, he spent a half minute or so examining the damage to the machine. The time of the flight was seven minutes and a half.[8]

Regardless of the bumpy conclusion of this flight, it was recognized immediately by all knowledgeable people throughout the world as the longest publicly ob-served flight in the history of powered flight. Just a month before in Paris, Léon Delagrange had made his public flight that had lasted 6 minutes and 30 seconds. Discounting the much longer flights claimed by the Wright brothers at Dayton in 1905 (which were still not publicly acknowledged at the time), Wilbur Wright had in this afternoon flight of May 14 set a documented world record. In all of the excitement, it was also overlooked that Orville Wright's flight with

Charles Furnas on board that same day had been the second longest recorded powered flight in history—at least at the moment it was completed.

The reporters who observed Wilbur Wright's solo flight that afternoon had been expecting from the first moment they learned of the new Kitty Hawk flights that one of the brothers would undertake what they called an "endurance" flight. That is, either Wilbur or Orville Wright would seek to set a world record for time and distance that would outshine their competitors throughout the world. It was this eager anticipation that led to speculative headlines that the Wrights might make a dramatic flight any day from Kitty Hawk to Cape Henry or to Cape Hatteras or to some other destination as a sheer demonstration of their skills and their plane's reliability. When Wilbur climbed aboard the plane alone on the afternoon of May 14, the reporters were sure that the moment had come for the much-discussed historic flight.

And this is how they described it, in almost euphoric and sometimes rhapsodic terminology: McGowan was perhaps the most inventive in his rendition of the flight after noting that "the American aeronauts, the brothers Wright, accomplished a world's record yesterday by flying in an aeroplane a distance of more than six miles." This flight, he wrote, had bested by far the teetering and uncontrolled flight of Léon Delagrange at Paris the month before (April 11):

Aeroplane history is being made [here] as the hours go by. . . . The aeroplane wobbled for an instant at the start, poised as if to mark its course, darted gracefully behind the west side of a sandhill, quickly came to view in a depression north of the brow, passed east of the next lower hill, turned westward when almost out of sight against the side of a third hill, and made a long straight lap to its starting point.

Then, without a moment's faltering, it came in a wide circle around the hill nearest Prospect Hill, where I was stationed, made a long straight lap northward, almost disappearing as before from my vision before turning. . . . Each straight lap is estimated at two miles, and the curves must add a mile or two more. . . . The precise time was seven minutes and forty seconds. . . . The beauty of the motion and the self-confidence of the driver were admirable. . . .[9]

William Hoster's story in the *American* was similar:

> Shortly after noon the aeroplane was once more got into condition and at twenty
> seconds past one o'clock the throbbing of her engines echoed across the beach
> and the machine rose gracefully into the air and at a height of twenty feet took a
> northeasterly course up the beach in the face of a twenty-knot breeze. Behind her
> floated a flock of gulls and crows that seemed at once amazed and jealous of this
> new thing.[10]

Another article that appeared in the *New York World* the following day, probably
written by Gilson Gardiner, summarized the historic flight perhaps most beautifully—giving more detail about the activity of the surrounding birds, which were
startled and spellbound:

> For the last week Wilbur and Orville Wright have made daily flights in the ma-
> chine, which they have spent years in developing. Every flight has been uniformly
> successful, and it was planned by the brothers to demonstrate to-day that the
> airship would perform all that they have claimed for it. The start was made from
> a point near the Kill Devil Hill Life Saving Station. The aeroplane glided down
> an artificial incline and rose into the air like a bird.
>
> In the teeth of a twelve-mile wind Wilbur Wright guided the wonderful ma-
> chine up the coast for a distance of two miles at a speed exceeding a mile a minute.
> With a graceful turn to the west the airship shot up above a small sand hill,
> dipped swiftly down between two others and glided off over the country at a mar-
> vellous [sic] rate of speed.
>
> A flock of crows attempted to follow in the wake of the motor-driven airship,
> but were soon left behind. Without diminishing the speed the aeronaut glided the
> machine in a series of circles, sailing around several sand dunes. After these suc-
> cessful evolutions, the flight was directed back to the starting point. Wilbur
> Wright followed the same course in returning, with the airship at all times under
> perfect control.[11]

And such was the dramatic story of the world's longest publicly observed flight in the history of the world at that time. At least it was the main story, until the sometimes hapless reporters got word of the great unwitnessed crash of May 14.

Readers of newspapers throughout the world on May 15 were greeted with a host of banner headlines reporting a disastrous crash of the Wright brothers' marvelous flying machine the day before. Both of the brothers had just completed historic flights of the plane with two persons on board. Wilbur then took the plane on the longest publicly witnessed powered flight in history to that date. He had completed two beautiful giant circles around the flying field at Kill Devil Hills, to the awe and admiration of the covey of reporters hiding in the nearby woods. This is what a reporter lived for—to be a witness to history being made and to be able to write the story not only for the next day's paper, but for the ages. James Hare had just gotten a set of very fine photographs of the plane in flight that would soon be in print. All of the reporters and Hare, the master photographer, watched as Wilbur and the plane completed a second wide circle of the flying field. At the end of this second circle, the plane flew behind one of the sand dunes where it quietly came to rest on the sandy surface. Obviously, from the reporters' vantage point, the plane must have run out of fuel or perhaps the engine overheated—both routine occurrences with Wright flights. Or perhaps a puff of crosswinds arose and Wilbur decided to land rather than risk the plane.

Whatever might have been the ending of this historic flight, the reporters had their story. There was no need to sit around and watch Wilbur, Orville, Furnas, and the lifesavers as they repeated the ritual of hauling the flyer back to the Wrights' camp. So they packed up their gear, their picnic baskets, and Hare's tripod camera and began their trek back to the sound, where some hired locals waited in gas launches to take the visitors back over to Manteo. There was no time to waste. They had stories to write, deadlines to meet, and all of that. They also dreaded the thought of having to stand in line again at Drinkwater's telegraph office, trying to get their precious words transmitted to New York, Chicago, Washington, and London.

Back on the porch of the Tranquil, the reporters each raced to one-up the others in completing their stories and getting over to Drinkwater's office. They were writing just as furiously as they had been the day before when a fishing skiff arrived at the Manteo wharf once again. Off the boat came one of the lifesavers from Kill Devil Hills (surfman William W. Midgett had been on liberty since 11:30 A.M.), and he proceeded from the wharf into town almost like a proud town crier announcing to any who would listen, "They crashed. The Wright boys crashed. It was awful. The plane was destroyed. And Wilbur was hurt."[12]

The reporters surely sat in amazement that for the second day in a row they had missed the most essential moment of the action—the crash, the wreckage, the carnage, the blood—and, yes, the headlines. Just as on the day before when they unwittingly put into print the rumored details of two passenger flights and looping flights across ocean waters, they were now faced with another headline story in which they had missed the most pivotal, newsworthy moment of the day. Just one day later, having already been burned, they were once more totally at the mercy of the lifesavers and their fantastic stories—essentially dependent on the biggest braggarts they had ever met. Somewhere between the apparent fact of a plane crash and the consequences, there was probably truth. But to what extent could they trust the story and take their details of the crash from the lips of a swaggering lifesaver?[13]

When the day was finally over, all of them had revised, overlaid, and filed or refiled their reports—all jumbled with at least three intermingled story lines: the historic two-person flight, Wilbur's longest flight on record, and the blood and gore of a great plane crash. As might be expected in the business of most news reporting, it was indeed the blood and gore—not the history—that ended up as the headlines of these published stories. The London *Daily Mail* at least mingled history and sensationalism in its large headlines:

WRIGHT BROS.' RECORD FLIGHT.
SIX MILES IN EIGHT MINUTES.
MACHINE SMASHED.

Such was not the case in the mega-headlines of the *New York Herald:*

WRIGHT DASHED TO EARTH AFTER 8 MILE FLIGHT
Aeroplane, Nearing End of an Epoch Making Voyage, Plunges to Destruction.
OPERATOR UNHURT BY THIRTY FOOT FALL

The rival, but usually more restrained *New York American,* followed suit:

WRIGHT AEROPLANE WRECKED ON BEACH
Lever Out of Order Forces Wonderful Machine to Crash to Earth.
ITS OPERATORS ESCAPE
Disaster Comes After Numerous Successful Flights; Useless for Further Tests.

The normally sober editors of the *New York World* at least raised the possibility of pilot error:

WRIGHT FLYING MACHINE WRECKED IN LONG FLIGHT.
After Sailing Eight Miles at the Rate of More than a Mile a Minute the Airship
Crashes Into a Sand Dune and Is Broken to Pieces.
PILOT TOUCHES WRONG LEVER BY MISTAKE.

The nearby Norfolk *Virginian-Pilot,* was perhaps the direst of all in reporting the damage done to the brothers' flying machine:

WRIGHTS' AIRSHIP IS TOTAL WRECK AFTER FLIGHT OF 8 MILES
Unmanageable Lever Plunged Aeroplane to Destruction On Beach At Kill Devil
    Hill But the Navigator Is Unhurt[14]

The news stories published beneath these blaring headlines—in the ultimate forms they took at the hands of the scrambling reporters and their eager editors—conveyed to readers of these and hundreds of other newspapers that the main event at Kitty Hawk on May 14, 1908, was not a historic flight, but rather a disastrous plane crash.

It was not the lifesavers' fault that the reporters and their publishers chose to emphasize gore over glory. But it *was* the storytelling of the lifesavers that created a misleading corollary to the crash story. According to one version in the *New York American*, which was replicated almost word for word in other newspapers: "The wreck was instantly screened from public view and to-night the pieces are being packed for shipment to the home of the inventors at Dayton, Ohio." This cloak-and-dagger version of what happened immediately after the crash was further elaborated in a follow-up story that appeared in the *Virginian-Pilot* a day later. Under the headline "DEMOLISH WRECK OF AEROPLANE TO KEEP THEIR SECRET," the article read as follows:

> All that was saved of the Wright Brothers' [*sic*] aeroplane after yesterday's accident was the gasoline engine. The rest of the parts of the wreck were cut up into fine bits so as to make it absolutely impossible for their ideas of aerial navigation to be discovered by others.[15]

Fully in line with the self-important understanding they had of their role in providing security for the top-secret mission of the Wrights, the uniformed lifesavers led the reporters to believe that the brothers were racing—in an almost Cold War–era fashion—to hide all evidence of their advanced technology.

The calamities of May 14 as set forth in newspapers did not go unnoticed—especially in the brothers' hometown. The news of the crash caused Bishop Milton Wright to put in his diary on May 15: "The 'Journal' reports that the "Wright brothers wrecked their machine yesterday.["] It also caused sister Katharine to send a telegram to Wilbur at Kill Devil Hills cryptically expressed as follows: "Newspaper reports compleet [*sic*] crash[?] if Posable telegraph."[16]

Two days later, after Wilbur sent a telegram explaining the crash and proclaiming that he was all right, Katharine wrote him a letter describing the situation in Dayton: "When we saw Friday morning's paper, we were worried although we did not believe that the smash-up was as bad as it was reported to be. The reports all said that the machine was broken into 'smithereens' but that the engine was saved." She then described the crisis the news reports had provoked at home:

You see Friday morning and evening papers and Saturday morning and evening papers all kept up the same report. Then we were besieged with friends and reporters and it required some nerve to keep saying that we supposed every thing was all right or we would have heard. I would be all right if I could be let alone. Daddy "done noble" this time. He kept up his spirits pretty well. Promise me that you will let us know promptly when there are serious accidents because we can't know what to believe.[17]

If the Wrights' immediate family was not sure what to believe about the events at Kitty Hawk—and they were in constant contact with the brothers—what must other friends, observers, and the general public have thought?

A very revealing window into the confusion and its causes surrounding the brothers' flights up to May 14 was provided by another journalist who arrived on the scene on May 15 to analyze the exciting events transpiring at Kitty Hawk and Kill Devil Hills. Zachary McGhee, a correspondent for the *Columbia State* of Columbia, South Carolina, arrived at Manteo on the fifteenth—after the last Wright flight at Kitty Hawk, but while all of the newspaper scribes were still present in Manteo. He was able to observe them in action as they tried to deal with the exasperating circumstances of having to rely on fishermen and lifesavers for information and on Drinkwater for transmitting their stories.

From the moment McGhee crossed into North Carolina, the entire region abounded with first- or second-hand information about what the Wright brothers were doing. Arriving in North Carolina from Virginia, he

. . . found the air full of the flying machine and the Wright brothers, not anywhere visible, but everywhere in the air audible. At Elizabeth City, on the boat going to Manteo, and, of course, in Manteo, nobody could talk of anything else. The monstrous performances over at Kill Devil Hill seemed to occupy the minds of all, men, women and children. Very few had seen it, though everybody claimed to be on intimate personal terms with the inventors. Accordingly I was entertained with the most wonderful tales.

When he arrived in Manteo, like most of the other reporters he checked in at the Tranquil House: "At the hotel in Manteo I met a whole bunch of newspaper men from Norfolk, Washington, New York, London." Their situation was pathetic, he thought. While they were dithering away at the hotel in Manteo, all the action was across the sound at Kill Devil Hills where none of them had been able to get closer than a half mile to the scene of the actual flights.[18]

Although the last flights had been completed, McGhee decided to head over to Kill Devil Hills anyway to investigate the scene for himself: "Chartering a fisherman's boat, propelled by a greasy chu-chuing, throbbing gasoline engine, I gathered a small party at Manteo and hied me away across Albemarle sound for Kill Devil Hill." The trip across had its usual adventures from the perspective of landlubber visitors: "After the usual experiences with the motor boat's engine, somewhat automobilious, you understand, and after climbing over a few sand dunes, marshes, quick-sands and things, we reached Kill Devil Hill." Since the flights had ended, McGhee found that the Wright flying machine had already been boxed up. However, that did not deter him from getting the story he was after.

McGhee decided to interview some of the locals who had seen the Wright brothers' flights and observed the flyers in action. He did not have to look very far: "The only 'natives' anywhere in the sight of the whole neighborhood were some six or eight lifesavers—technically or professionally so-called—at the United States life saving station beside the roaring sea, a short distance from the camp." In talking to the lifesavers, he found that some of them had been around almost from the time the Kill Devil Hills Station was opened in 1878. But, McGhee wryly observed: "Their specialty seems to be, not to save life, but to kill time. This may be another reason for calling the place Kill Devil Hill, Old Father Time being the devil, as many folks are quite willing to attest."

Then McGhee described the impact of the Wright brothers' arrival and their flying antics on the sleepy lifesavers:

The flying machine was a boon to these poor fellows away there on the desolate uninhabited shore, who had nothing to do all the live long but to sit and look at one another, stare at the ocean or make toad frog houses in the sand. They watched the wonderful performances of the flying men from the top of the sand dune. Each one of the life savers could tell wondrous things about it, and they each had a theory about the puzzling Wright brothers and the problem of flying.

But as McGhee also reasoned, "At last I had reached folks who had actually seen it." The lifesavers, he found, were very willing to talk with authority about the Wright brothers' flights: "And these life savers or time killers told me about it, what was, what had been and what was going to be, not going it particularly strong, however, on the last, . . . in spite of their intimate association with the mystic and majestic sea." But the lifesavers, he learned, could do a very good job of embellishing a story, which is what they had done with all of the reporters they encountered.[19]

As a result of the stories of the lifesavers and the impossibly close deadlines by which the reporters had to file their stories, virtually everything about the Wright brothers that came from the Outer Banks was a jumble of fact, fiction, and fantasy. In the end, newspaper readers would certainly remember that the Wright brothers had a spectacular smash-up somewhere down on the coast of North Carolina. But would they remember that on May 14—the same day as the crash—Orville Wright completed a spectacular two-person flight, carrying his mechanic Charles Furnas in a beautiful circle over the sands and among Kill Devil Hills? And would they remember that on that date, Wilbur Wright also completed the longest powered flight in history that had been observed by reporters? Or that on the same day, a news photographer snapped what would become the first published picture of a Wright plane in flight? Regardless of what the newsmen reported, on May 14 both Wilbur and Orville Wright showed the world that they could fly almost at will, with no more room for speculation. In the process, the brothers set in motion the dramatic sequence of events whereby, in the space of a few short months, they would teach the rest of an eagerly awaiting world how to fly.

Chapter Five

AFTERMATH
THE ELUSIVE WRIGHTS

Reporters Spying on the Wright Brothers' Secret Kitty Hawk Flights
Ace reporters from the New York Herald, the London Daily Mail, and Collier's Weekly lurked in nearby
woods at Kill Devil Hills on May 14, 1908 hoping to provide the world's first press reports of the Wright
brothers making powered flights.

While the group of journalists who gathered at Kitty Hawk in May 1908 missed many opportunities and made an alarming number of factual and interpretive mistakes in reporting these secret flights of the Wright brothers at Kill Devil Hills, they proved to be much more adept after the fact in explaining to the world what the brothers had done. This was because, for all of their misadventures, they quickly realized that they had just witnessed some of the most important events in the evolution and ripening of flight.

Through the end of the day on May 14, the reporters had been limited by the difficult environment of the Outer Banks of North Carolina where the Wright brothers chose to operate. They had been handicapped by the firm rules established by the brothers to avoid the presence of prying reporters during their flight tests. Perhaps most difficult of all, they had been captives of a unique culture in which most of their information—rarified and embellished as it was—came from a cadre of carefree fishermen and uniformed lifesavers who were savoring a brilliant moment in the limelight. It was an opportunity to play out a role that would not come again in any of their lifetimes. Beginning on the morning of Friday, May 15, 1908—understanding that the Wrights would probably not be conducting further tests—the reporters at Tranquil House were ready to reassert their independence and seize the prerogatives and responsibilities of their profession. They would investigate just what had happened at Kill Devil Hills on the preceding days and explain it fully to the world.

What had happened there—at least from the point of view of the Wright brothers—was reported by Wilbur Wright in his diary. Following the last flight—the unobserved crash on the fourteenth—the Wrights began the slow process of manually cleaning up the mess. Since, owing to the crash, they had no operating engine or propellers to help drive the plane back to their camp, they had to recover the machine piece by piece—a process that would become thoroughly routine in the case of such mishaps during the succeeding era of flight:

We tore the machine apart and put the lower surface on our trucks with the engine in place, and piled on the transmission & a few other parts, between four &
five hundred pounds in all, and the three of us dragged it back to camp, a distance
of about a mile and a quarter. The heat had become almost unbearable and we
barely escaped collapse before reaching the camp. After dark we went over and
got the rudders and radiators. We went to bed completely fagged out.[1]

Early the next morning, the transporting of the rest of the broken plane continued:
"The heat was intense . . . but we went over to the scene of the wreck and hauled
back the wing tips, uprights, &c." To assist in the hauling, the brothers devised a
one-man harness for use in pulling forward their wide-wheeled trucks. In the hot
sun, Orville donned a bonnet to protect his bald head, making the brothers and
Charles Furnas a curious sight trudging across the bright sand.

As they approached their camp, they saw that their buildings had been infil-
trated by several reporters. In the absence of the brothers and Furnas, the intruding
journalists had examined the buildings inside and out and were on the verge of taking photographs when the brothers arrived on the scene. The reporters—who turned
out to be Gilson Gardiner from Washington, currently writing for the *New York
World*, and P. H. McGowan of the *Daily Mail*—had pulled out the tattered remnants
of the Wrights' 1902 glider and had pieces of it propped up against the building with
a tripod camera in place to take pictures when the brothers approached.

Caught in the act of photographing wings, tools, and engine parts, the surprised reporters sheepishly turned the tables on the Wrights and asked to photograph them in their somewhat ridiculous hauling outfits. Wilbur jokingly wrote in
his diary of the incident: "They wished to take a picture of Orville in his 'Merry
Widow' bonnet and me in my dog harness hitched to the trucks, but finally de-
sisted. It would have been an amusing picture for private use but not such as we
cared to have spread broadcast."[2] While the reporters, who must have been accompanied by Hare, the photographer, said that they had taken no pictures before
the brothers arrived, Orville reported to their father the same day: "They had visited the camp in our absence and had taken a few photographs of the outside but
claimed to have no picture of the interior."[3]

Evidently only Gardiner and McGowan took it upon themselves to approach the Wrights directly on the fifteenth, supposedly seeking to get a postmortem directly from the horses' mouths. Most of the other reporters remained in Manteo for a few more days gathering additional information, writing up more reflective articles for their newspapers, or taking a look at the local sights. Gardiner and McGowan were the only journalists to publish exclusive postflight reports from a direct meeting with the Wrights at their camp.

McGowan's report appeared the next day in the London *Daily Mail*. His piece corroborated both the details and the playful discussion reported by Wilbur Wright in his diary. McGowan found the brothers "hauling the fragments of the dismantled machine on a truck to the barn." His description of the scene was light and graphic:

> Mr. Orville Wright smiled from beneath a huge "Mother Hubbard" straw hat lightly tied under the chin. He and Furnass [*sic*], the mechanic, dropped the handles of the truck, but Mr. Wilbur Wright remained in the rope harness which he had been pulling. He showed no hurt from yesterday's accident except abrasions on the nose.

Unlike every other moment of their time at Kitty Hawk until then, McGowan found that "to-day they talked leisurely, though maintaining the reserve which has always characterized them."[4]

McGowan was actually able to engage the brothers in an informative conversation. Wilbur acknowledged that the crash the day before was due to "my personal error, the human elements." His explanation of the situation was very Wrightesque: "It was just such a thing as might happen to a bicyclist or a chauffeur, if his mind were engaged with as many things as mine was." In the process of "practicing with the new steering-gear and observing the machine's motion," he forgot to keep a safe and steady height and thus swooped into the ground. But the crash would not affect any of their plans, the brothers averred, or their schedule for demonstrating in a few months that they could fulfill the requirements of their contract with the U.S. government.

Orville acknowledged that the plane they had just crashed was actually a renovation of the flyer they had used at Dayton in 1905 and that they had already fabricated additional planes for the upcoming flight trials in August both in France and in America. For their demonstration that they could keep two passengers airborne for one hour and fly distances of 125 miles and longer, they would be using entirely new planes. In answer to McGowan's question about why they were flying at Kitty Hawk and not in Dayton as they had in 1904 and 1905, Orville responded, "We came here principally because Dayton lacks wind, and here we find steady breezes. We have been flying [here] in winds as strong as twenty miles an hour."[5]

For some reason Gardiner's article resulting from this interview did not appear in the *New York World* until three days later, on May 18. His analysis—except for the comedic appearance of the Wright brothers hauling their broken flying machine—followed along the same lines and repeated the same comments as McGowan's article. However, Gardiner was a more steadied and philosophical writer than McGowan, and he was able to pick up on a couple of additional hints from the Wrights that did not find their way into McGowan's story. Both McGowan and Gardiner reported that "Orville and Wilbur smiled confidently and confessed that yesterday['s flights] dispelled all lingering doubts among many competent American judges" as to their ability to fly for long periods and great distances.

It was Gardiner, however, who savored Wilbur's classically inspired characterization of the brothers' flights in comparison to other inventors who were creating kite- or drone-like planes. He specifically referred to Alexander Graham Bell's simultaneous testing of a tetrahedral wing in Newfoundland. Gardiner quoted the elder brother as saying that he and Orville were vitally interested in speed when it came to flying: "I thought of the kingfisher, which darted from the empyrean near my launch yesterday, dived to the bottom of Albemarle Sound, rose with a fish and disappeared in the woods, with a few graceful sweeping strokes." No mere mechanic, Wilbur Wright here mixed and matched a complex set of allusions to theology, mythology, and natural history that surely flew over the heads of most of the *World*'s readers, but that revealed to some the contemplative and well-informed structure of his special vision of the world.[6]

After being the focus of a swarming herd of reporters for seven memorable days, Saturday, May 16, was for Wilbur and Orville Wright a day of deceptive quietude. The reporters were gone. The lifesavers who had been daily visitors and aides-de-camp for the brothers were starting their weekend of fishing and visiting, mainly away from the Kill Devil Hills Station. While the brothers needed the day to continue packing up the remains of their spent flyer, there was time for each of the brothers to do what he was most inclined to do. Wilbur, in his diary, revealed Orville's basic habits during such a moment of free time:

> In the morning Orville spent some time experimenting with the two anemometers, holding them together letting them run equal times simultaneously and comparing the records. He found that on the average the Richard anemometer recorded 930 m[eters] while the English instrument was recording 3,280 ft., thus being about 7% slower than the other. The wind on top of the Big Hill [pursuant to Orville's observations and measurements] was almost double that at camp.[7]

Wilbur, meanwhile, was already focused on the next stages in the shared career of the brothers. He sent a special delivery letter to Katharine on the thirteenth asking her to pack up a trunk for him, as he was heading immediately to Europe. This was followed by a telegram on the sixteenth requesting that she forward the trunk to New York City, where he would go directly from Kitty Hawk. From there he intended to proceed immediately to Europe to prepare for the scheduled test flights that would begin in August somewhere in France.[8]

This Saturday turned out to be so peaceful at Kitty Hawk that the Wright brothers did not yet realize how their historic seven days in May 1908 in North Carolina had touched off a veritable firestorm across the Atlantic and elsewhere in America. Aside from the confusing stream of misinformation that had gone forth from Manteo concerning their activities between May 8 and 14, a tidal wave of excitement radiated from Kitty Hawk far greater than anything associated with their first powered flights in December 1903 or their subsequent Dayton trials in 1905.

Those were mere arcane footnotes to history compared to the seismic impact of these most recent flights.

As a result of the almost instant transatlantic messaging that had come to be employed by the world's news media at the turn of the twentieth century, the articles covering the 1908 Kitty Hawk flights produced instant responses across Europe. The European nations—namely the United Kingdom, France, and Germany and, to only a slightly lesser degree, Russia, Italy, and Spain—were engaged in lockstep national rivalries for economic, technological, colonial, and military supremacy. Those same nations—with the addition of the United States and Japan—had already launched an arms race that would pervade much of the twentieth century. At the moment of the Wrights' flights in 1908, the British considered themselves the leading naval power in the world. French citizens, meanwhile, viewed their government as the leader in all matters relating to flight—particularly powered airplane flight. And German military leaders were in the process of establishing their country as the world's leader in the development of airships—both dirigibles and gigantic Zeppelins that were currently being launched from airfields around Berlin. Italian fliers—little noticed outside their recently united kingdom—also saw themselves as being on the cutting edge of innovations in flight and the design of new armaments.

It was thus not surprising that the audacious, though confused, news stories about the Wrights' flights at Kitty Hawk should touch reactive nerves all over the world. Since the London *Daily Mail* had a correspondent on site at Kitty Hawk, it was natural that one of the first editorial reactions to the new Wright flights should come in the very pages of the *Daily Mail*, while the Wright brothers were still quietly playing with their gadgets and packing up to leave Kitty Hawk.

On May 16, the *Daily Mail* published an article on the Wrights' activities titled "The Mysterious Wright Brothers" that was most assuredly not a news article. It was more of a thought piece or opinion column about how the world might come to an understanding of what the quiet innovators had just accomplished in North Carolina. The author—who was probably the same P. H. McGowan writing from a desk at Tranquil House—promised to provide "a personal sketch of the men who have learnt to fly." His lead sentence nicely summarized the milestone of history in one short statement: "The Wright brothers, those mysterious Americans, who for years have kept secret the details of their discoveries, have at last accomplished what is undeniably the world's record by flying in an aeroplane a distance of more than six miles."[9]

McGowan—assuming that he was indeed the author—then launched into a brief essay on the personalities of the brothers: "they are modest thoughtful, rather reserved young men, full of energy and enthusiasm where the work of their life is concerned." His real focus, however, was on the question of why the world had not previously heard more about their achievements in flight. He questioned why "much has been heard of their experiments in flying, but very little has been published" about them or their flights—especially a flight in 1905 claimed by the brothers to have covered twenty-four miles over a period of thirty-eight minutes. Although the Wrights maintained that they had pictures in hand to document the facts of this and all their other flights, they had withheld the photographic proof for a very fundamental reason:

> They claim that scientific spectators would quickly understand the simple device that gives almost perfect equilibrium in the air, and that an intrusive man with a camera would also swiftly reveal to the world what, in their own interests, they must keep secret for the present.

The Wrights' primary goal, according to McGowan, was to learn how to fly. Thus, he wrote, "their patience has been the sublime patience of scientists who knew that the end sought after would be attained some day, somehow."[10]

While the *Daily Mail*—based on the eyewitness observations of their own reporter—concluded that the Wright brothers had indeed broken the barrier of sustained flight, the reaction across the English Channel was far different. There, French observers had also been provided with a constant diet of articles about the Wrights through the Paris edition of the *New York Herald*. But no one in France was ready to believe what had been written about the flights at Kitty Hawk. In fact, pilot Henri Farman, British born but having done his flying in France, had soon had enough of the wild stories about the Wrights that were appearing in the pages of the *Herald*.

Winner of the celebrated Deutsch-Archdeacon Prize of $10,000 for the first *public* circular flight in history, Farman filed a letter with the Paris office of the *Herald* on that same day expressing his skepticism and more:

To the Editor of the HERALD:—

DEAR SIR—For some time I have seen in the papers that the brothers Wright are establishing new records, and the following day everything is denied. For my part I believe the brothers Wright are very expert in the matter and able to execute fine flights.

However, my experience in aviation permits me to assert that present reports at least and even former ones are absolutely inexact. Among other examples I cite the fact which has appeared in a report that three or four miles were covered in fifteen minutes or something approaching that period. Now, it is absolutely impossible to fly so slowly.

I am, moreover, ready to challenge them to a speed and distance contest, to be decided in France. I can propose 25,000f [French francs] ($5,000) as stakes at once, and I am certain of being able to get together a larger sum if the brothers Wright will accept.

I propose this match with full knowledge of what I am doing, for I have made more than a hundred flights and have covered a distance of about five kilometers, remaining five minutes in the air above ground, which is too small and which obliged me to make numerous turns. Moreover, I was hampered by spectators.

My present apparatus, such as it is, can remain twenty-four minutes in the air at a speed of eighty kilometers an hour, and with modifications which I shall make in it I am certain in a short time I shall not be far from establishing a record for an hour, but it must be understood not at Issy-les-Moulineux [where the crowds interfered].

H. FARMAN.[11]

The very next morning Farman's challenge to the Wright brothers appeared both in the *Herald* and in hundreds of other newspapers in Europe and the United States. And so did the most recent confusing articles about the Wright brothers' flights—arriving almost instantaneously in Paris from Manteo for the next days' publications.[12]

Wilbur and Orville arose in utter peace on the morning of Sunday, May 17, 1908, oblivious to having been the subject of so much international attention on the previous day. While Drinkwater's telegraph machine in Manteo hastened the outflow of information for the world press, there was no comparable inflow of the resulting newspapers to the Outer Banks or in Manteo to provide interesting Sunday reading for the Wright brothers. According to Wilbur's diary, "Left camp about ten o'clock and went over to Manteo with 'Uncle Benny' O'Neal"—one of the faithful and very helpful lifesavers from Kill Devil Hills.[13] Neither Wilbur nor Orville noted at the time—they could not know and would not have believed—that this was their last night and morning together in North Carolina, at the place where they had originated flight and where they—as it would soon become clear—had literally just sent the world soaring in powered flying machines. While Orville would return without Wilbur for further test flights in 1911, and on many other occasions to commemorate their flights and consecrate monuments until his death in 1948, this was the last day they would ever spend together at Kitty Hawk.

While Orville stayed behind to close their camp, finish the process of packing their goods for shipment back to Dayton, and further analyze the remains of their 1905 flyer for clues about its failure on May 14, Wilbur was, in essence, catapulted from Kitty Hawk and Kill Devil Hills onto the world's stage. He would not return to Dayton at this time. As hastily planned, he proceeded directly from Kitty Hawk to Manteo and on from there to Norfolk and New York as momentary stopovers on his way to Europe. His next destination would be Le Mans, France, where he would astound Europeans, gathered from virtually every nation, with flights between August 8 and December 31, 1908. From there, he would continue to increase the duration of his flights dramatically until he flew nonstop for a period of 2 hours and 20 minutes on the last day of the year.

From Le Mans, Wilbur would proceed in January 1909 to Pau, France, where he would amaze even more Europeans—especially Britons and Spaniards who vacationed in that southwest corner of the country—with his daring flying feats. He would do the same in the presence of Italians while flying at Rome between April 15 and 27. Over the twelve-month period following his departure from Kitty Hawk, he flew—just as he had imagined on his way to Kitty Hawk—in the presence of kings, dukes, dames, duchesses, and throngs of thousands of observers, single-handedly demonstrating to an enthralled world how the Wright brothers could fly. His feet would not touch American soil again until May 1909, on the first anniversary of the historic Kitty Hawk flights. He arrived in New York for a hero's welcome on May 11 and reappeared in Dayton on May 13—precisely twelve months after the start of the worldwide stir he and Orville had launched.

This yearlong whirlwind tour seemed only a remote possibility as Wilbur proceeded from Kill Devil Hills to Manteo on the morning of May 17, 1908. He wished to advance from North Carolina to Europe via New York as soon as possible, but he was also interested in determining the identities of the reporters who had been dogging the brothers' path for the last week or so. As soon as he arrived at the Tranquil House in Manteo, he got his answer. The wide-open hotel register showed the comings and goings of all of the reporters except Gilson Gardiner. Bruce Salley had been there from May 4 on; Hoster and Newton arrived on the eleventh; Hare, Ruhl, and McGowan on the twelfth. By the seventeenth when he came to spend his last night in North Carolina, also at the Tranquil, all had departed except Hare—who was still around trying his hand at fishing and snapping more photos.[14]

It was a Sunday, however, and, as always, for the Wrights, it was a day of rest, contemplation, and writing letters. Now it was Wilbur's turn to sit quietly on the porch at the Tranquil, pen a few letters, and gaze into the future. One letter was to Orville who, of course, he had just left an hour or so before. He sent his brother a report on what he had learned about the activities of the reporters in Manteo. He wrote another letter to sister Katharine, summarizing recent events and using her, as he sometimes did, as a sounding board for what he was thinking.

He could be officious with her, but this time he was almost confessional. He wrote, "I cannot remember just when we wrote last but think it must have been nearly a week." There followed a recounting of the events of the historic day of

May 14—when both brothers took Charles Furnas on flights and Wilbur completed the solo flight that amazed the onlooking reporters. Rather than dwelling on the historic importance of the occasion, Wilbur used his sister as his confessor to admit that he and Orville had been too rushed in their flights and that he had erred in using the new control system on the last flight, causing the disastrous crash. He also lamented leaving Kitty Hawk without repairing their plane for further flights. It could easily have been done, he wrote.[15]

But there were places to go and things to do. And there was, alas, a lifetime thereafter of unsought and unwanted intrusions from inquiring reporters. Feeling as if he were in the midst of a well-deserved holiday, Wilbur was suddenly presented late on the seventeenth with a copy of the Associated Press dispatch containing Henri Farman's challenge for a flying duel with the brothers to be held in France. Since Alpheus Drinkwater had by then made himself a virtual Associated Press contact in Manteo, the inquiring party might have been Drinkwater or perhaps the Tranquil House's innkeeper on Drinkwater's behalf. Wilbur did not mention the incident specifically in his diary or letters, although this may have been what he was referring to in his letter to Orville that day when he wrote, "I enclose an amusing telegram from Salley which you have no doubt already received from the K. D. Station."[16]

Wilbur evidently decided not to respond to Salley's telegram, but he must have made a gruff comment to either Drinkwater or the innkeeper agent, for the incident led to an article that went across the world through the Associated Press. One version, datelined Manteo, was in the guise of a first-person voice representing the London *Daily Mail*. On May 19 the paper published a brief blurb said to be from "Our Special Correspondent"—most likely Drinkwater, since McGowan had already departed: "When I told Mr. Wilbur Wright of Mr. Henry Farman's challenge to a flying match for £1,000, he merely replied: 'Thanks.' Urged to say whether his answer would be an acceptance, he said there would be no answer."[17]

Another version of this abrupt conversation was datelined "Norfolk" without attribution. According to this article, which appeared in the *Charlotte Observer*, the incident was indeed brief: "Wilbur Wright, . . . when shown last night's Associated Press dispatch from London to the effect that Henry Farman . . . has issued a challenge to the Ohioans to an aeroplane contest in France for a stake of $5,000, refused to make any statement on the subject." Nor would Wilbur "say whether or not he had received Farman's challenge through another source than the Associated Press dispatch." In fact, according to the release, Wilbur stated, "I will talk to you on any subject except aeroplanes or my plans for the future."[18]

It was on this abrupt and none too kindly note that Wilbur Wright lay down that evening to spend what must have been a somewhat troubled night in the Tranquil House at Manteo—his last ever in North Carolina. But even as Wilbur had begun his last bit of sleep at the Tranquil House, other reporters were trying to get a comment on the Farman story back home in Dayton. Katharine Wright described what happened late on the seventeenth: "Last night at ten, a newspaper reporter, named Glass, called up, saying that he had a telegram from the New York World asking him to interview one of you on Farman's challenge." A Philadelphia newspaper had an article quoting both Farman and Léon Delagrange—another French flyer—both questioning the Wright brothers' achievements. In Katharine's opinion, "Delagrange is very patronizing—so is Farman—from published interviews." Serving as young sister and cheerleader for her older brother on his way to Europe, Katharine wrote, "Show 'em a few things, Jullam."[19]

Wilbur arose long before dawn on Monday, May 18, and bid his last adieu to the Tranquil House. He only needed to travel a few yards with his baggage to the wharf in Manteo where the 65-foot shallow-bottomed *Hattie Creef* waited to take him across Albemarle Sound to Elizabeth City one last time. The boat, originally built as a sailboat in 1901, but equipped with a gasoline engine in 1903, left promptly at 5:00 A.M. and made a quick passage in just four hours, ending at the dock in Elizabeth City at 10:20 A.M.

On this boat, which made daily runs between Elizabeth City and Manteo for decades, was also Zachary McGhee, the South Carolina reporter for the *Columbia State*. Wilbur liked this particular reporter's manner and point of view. He also learned that their paths had crossed the day before as McGhee was headed to Kill Devil Hills while Wilbur made his way to Manteo. Since McGhee had arrived in Manteo while the gaggle of reporters was still in town, he was able to fill Wilbur in as to who they were and where they were from—and the fact, which Wilbur very much enjoyed, that the reporters knew nothing of his crash on the fourteenth until they were informed by the lifesavers arriving in Manteo.[20]

McGhee chortled with Wilbur about the fact that the high-powered reporters had written about the crash and other scenes as if they had been eyewitnesses. This made Wilbur warm up to the young reporter even more. When he wrote Orville a couple of days later about his time with McGhee, he gloated about the reputation the two of them had gotten with the newspapermen. About the wreck on the fourteenth, he wrote, "If the life savers had not been crazy to spread it so soon it would have attracted no attention in the papers." He also added a telling lesson: "It seems we had the newspaper men thoroughly convinced that if they attempted to approach at all closely that we would not fly. *It is a good thing sometimes to have a fierce reputation, like a school teacher.*"[21] The joke between the brothers, of course, was that they would have flown whether or not the reporters had been there— since their most important goal was to make sure that their new control system was working as they had hoped and that they could carry the additional weight.

While Wilbur was making his way across the waters of Albemarle Sound and through the dark thicknesses of the Great Dismal Swamp via rail from Elizabeth City to Norfolk—a rather quiet, somewhat desolate, and contemplative portion of the world—things were hopping at home in Dayton. At 9:30 that morning Bishop Wright inscribed a breathless letter to Orville at Kitty Hawk describing the mayhem back home. "This morning's mail brought your letter, dated the night of the 13th to Katharine." While the good Bishop did not mention it in his letter to Orville, in his diary he wrote, "I took Katharine's lunch basket to her at school"— with Orville's letter, of course, tucked into the container of food.[22]

The Bishop's diary continued with the story of exciting times that day:

The Scranton *Republican* came this morning (addressed to Wright Bros.) containing an editorial saying that for the destruction of your aeroplane the Wright brothers will have "world-wide sympathy," and saying that "there is reason to be devoutly thankful that the men who devised the mechanism are unhurt," and also predicting increased success. The Sunday Philadelphia *Press*, contains a little over a long column about you and your machine—all complimentary. It says that you are "slim, sedate and placid," "the very antithesis of one's idea of what an airship sailor should be;" "nothing daring, nothing devilish about them," "They look like a pair of clerks in a village hardware store, whose pleasure it is to attend the Wednesday night prayer meeting,"[illeg]. How sadly they miss the devotional tendency! Yet largely you owe your training and standing to the church. *Saturday Evening News* has a 14 inch quotation from Hearsts newspapers on your flights; and this morning's *Journal* has an 8 inch, first page report: "Wrights O.K. Won't be Home," (Interviewed Katharine).

In addition to all the attention the brothers were getting in the press, their father reported that the local Presbyterian clergyman, the Rev. Merle Anderson, had talked about them in his Sunday sermon: "On treating of the achievement of the impossible, [he] referred to Columbus, Fulton &c. and wound up on the achievements of the 'Wright brothers.'"[23]

Before that long Monday ended, Wilbur's train finished its journey through the Great Dismal Swamp and chugged into Norfolk. As soon as the train arrived at the station, Wilbur saw a familiar face. D. Bruce Salley was waiting on the platform, hoping to get a real interview with Wilbur as a capstone to his sleuthing in Manteo and Kill Devil Hills over the last two weeks. Wilbur was headed to the Monticello Hotel, where the brothers always lodged when visiting Norfolk. Salley insisted on buying Wilbur's dinner at the hotel. Wilbur, who—despite his protestations to the contrary—had not yet gotten his full diet of reporters, agreed to the proposition. Besides, he wanted to learn more from Salley about what the reporters had been doing around Manteo. He was also interested to know what reporters were saying about the recent flights, which were presently, he learned, being bantered about all over the world.[24]

Now that the big city reporters had returned to their dens, Salley was once again *the* man on the spot and in a perfect position to gather up a unique story. He had been overshadowed and supplanted by the other reporters who had descended on Manteo and Kitty Hawk. But on this evening he was able to spend some quiet time conducting a real interview with the elder Wright. From their dinner conversation he was able to produce two important stories—one that he broke immediately and the other resulting in a deeper reflection on how the Wrights were being affected by their new fame.

As soon as they finished dinner, Salley sent out a special dispatch that was picked up and published the very next day by the *New York Herald*. From his interview, Salley reported that he had asked Wilbur if he and Orville were happy with their recent flights at Kill Devil Hills. Wilbur, he said, "replied laconically:— 'Yes, quite.'" Asked whether the brothers had now solved the problem of flight, Wilbur responded: "We consider we did that several years ago. Our recent experiments had no connection with that problem, but were made to better understand the operation of our machine."[25] The *Herald* was satisfied with this brief news flash, for the editors knew that Wilbur was on his way to New York and were confident that they would get a bigger and better story once he got to the city.

Salley's second story from the private dinner was published by the *New York World* on the twentieth, and here Salley was able to make full use of his relaxed conversation with Wilbur. Up close and without the usual cap that Wilbur wore at all times out of doors, Salley could easily see the marks left by the crash on May 14: "As souvenirs of the mishap, Wright bore a rapidly healing scar on the bridge of his nose and a bruise on his partly bald head." After repeating the lusterless remarks already covered in the *Herald* piece, Salley branched into some of the brothers' more deeply revealing thoughts and observations—moments that could only have been captured in conversation, not at a press event.

On the subject of the vaunted crash Wilbur said: "You fellows exaggerated the injury sustained by our machine when it was wrecked. As a matter of fact the total damage did not amount to more than $50." When Salley delved into the topic of the challenge from Henri Farman for a flying duel in France, Wright said, "I have nothing to say about that." But Salley followed this with a further observation: "From what Wilbur Wright said later it would be inferred that he does not consider Farman in the same class with himself and brother as navigators of the air. He evidently does not think Farman has ever accomplished much."[26]

While Salley found Wright, as usual, reticent to speak about the next moves the brothers would make in the international chess game of spreading the power of flight throughout the world, he definitely tapped into the brothers' deeply held feelings that they had figured out before anyone else on earth how to fly and that it was their turn—at long last—to demonstrate their unique discoveries before a world audience. He and Orville had carefully selected their venues, and they were not about to be deterred from their impending rendezvous with history and fate.

At 7:00 A.M. on the next day, May 19, Wilbur was on the train headed from Norfolk to New York. Since Salley had been in contact with the *New York Herald* about his own story, he was able to warn Wilbur about what he was likely to face when he arrived in the big city. Wilbur described the reception when he wrote Orville on the twentieth: "When I got to New York a *Herald* man met me at the train having been warned from Norfolk. He acted very decently and gave a fairly good report of our talk, though he got all balled up on the motor question." The reporter accompanied Wilbur to the Park Avenue Hotel where they continued their conversation for quite a while—until the reporter left to write his story.[27]

After this conversation, Wilbur apparently learned that the New York offices of Charles R. Flint—where he was headed at the moment—had been besieged all day by reporters demanding to see the elder brother. Flint, an international munitions dealer and a domestic financier and creator of monopoly corporations, worked with the international syndicate chosen by the brothers to sell their planes in Europe. As an object of curiosity to reporters himself, Flint had some experience in deflecting eager journalists. Seeking to save Wilbur from having to deal with the New York press, he quickly devised a diversionary tactic to protect the suddenly world-famous aeronaut. Rather than risk a confrontation either at the Flint and Company offices or at the Park Avenue Hotel where Wilbur had a room waiting for him, the savvy Flint decided to move Wilbur to the City Club of New York after dinner at the hotel and pretend that the celebrity flier had already left the country. Wilbur wrote to Orville the next day: "I am now staying at the City Club, and have a splendid room with bath &c." As for the reporters, they were told that Wilbur had made his exit the day before.[28]

As it turned out, this was only one layer in a multitude of subterfuges going on at that moment. Wilbur was refusing to deal with the press. Charles Flint wanted to protect his new star client from unwanted encounters with the press. And on the side of the press, every major newspaper had challenged its reporters to get the true story of what had really happened at Kitty Hawk and to find out what in the world the Wright brothers would be doing next. There had been conflicting stories out of North Carolina about long flights over ocean waters, soaring flights to great heights, and traverses to capes and islands many miles away. Moreover, some of the biggest newspapers and magazines in the United States had spent good money to send well-paid reporters to the Outer Banks of North Carolina, and they came back with neither photographs nor detailed descriptions of what were said to be the greatest flights in human history. The curse of the swaggering lifesavers was beginning to cause some frayed nerves in the news media capital.

One of the casualties of this stampede to get better and more revealing stories on the Wrights was Byron Newton, the *Herald* reporter who had been on site at Kitty Hawk and who had written some of the most accurate and well-documented articles that emanated from the telegraph office in Manteo. On either May 18 or 19—probably his first day back in the *Herald* offices in New York and fresh from the wilds of the Outer Banks, Newton was called on the carpet for the timidity of his stories from the scene of the flights. Why could he not get more information on the long flights in the sensational stories the *Herald* had received at first? Why could he not describe the crash scene on the fourteenth? Did he really personally witness the two-person flights that were reported on the thirteenth, but that had evidently not really happened until the fourteenth? Newton was told, in essence, that he either had to up the ante in his stories with real facts or face the consequences. Claiming later in a letter of June 11 to Orville that he refused to be intimidated by his editors, Newton resigned on the spot. As he explained, "I regret to state, however, that after eight years of very pleasant association, The New York Herald and I have been obliged to part company, on account of widely differing views about the way aerial navigation matters should be handled."[29]

When Wilbur arrived in New York and was greeted by "a *Herald* man," it was not the genial Newton who had been to North Carolina and who knew and understood what had really happened there. The unnamed *Herald* reporter who met Wilbur at the train station and accompanied him to the Park Avenue Hotel pummeled him with the same questions he had previously gotten from McGhee on the *Hattie Creef* out of Manteo and from Salley in Norfolk. The resulting article, which appeared the next day, May 20, provided almost no new information on the Wright brothers' activities—but it did give readers a little more insight into the character and appearance of Wilbur Wright. The reporter described Wilbur as "a man of medium height, well set up and clean shaven" who was "tanned to a deep brown by the North Carolina suns." He noted that "his hands are scarred and minus several patches of skin, lost in the course of his work with the airship at Manteo."

But he also found that the elder brother was unwilling to make many substantive comments. Why was he in New York? "Business," Wilbur replied. Would he and Orville accept the challenge issued by Henri Farman? "I have not seen his challenge," he said—"Down in Manteo we did not get the papers and I have fallen behind of late as to recent developments." Could he add any additional information on the results of the brothers' flights in North Carolina? "I can say nothing now more than is generally known," Wilbur stated. But without further prompting, Wilbur added to his virtual "no comment" performance a further spike for the press:

> It is probable that in a few days my brother will give out a formal statement for the public, but even this has not been definitely decided on. In declining to tell now what we accomplished or did not accomplish, I do not want to be misunderstood. At all times we have given such information as would not interfere with our plans. We appreciate the interest shown in our work by the public, but it has happened more than once that well intended publications have worked serious injury to us. . . .

Since he was not able to gather concrete information on the brothers' plans, the reporter wrote up a couple of general comments made by Wilbur on the prospects of the airplane as a military tool and on the future design of airplanes. It was nothing sensational, however—nothing worthy of new headlines.[30]

Still, the editors and publishers of the *Herald*—unable to get a story from Wilbur Wright and having severed their ties with Byron Newton, who had been their only envoy on site at Kitty Hawk—had another set of ideas about how to make headlines concerning the Wright brothers. They planned to publish their surprise simultaneously with the exclusive interview obtained by their reporter on the nineteenth—the first such interchange with Wilbur since he arrived in New York. It was also the last contact he would have with the press before departing New York for Europe on the twenty-first. But since he stayed in the news metropolis of the United States for one more day, Wilbur was able to read the newspaper headlines on the twentieth and twenty-first and to experience the first taste of what being a recognized newsmaker would be like for the rest of his foreshortened life.

The *Herald*'s first great surprise appeared alongside the rather innocuous news article produced by the reportorial staff. The editors placed beside that article a picture of one of the Wrights' recent historic flights in North Carolina. There thus appeared for the first time in print anywhere in the world a picture that was said to be a faithful photograph of one of the Wright brothers' recent flights at Kitty Hawk. The combined headline and caption laid out the claim as follows: "*The Wright Brothers' Aeroplane at Kill Devil Hill, N.C./Photographed by a N. Y. Herald Photographer. Copyrighted 1908 by the New York Herald Co.*" A short explanatory statement with the photograph elaborated on the remarkable claim: "The picture of the Wright brothers' aeroplane printed in to-day's HERALD is the first photograph of the flying machine ever published, if in fact it is not the first ever made." Supposedly the "photograph" had been "snapped last Thursday [May 14] at Kill Devil Hill, North Carolina, just after the famous brothers had started on what was intended to be a fifty-mile flight, but which ended in disaster after eight miles had been covered." As to why there had never been another photograph published of a Wright powered flight, "the brothers have successfully, up to this time, avoided photographers."31

The published picture, presented as if it were a faithful image made from a photographic negative, was not a photograph at all. It was rather what can only be described as an "illustration" based on a photograph. The image used to create the illustration was one of those that had been taken by James H. Hare at Kill Devil Hills on May 14 and that would soon appear in *Collier's Weekly*. What the *Herald* published was a doctored version of Hare's photograph—almost a century before the introduction of digitally manipulated photographic images. The *Herald*'s editors explained that the original photograph "was taken from a distance of but a few rods and gives an excellent idea of the appearance of the aeroplane as it swung in and around the immense sand hills near Manteo, N.C." It does not require an experienced eye to determine that the printed image lacks the fidelity and clarity of a photograph.

Although Wilbur saw the *Herald* issue that day, he made no immediate comment on its creative illustration. Instead, he spent the day dodging reporters, modifying his lodging plans, and doing a number of things that would spur even more speculation about both his mission in New York and the Wrights' plans for the immediate future. On the subject of the press, he wrote in his diary, "Reporters and Aero Club men besieged the hotel and Flint's office but I refused to see anyone." In one of his two letters written to Orville from New York on the twentieth, he commented that there were a dozen reporters on his trail that day.

His actual path on this day was quite curious. It could not have been better designed to fuel speculation on the part of reporters when they got hints and patches of where he went and who he saw. His plans were to do one thing: "Arrangements had been made for a trip by automobile to Orange [N.J.] to visit Mr. [Thomas] Edison in company with Mr. Flint and Wu Ting Fang, the Chinese ambassador, but rain prevented it." Flint had organized this outing, which had to be canceled because of the inclement weather. Instead, Wilbur met with General Nelson A. Miles of the U.S. Army concerning the Wright contract to produce an airplane for the U.S. government by the end of August. He also conferred with Flint and one of Flint's associates, Frank R. Cordley, concerning his pending trip to France. Sometime during the day he also saw Charles Levee, a member of the Aero-Club de France, whom he had met while in France in 1907.[32]

New York reporters were almost going mad in their search for Wilbur and further comments from him on the experiments at Kitty Hawk and the brothers' pending plans for flights in the United States and France. While Wilbur avoided direct encounters with roving journalists, he ultimately left so many crumbs about his activities and whereabouts that he ended up feeding rather than quelling the frenzy. One of the *New York Herald* reporters knew that Wilbur was meeting with the Flint Company and was able to corner Charles Flint and ask him: "Are you negotiating with the Wright brothers in the matter of their airship plans?" To which the urbane Flint responded, "I have nothing to say about this." This led to the further question, "Is it to be understood from your refusal to discuss the subject that you have not been or are not negotiating with the Wrights?" Flint reiterated his comment, "I have nothing to say."[33]

Another *Herald* reporter—or at least someone writing a story that was bought by both the *Herald* and the *Virginian-Pilot*—came up with a much more fanciful story on the day's events. Both articles reported that the quiescent Flint was organizing the meetings of his clients (the Wrights) with Edison and the Chinese ambassador. The purpose of the meeting with Edison in his laboratories was "to confer with the 'Wiseard,' as to the adoption of an electrical contrivance for the airship." As for meeting with the Chinese representative, it was "leaked out" that Wilbur had been meeting with him for several days:

> The nature of these conferences is a diplomatic secret, but Mr. Wu has shown great interest in the meeting with the aeronaut and has given the latter practically all his time for the past three days. It is stated by those claiming to have known[,] negotiations are pending for the sale of the secret to the aerial ship to China. Confirmation of this, however, is unobtainable, as Mr. Wright and Mr. Flint refuse to talk on the subject.

In addition to clandestine meetings with Edison and Wu, neither of which actually happened, these same papers also reported that Wilbur Wright "held a number of consultations" with J. M. Flannery, general manager of the American Vanadium Company of Pittsburgh, Pennsylvania. These stories held that the Wrights were about to embark on the use of Vanadium steel in the construction of their airplanes. The use of Vanadium, described as "a flux in the hardening of metals" including steel or aluminum, would result in machines "much lighter than the one with which the flights were made at Manteo" and therefore "much easier to keep in the air."[34]

These articles, which appeared in many similar versions throughout the United States on the morning of May 21, also reported that the older Wright brother would "begin experiments with the flux [Vanadium] as soon as he can finish his business in New York and return to his workshops in Dayton." What the newspapers did not know was that Wilbur had sailed out of the port of New York at 10:00 that morning on board the SS *Touraine*—noted in his diary that day as a ship of 9,000 tons and 12,000 horsepower—bound for Le Havre, France. His real destination, of course, was Paris. For the next seven days, as Wilbur observed in a letter to his father on May 28, "On the steamer . . . we have no news of importance to occupy our minds, and few distractions of any kind." There were only about sixty passengers in the first-class cabins where Wilbur took passage and only "a dozen or so talk English, so life becomes a little monotonous." Wilbur was, in essence, out of the limelight and out of touch during one of the most critical weeks in which the Wright brothers unexpectedly emerged from the relatively peaceful existence they had known during all their years of pursuing the grail of flight. He would not reenter the world of news and news making until he arrived in Paris on Friday, May 29, at 10:00 P.M.[35]

By departing at this critical moment, Wilbur did something very uncharacteristic of him—something he avoided doing throughout most of the joint career of the Wright brothers. He placed the responsibility for their public relations entirely in the hands of Orville. Since Orville suffered throughout his life from a fear of public speaking and a certainty that he could not write a coherent sentence, this was a role he was thrust into abruptly and unwillingly. However, he had little choice in the situation: while the Wright brothers were totally equal partners in the invention of flight, they were unequal partners in making decisions about business and publicity. Wilbur handed out orders to Orville as if he were general and the younger brother a lieutenant. Almost always, Orville took such orders in stride and did his best to carry them out.

On May 20, the day before he departed from New York on the *Touraine*, Wilbur was in a typical barking, commanding mood. In two letters written to Orville on that date he ordered his brother to bring his watch and "also my Derby & straw hats & the meteorological reports & the French money which is probably somewhere about my washstand" when he followed him to Europe, as was the plan at that time. This was doable, but Wilbur also gave his younger brother some other, more complicated assignments. Believing that the time had come for the brothers to assert their claims as the world's originators of controlled flight, Wilbur gave two instructions.

First, he assigned Orville the responsibility of writing the brothers' first official article in which they would explain their accomplishments to date in innovating flight. This article would also be the place where the Wrights intended to publish for the first time ever the historic photograph of their first powered flight on December 17, 1903. Secondly, given the plethora of confusing and misleading articles published surrounding their recent flights at Kitty Hawk, Wilbur told Orville that he should prepare a statement for the press explaining precisely what they were attempting to do and what they had actually accomplished while in North Carolina.[36]

After they had gotten many, many requests from newspapers and magazines to tell their own story and, more important, to display photographs in the pages of this or that exquisite publication, the Wrights had settled upon *Century Magazine* as the place to tell the whole story for the first time from their point of view. Wilbur had intended to write the article, as he had previously prepared well-honed speeches that became articles in *Scientific American* and in various engineering journals. But in the rush to create, build, and sell planes, there had not been time for him to write what would be the most important article ever published by the Wright brothers on their flying experiments. He turned to Orville, writing, "it is my opinion as firmly as ever that we need to have our true story told in an authentic way at once." "It is important to get the main features originated by us," he continued, "identified in the public mind with our machines before they are described in connection with some other machines." Nervously entrusting his brother with this crucial task, he added, "I strongly advise that you get a stenographer and dictate an article and have Kate [their sister] assist in getting it in shape if you are too busy."[37]

Despite misgivings about his abilities to do as instructed in this particular instance, Orville would faithfully attempt to carry out the complex set of assignments. Orville had now become the principal agent for advancing the brothers' American business, while Wilbur sought to establish their European ventures. A crucial factor on both of these fronts was to figure out why their plane had failed prematurely during Wilbur's last flight on May 14.

The brothers could ill afford for this to happen again when they began their public flights in France and the United States. Yet they were mystified as to what might have caused the plane to halt in midair and then plunge downward into the sand. Wilbur told the press that he had made a mistake in operating the control system. But both he and Orville knew that the real cause was a mechanical malfunction, not human error. Wilbur expected Orville—as the mechanical engineer in their partnership—to diagnose the problem and to find a solution. Also, dates for test flights had to be scheduled both in Europe and the United States, and two of their new planes had to be prepared for flights in each place. Wilbur would handle Europe, but Orville had to make all things happen in the United States.

Beyond the demands set by Wilbur, there were extraordinary additional pressures that fell upon Orville at this time. The challenge from Henri Farman delivered by reporters to Wilbur as he was leaving North Carolina was one of them. Wilbur had, of course, decided to effectively ignore the challenge. But one of the great American publishers—Robert J. Collier—decided to step into the breach to see what he could do to produce a spectacle in flight comparable to an international prize fight between two celebrated and undefeated heavyweight boxing champions. Through Arthur Ruhl, the reporter *Collier's Weekly* had put on the scene at Kitty Hawk to interview the Wrights, Collier initiated an exchange of correspondence that would presage a newsmaking article soon to appear in the pages of *Collier's*. Ruhl had composed a brilliant article on the Wrights' achievements at Kitty Hawk, and James Hare had been the one to snap a monumental photograph of the Wright plane in flight. What could be better than for *Collier's* to organize a challenge match between the two parties claiming to be the greatest aeronauts in the modern world?

In a letter addressed to the brothers at Dayton on May 21 and followed by a telegraph sent to Orville the same day, Ruhl reminded the brothers that he had intruded into their camp at Kill Devil Hills on behalf of *Collier's Weekly*. At that time, he said, they had discussed the challenge that had been issued by the London *Daily Mail* to the Wrights and delivered to them in person by P. H. McGowan, the *Daily Mail* reporter on the scene. Later, a second challenge by French pilot Henri Farman had appeared in the *New York Herald*. Although Ruhl knew nothing more of either of the challenges "than has been given in the newspapers," he told the brothers that his boss, Robert Collier, would like to organize and produce the contest:

> He would like to accept Farman's challenge for you, putting up, himself, the nec-
> essary stake and paying all your expenses for the race. If you wish—and I sup-
> pose there is no doubt whatever that you would win—whatever prize, or stake,
> etc., there is, will come to you. If you or Farman should afterward want a return
> match in this country, he would be glad to back you in the same way.

Having heard that Wilbur might be in New York at that moment and might be available for a meeting at the *Collier's* headquarters, Ruhl addressed his telegram specifically to Orville with the message, "Mr Collier very anxious to make propo-sition about race with Farman[.] can we see willbur Wright here[?]"[38]

Much to Ruhl's chagrin, Orville did not respond to this urgent plea on May 21, nor on the twenty-second or the twenty-third. Indeed, Ruhl would not be able to rouse a response from the much slower and more deliberate Wright brother until he followed up with another communication a week later.

While Wilbur had made his way to New York, pausing there to become the elusive sensation of city reporters, and then sailed away to Europe, Orville remained at the Wright camp at Kitty Hawk. There was much to be done to close out the 1908 camp and the testing season on the Outer Banks. The broken flying machine needed to be crated up and shipped back to Dayton. They had brought an endless stream of tools, parts, and equipment that needed to be returned as well. Both of the brothers were still very eager to investigate what had happened on that last flight on May 14.

After Wilbur headed off to Manteo on May 18, Orville spent three days tak-ing care of these matters until he could leave on the twenty-first. In addition to taking a good look at the engine that had failed on the fourteenth, Orville and Fur-nas also drew up a map of the flight paths the brothers had followed in their test flights—particularly Wilbur's last flight. Using this map, he was able to gauge more accurately the distances covered and calculate the speed of their flights—including the plane's speed in the final test, which was approximately 30 miles per hour. As usual, Orville was the master of the post mortem—what had happened and why—while Wilbur was charting the future. The mapping exercise did not fully explain the failure, but it would be helpful in doing so.[39]

When Wilbur sailed from New York on the morning of May 21, Orville was making his way over to Manteo and on to Norfolk. At Norfolk, he boarded a night boat that took him on to Washington, D.C. But before Orville was able to make his way onto the boat, he was intercepted by the intrepid Salley. The insatiable reporter met Orville at the same train station where he had previously tracked down Wilbur. Although he had been off the Wright brothers' track for the past week, he was still attempting to sell stories. According to Orville, "I had a time getting away from him without giving away where I was going." Evidently he was also tight-lipped about other Wright activities and was able to shake the persistent reporter off his trail, for it does not appear that Salley was able to wangle enough information from him to post a news story.

On the morning of Friday, May 22, Orville's night boat from Norfolk arrived in Washington, where he planned to make an inspection tour of the U.S. Army base at nearby Fort Myer, Virginia. This was the narrow field chosen by the Army Signal Corps for the Wrights' flying tests scheduled for August and September. But just as Wilbur's ship had encountered thick fog and stormy weather as it departed from New York on the twenty-first, Orville's path took him into the heavy rains of the same weather system that hugged the Atlantic coast from the south to the northeast. The driving rain he faced all day on the twenty-second hampered the progress of his boat out of Norfolk and made it impossible for him to do a thorough inspection of the cramped grounds at Fort Myer. Orville told Wilbur following his visit, "That is about as tough ground to fly over as one could well expect."[40]

Following his weather-impeded visit to Fort Myer, Orville returned quietly by another night boat to Norfolk late on the evening of the twenty-second. Since he kept no record and did not otherwise mention a secret meeting with a French agent in Norfolk on either the twenty-first or the twenty-second, Orville apparently barely missed an encounter that provided one of the curious outcroppings of the Wrights' already renowned recent activities at Kitty Hawk. On the twenty-second, while Orville was making his rain-soaked round trip from

Norfolk to Washington, there appeared in Norfolk a mysterious Frenchman by the name of Jean Jardin, who represented himself as Henri Farman's official agent. His mission, though shrouded in mystery, was to arrange the much-publicized flying duel between the Wrights and Farman. Somehow this man, who does not appear elsewhere in the Wright-Farman story, encountered a writer for the *Virginian-Pilot* and was interviewed on the twenty-second on the subject of a possible Farman-Wright challenge match.

The man was just as coy with the reporter as Wilbur had been just a few days earlier on the same topic. But because Jardin was carrying "several telegrams, dated Paris and addressed to himself in New York" and signed by Farman, his story was given much credence. He explained that his instructions were to convey Farman's challenge directly to the Wright brothers "while tapping the cablegrams he held in his hand." Since Orville's secret maneuvers had probably frustrated his great mission by the evening of the twenty-second when he was interviewed, his statement for the press was brief and elusive: "It is a matter of very great secrecy. I can say that in the near future there will be made some very startling sensations in the way of aerial flights, and if the problem is said to be solved now it will be to a greater extent when these flights take place." Since no direct set of challenge matches between the Wrights and Farman ever occurred, Jardin did not succeed in his mission—even if he eventually did by some chance make direct contact with Orville on the twenty-first or twenty-second.[41]

Apparently knowing nothing about Jardin's clandestine visit, Orville proceeded from Norfolk to Dayton on the morning of Saturday, May 23, arriving home about noon. Katharine Wright, who was expecting him to come on a train from Washington, described his odd appearance:

> Orv came home Saturday noon. I met him—in the most comical way. I thought
> he would come from Washington and so went to meet the 12:05 Pennsylvania.
> At exactly 12:05 he walks off of a C.H.& D. from Cincinnati! He had left his bag-
> gage at Norfolk, went up to Washington, by one night boat, spent the day in
> Washington, back again to Norfolk by another night boat and came home over
> the C. & O. So I met him all right.

According to Katharine, Orville "looks thin and worn." She thought the physical and emotional ordeal of flights and trailing newsmen was taking a toll on him and wrote, "I can't wait until this summer is over. It is getting to be such a worry to us all."[42]

The home folk were nevertheless jubilant to see at least one of the pair of the overnight celebrities back home. After a round of welcomes and some good home cooking, Orville eventually sat down to read Wilbur's letters of instruction from New York and to look through another pile of mail awaiting him. He could easily have become overwhelmed. As he shortly wrote Wilbur, "our mail has increased about tenfold." And with all of the assignments from his brother looming, he was completely swamped: "It has been a hard job to get work done since I came back on account of everyone wanting to talk." Whenever he encountered local folk around Dayton, he found that "the wreck [on the fourteenth] was the talk of the street the morning after it happened."[43]

Since Wilbur was still at sea on the *Touraine* and inaccessible even via telegraph—which the brothers used frequently when they were on separate sides of the Atlantic—Orville had to devise his own strategy for answering the endless inquiries about what really happened at Kitty Hawk. He was surely spurred further into action when he opened the pages of the *Scientific American* for May 23 and saw that even this prestigious weekly—which prided itself on providing accurate information on new developments in aeronautics—contained faulty information about their flights. The great news journal on science had also relied on the extravagant news reports that had come from the hands of Drinkwater and the *Virginian-Pilot*. Despite the conflicting stories, however, the *Scientific American* did declare from the muddle of reports that "in view of these semi-public demonstrations, there can be no further doubt of the claims made by the brothers as to their ability to fly." That was an assuring perspective coming from the highest court of science in America, but for Orville—who was a lifelong stickler for absolute accuracy in every detail—the persisting errors in documenting the nature, distance, and duration of their flights at Kitty Hawk was galling. He found this so troublesome that he decided to wage a one-man battle to get corrections published in all the venues where it really counted.[44]

On Sunday, May 24, with Orville in Dayton and Wilbur still inaccessible in the middle of the Atlantic Ocean, Milton Wright went to church and wrote in his diary that he heard a prophetic sermon from the lips of the Rev. Asa McDaniel. The text was from Matthew 13:31–32; it was the story, he wrote, of "The Mustard Seed." From the tiny, almost microscopic seed arose a great tree. Bishop Wright could not help but draw a parallel with the amazing works that had suddenly emerged from the quiet ruminations and rehearsals of his two creative sons. Without drawing out the parable of the seed, he simply recorded the fact that May 24 was in every way a "Beautiful day."[45]

Wilbur remained at sea on the *Touraine* on May 25, while Orville—against his basic nature—spent nearly the entire day at his desk, compiling the data the brothers and Furnas had recorded on their work at Kitty Hawk. Orville would have preferred to be tinkering with mechanical tasks—especially examining the engine that had failed at Kitty Hawk—but the crates containing the machine had not yet arrived in Dayton. They were supposed to be taken from Kitty Hawk to Elizabeth City on May 22 by Captain Franklin Harris Midgett for shipment to Dayton. But as Orville knew, Captain Midgett was an archetypal Outer Banker who operated on his own schedule and inclinations. The grumpy captain would eventually ship the crates over, but in his own good time. For the time being, the mystery of the failed engine would have to wait.

Chapter Six

THE BROTHERS WRIGHT
ON SEPARATE SHORES

Wilbur Making the Wright Brothers' First Public Flight Ever—at Le Mans, France in August 1908
It was the Wright brothers' intention that they would fly publicly for the first time in August 1908—
Wilbur in France and Orville in the United States. Wilbur made his debut at Hunaudières Race Track
(pictured here), at LeMans, France, on August 8; Orville's first flight was at Fort Myer, Virginia, outside
Washington, D.C., on September 3.

On May 26 the *Touraine* was finally nearing Europe, but Wilbur was still out of touch. The responsibility for supplying information to the news media and for answering the letters and queries of all inquisitors rested entirely with Orville. On this second workday following his return from Kitty Hawk, Orville had already decided what he was going to say about the North Carolina flights and to whom. He had also figured out how he would respond to some of the many and conflicting demands being put to him by the press.

What he would say was reflected in a letter he wrote on the twenty-sixth to the brothers' old friend George Spratt. Spratt was practically the only person outside their family circle in whom they confided their inner feelings and plans for the future. Spratt had been in the Wright camp at Kitty Hawk every year from 1901 through 1903 and knew the brothers—as inventors and friends—probably better than anyone else. Orville told Spratt, "We would have enjoyed your company with us this year as of old." But their 1903 camp had been destroyed and their new building would not have accommodated the additional observers they had been accustomed to welcoming and hosting in earlier years.

As for the stories published about their crash on the fourteenth, Orville wrote Spratt, "The damage done our machine was nothing compared to that described in the papers." "A few days would have put it in good shape again," he continued, "but we had already over-stayed our time so we discontinued the experiments." On the topic of going from a single person to two passengers on a plane, he wrote, "We carry two men and a lot of additional weight without trouble." Obviously in a positive and upbeat mood when he wrote this letter, Orville was probably better prepared to face the press and all comers after testing his storyline on Spratt.[1]

As Orville was preparing to talk to the press, he worked closely with his beloved sister, Katharine, to whom he naturally migrated for support and assistance whenever Wilbur was not around. After the two of them discussed the reaction of the local press, Katharine wrote a letter to Wilbur with her assessment of the situation:

> The Dayton papers certainly tried to treat you white [i.e., good]. They can ex-
> plain every thing about your not having done more [in the flights at Kitty
> Hawk] . . . Most of the papers have been very decent. The Journal remarks that
> "for men who have made no effort to break into print, the Wright Brothers are
> getting more free advertising than any other men on earth."[2]

In truth, the entire Wright family was energized by the press coverage the brothers were getting, and they constituted a solid, unswerving support system for both
of them as they were transformed from local celebrities to international stars.

On the morning of Wednesday, May 27, 1908, Orville began making public
pronouncements about the recent flights and even granted an interview with a few
reporters. His first public statement was issued at Springfield, Ohio, from the offices of the Wrights' longtime patent attorney, Harry A. Toulmin Jr. In the carefully drawn statement, which was picked up and sent abroad by local reporters,
Orville put most of his efforts into clarifying erroneous stories that had been published about their flights.

He described the North Carolina flights as "entirely satisfactory" and totally
"successful."

The Wrights had not, according to Orville, attempted to make any lengthy
flights or flights to great altitudes. Their main purpose was to try out a new steering mechanism, making use of their old and reliable 1905 flyer. He also explained
how the reporters had been led astray with misinformation provided by the locals
on the Outer Banks:

> There were stories of flights over the sea at an elevation of three thousand feet.
> That story was written before we had made a single attempt at flight. There were
> a lot of reporters hanging around travelling [sic] back and forth asking questions
> of all whom they might meet. Some one on the boat between Elizabeth [City] and

Manteo told them that story. We did not attempt lofty flights. We did not go there for that purpose.

Orville knew full well that the lifesavers and boatmen plying the waters around the Albemarle Sound of North Carolina were hardly reliable sources of factual information, and that they could be depended upon to spread the tallest of tales.[3]

In addition to attempting to rectify faulty news accounts, Orville was also prepared to speak on the subject of challenge races and contests—particularly the outstanding invitation from Robert Collier to meet Henri Farman at the expense of *Collier's Weekly*. He was prompted to respond to this on May 27, when Arthur Ruhl sent another telegram to Dayton urging a response: "When may we expect answer to letter are you sufficiently interested in contest with Farman for us to send man to Dayton to arrange details." Before the day was very old, Orville sent back a firm response. Asking Ruhl to thank Collier for "his generous offer" and congratulating him on his "sportsman-like spirit," Orville politely declined the invitation to compete:

> Our position in regard to races and prizes is unchanged from what it was when we saw you at our camp at Kitty Hawk. While it would be a pleasure to enter into these contests, our present business contracts will engage so much of our time for the next five or six months that we can not undertake any further engagements at the present time.

He further indicated that "my brother would join with me in thanks, if he were here."[4]

Try as they might to clarify matters in and through the press, however, Orville and Wilbur Wright were learning that while they could control the direction of their airplanes most of the time, they could almost never exert any similar guiding power when it came to the press. The *New York Herald*, in an effort to underscore its commanding role in breaking news stories on worldwide flight, decided to make a bold move. The editors chose Thursday, May 28, to announce that the paper had discovered the secrets of the Wright brothers. Most observers of the rapid evolution of flight were persuaded that the Wright brothers had indeed demonstrated at Kitty Hawk that their flight capabilities exceeded those of anyone else on earth. And the editors of the *Herald,* disgusted that their reporter on the scene in North Carolina had not discovered the brothers' true secrets of flight, chose in essence to *make* news on one of the hottest and most engaging topics of 1908. Having provoked the resignation of their ace flight reporter, Byron Newton, who refused to participate in the ruse, they went ahead with a publicity plan for the Wright story that was cleverly designed to sell newspapers.

On May 28, in the same issue of the *Herald* that contained Orville's modest statement issued from their attorney's offices at Springfield the previous day, the publisher inserted a banner advertisement on page two of the paper covering a full third of the large sheet. It blared forth a bold notice:

WRIGHT BROTHERS' SUCCESS
In The AIR NO LONGER A SECRET
Builders of the AEROPLANE
Reveal Their Plans to the Public.
Original and Authentic Draw-
ings and Plans, with Description
Written by the Inventors.
IN THE NEW YORK HERALD
TO-MORROW, FRIDAY, MAY 29

Alongside the short news story itself the editors included a boxed notice of the forthcoming issue: "The HERALD will give to the world to-morrow morning the first authentic drawings and description of the Wright brothers' aeroplane. The veil of secrecy has been lifted and the machine in all of its simplicity will be fully described." The publisher also blanketed New York City with its fleet of horse-drawn newspaper wagons bearing the same banner. According to reports coming to Orville, the sensational display "stirred up considerable commotion by advertising on its wagons in big letters that it would the next day—May 29th—give a full description of the secrets of the Wright invention."[5]

Before the story could appear the next day, Orville relayed to Wilbur, "all of the other papers began telegraphing trying to either get something for themselves or [something] to discredit the *Herald* story." Katharine, in a separate letter to Wilbur, observed:

> Thursday was our busy day. On that day, the N.Y. Herald announced that on Friday it would "lift the veil of mystery and publish the secret of the Wright Brothers flying machine." Then the fun began. Telegrams and reporters! There hasn't been much let up since.

While the world was already beating a fast path to the Wright brothers wherever one or the other of them happened to be, the *Herald* had now ratcheted up the intensity several more notches for both its readers and its competitors.[6]

Byron Newton, just severed from the *Herald*, declared to his colleagues at other papers that he did not have a clue what his former bosses would be publishing. Ernest La Rue Jones, editor of the weekly newsmagazine *Aeronautics*, for which Newton was already busy preparing an article on his North Carolina observations, protested that Orville now seemed to be giving out exclusive information to the *Herald*, going back on his earlier promise to give out a single statement to all inquiring agents of the press. Jones wrote Orville that the *Herald*'s bold campaign

> was rather startling this morning and, as you can see, produced some cause for wonderment, as I could see no reason why they—the *Herald*—should be able to publish such a statement, having in mind the policy which has been yours from the beginning.

Arthur Ruhl, on behalf of *Collier's Weekly*, registered a similar complaint since that magazine had also advertised that it would be giving the inside story of the Wright brothers' activities at Kitty Hawk in its own issue of May 30—due out the very next day.[7]

On the morning of May 29, the *New York Herald* published and distributed its much vaunted and specially advertised paper containing the "secret" story of the

Wright brothers. It was sensational indeed. The banner headline was spread across the entire length of the front page and it was followed—as was typical for newspapers of the day—with an additional set of headlines that read almost as a miniature story in themselves:

SECRET OF THE AEROPLANE OF THE WRIGHT BROTHERS LIES
IN THEIR METHOD OF BALANCE IN UNSTABLE AIR CURRENTS
THE HERALD REVEALS THE MYSTERY OF THE AIRSHIP AND TELLS
    WHY IT FLIES
Technical Diagrams as Presented Herewith Are Reproduced from the Original
    Drawings of the Inventors, Placed on File in France.
DESCRIPTIONS ACCOMPANYING PICTURES ACCURATE TRANSLA-
    TIONS IN ALL DETAILS
Feature Which Chiefly Differentiates the Wright Aeroplane from Its Rivals Is So
    Simple as to Amaze Scientific Men Who Have Studied Aerostatics.
IN SOLVING THE RIDDLE OF AIR CURRENTS HAS LAIN THE CRUX
    OF THE WHOLE PUZZLE
And in the Apparent Solution, by an Easily Explained Device, of This Difficulty
the Ingenious Americans Have Taken an Important Step in the Right Direction

The *Herald* thus promised that its pages that day would boldly carry its readers into the incredible new world just recently unveiled at Kitty Hawk—fully observed by an inquisitive band of reporters who began breaking the epochal story.

Between the first line of the headline and the subsidiary lines appeared five images, which took up fully one-third of the newspaper's front page. All of the pictures except the first—a somewhat dark and blurred image of a Wright glider said to represent the type of machine used by the Wrights from 1895 to 1903—were accompanied with a copyright symbol and declaration by the New York Herald Company. Two of the images were excellent portraits of the slight but handsome and serious Orville and Wilbur Wright—presented here and in other places in alphabetical order—by editors and publishers who did not understand sufficiently the dominant role played by the older and much more driven brother. The fourth

image was a reprint of the retouched James Hare photograph, which had been first
published by the *Herald* on May 20.

But it was the fifth image that was to be the focus of this story. It was a set of
line drawings—clearly of some kind of flying craft—described by the accompanying caption as "Working Drawings of Wright Brothers Aeroplane as Improved
Up to Last January. From Specifications Filed in the French Patent Office." A further bold headline under the image promised: "THESE DIAGRAMS ARE EX-
PLAINED IN DESCRIPTIVE ARTICLE ON THE FOLLOWING PAGE." The
long-hidden "secret" of the Wright brothers would thus be unveiled for the first
time from drawings that had been submitted in person at the French patent office
by Orville on November 18, 1907—the same day he saw Henri Farman make a
demonstration flight in Paris. The plans had presumably been available for inspection by anyone in France from the day the patent had been granted on January 27, 1908.[8]

The *Herald* was, indeed, the first popular newspaper to turn to foreign patent
office files—it cited both French and British patent records—to seek answers as
to how the Wright brothers had achieved an apparent precedence in their ability
to fly. As demonstrated in North Carolina, they could fly almost at will. No one else
on earth could equal these feats. Although similar drawings and descriptive expla-
nations had been filed by the brothers with their successful U.S. patent application
on March 23, 1903, and finally issued on May 22, 1906, it evidently did not occur
to the news media gurus that the Wrights had been talking about one and the
same flying machine since early 1903—even prior to their first powered flight.
News reporters and all other observers of the period were so focused on a flying machine with a motor that they did not understand or appreciate the genius and simplicity of the Wright brothers' innovative and revolutionary advances. Their true
secret was the invention of an airworthy and fully controllable flying device—with
or without an engine.

The Wright brothers and other knowledgeable students of flight at the time
ridiculed the *Herald* for fabricating headlines out of records that had been available
for quite some time. But as the leading international newspaper of the day, the paper
was, in its crude way, providing a considerable service to its readers and to the world

at large. The *Herald* was in the vanguard of those who sought to explain to the world for the first time in history that human flight was no longer a fantasy. Now the Wright planes were not only pictured in flight; they were also portrayed against the backdrop of an eerie, almost extraterrestrial surface at legendary Kitty Hawk and in the surreal presence of Kill Devil Hills. The almost moonscape environment where the Wright brothers had been flying since 1900 added additional drama and mystery to the new world that was just fully dawning in human consciousness.

In that the Wright brothers were still—and persistently so—making it clear that they had secrets to hide and would not discuss their methods of flight publicly, the leading news outlets of the day felt directly challenged to discover these secrets. Since the brothers also refused to allow anyone to take a photograph of their plane either on earth or in the air, newspapers such as the *Herald* and illustrated magazines such as *Collier's Weekly* were driven to find some other way of getting a picture in print. On May 28, the *New York Herald* thus made great advances in hinting that it could demystify what was previously unknown about the Wrights and their flying machine. Between the *Herald* and *Collier's*, the Wright story was indeed finally and fully in the open.

Although the newly assigned reporters at the *Herald* lacked the knowledge, experience, and suave writing style of the recently expunged Byron Newton, they did a reasonably good job of isolating—among their thousands of other rambling words—what they called the "crux" of the Wright achievement. As the writer of this bold piece explained:

> The seemingly insuperable difficulty [of successful flight] lay in perfecting some
> device that would enable the operator to maintain his machine in stable equilib-
> rium when subjected to the toss and strain of ever shifting air currents of vary-
> ing direction and strength. In this has lain the crux of the whole puzzle, and it is
> in the apparent solution of this riddle that the enterprising American brothers
> have taken a long step toward the ultimate conquest of the air.

While the reporter used the expression "stable equilibrium," the Wrights described it simply as "control." This had, in fact, been the ultimate objective of their years of research—control of the flying craft in any environment—and the *Herald* finally understood and reported this essential fact. The Wrights' ultimate scientific and engineering achievement had little to do with engines, power, the push of wind, sleek design, athletic prowess, heroic ventures, or daredevil stunts—just crafty manipulation and maneuverable control in any given atmospheric and wind conditions.

In this extended story, The *Herald* did not take much notice of the other major ingredient in the Wright brothers' prior successes at both Kitty Hawk and at Dayton—repeated practice and near infinite patience. The big story was the design of the Wright flying machine, and what an airplane of such structure and malleability could accomplish. While it took the *Herald's* writers thousands of words to try to explain years of innovation and refinements in the Wright flying machine, they did a credible job. So believable, in fact, that the other competing media felt they had been scooped and that the Wrights must surely have cooperated with the *Herald* in developing an article that was designed both to create a sensation and to provide exclusive information about their methods of flight.

Arthur Ruhl, who had been engaged in writing the separate article for *Collier's Weekly* that would appear two days later—with the undoctored photographs taken by James Hare at Kitty Hawk—was incensed that he was being scooped. After seeing the *Herald* article that morning of May 28, he wrote a mildly protesting letter to Orville:

> The drawings and description of the machine in the *Herald* this morning naturally make us regret that we should not have been the first to make such an announcement—the very thing that we wanted to do when I came out to Dayton last year. As near as I can gather, however, the *Herald* obtained its "story" not from you but from the French Patent Office. Should you at any time contemplate making a further announcement, I hope that you will remember *Collier's*.

Poor Wilbur, meanwhile, was totally oblivious to the fray going on in America surrounding the brothers' recent activities at Kitty Hawk. He was also without a clue on the trials and tribulations his brother Orville was facing. After being silent for an entire week and perhaps enjoying the amenities of the *Touraine*, he began ex-

ercising his writing hand more as the ship neared its destination at Le Havre on the
north coast of France. On the twenty-eighth, he wrote a newsy letter to his father
about the ease and comforts of this trip across the Atlantic: "I have been unusually well on this trip, since the first day, and will not be worn out at landing as I usually am." The *Touraine* turned out to be a quiet and restful ship: "Owing to its low
power the ship vibrates less than those I have been on before"; and "the table [food]
is better than on English boats."9

Despite the pleasantries contained in this respectful letter, Wilbur returned the
next day to his habit of lording it over Orville in a letter filled with pointed re-
minders to his younger brother. He would be expecting a full and complete letter
from Orville when he arrived in Paris with a total briefing on all matters he had
missed in the intervening period. He wanted to make sure Orville had shipped
everything he would need to France. Orville should send plenty of extra parts for
the plane in France, but he should not get fancy and redesign any of them—as
Orville evidently was wont to do. Just send standard, regular parts, Wilbur asked.

The mystery of the plane's sudden fall on the last day at Kitty Hawk still continued to bother Wilbur as a nagging piece of unfinished business. He was eager
to get to the heart of it since he was more and more convinced that it was not pilot
error, as he had so blithely stated to the press following the accident, and wrote to
Orville:

> The more I think of the circumstances immediately preceding the accident at
> Kitty Hawk, the less I can account for it. I cannot remember that there was any
> indication of the approach of any disturbance such as I had noticed at other times.
> I do not think there was any upward turn such as had preceded some of the darts
> at Simms. On the other hand I feel pretty sure the trouble did not result from
> turning the rudder the wrong way; however it happened so quickly that there
> was little time for taking observations.

He had several suggestions for modifications that might help to avoid the sudden
fall, but he was not sure that any of them were correct. He was depending upon
Orville to come up with a more cogent answer.10

But Wilbur was to be disappointed that day and for several days thereafter. The *Touraine* arrived at Le Havre at 4:00 P.M. on May 29. He proceeded immediately to Paris where he arrived at 10:00 P.M. Much to his disappointment, there was neither letter nor telegram nor any kind of message from Orville, Milton, or Katharine. He could not believe that no one had bothered to keep him in the informational loop that normally operated very efficiently within the close-knit family.

Beginning on Saturday, May 30, Wilbur was back on solid earth in Paris where he could read the newspapers, including the international edition of the *New York Herald*, which was normally timely and thorough in its news reporting. He also had access to the London *Daily Mail* and other English-language newspapers and magazines. So he could at least read about what was going on in America, even if he had not gotten any mail from the family and did not have access to some of the other media in which more measured assessments of the events at Kitty Hawk had begun to appear.

Also, on May 30 it became immediately known both in America and in Europe that Wilbur was in Paris and not in New York, Dayton, or anywhere else. Indeed, the evening editions of some papers in the United States on the twenty-ninth revealed Wilbur's whereabouts in headline stories. As Katharine reported, "The news had big head-lines Friday night 'Wilbur Wright in Paris.' So we suppose you are there all right." Since Paris was the recognized center of the aeronautic world at the time, Wilbur was almost certainly in for a busy season. But since he smugly enjoyed all of the attention, he was just where he wanted to be.

On the morning of May 30, Wilbur had his first business meeting in France at the office of Hart O. Berg, a business associate of Flint and Company who was responsible for selling the Wrights' planes in continental Europe. To satisfy the keen interests of Paris-based reporters, Berg arranged for Wilbur to meet some of them that very first morning—Howard Thompson from the Associated Press and a French correspondent for the London *Express* identified only by the name of Raphael. A *New York Herald* reporter, George P. Dickin, was also assigned to track Wilbur wherever he went in France. Before the end of the day, Wilbur had granted Dickin an interview and quickly came to the conclusion that he would have to get along with this intrepid representative of the press.[11] Of course, Dickin was also in a position to keep Wilbur posted on the new outpouring of articles in the American press analyzing the recent activities at Kitty Hawk. As either a reward or in resignation to his persistence, Wilbur would later in 1908 take Dickin on a short flight, making him the world's first journalist passenger.[12]

Even Dickin, however, did not have access to the full raft of new articles on the suddenly-famous Wrights that had begun to emerge throughout America. In contrast to the hastily assembled news stories that had been rushed out through Drinkwater's telegraph key, these new pieces were often reflective essays written by reporters who had been on the scene and were now trying to give some perspective to the historic events they had witnessed. Among the most important of these articles was, of course, the thoughtful eyewitness story written by Arthur Ruhl for *Collier's Weekly*, which contained the commissioned photographs taken by his colleague James Hare.

While Wilbur was still getting his land legs in France on this Saturday, May 30, Orville, Katharine, and Milton Wright were all sitting on the front porch on Hawthorne Street in Dayton savoring every word of Ruhl's entertaining tale. It was perhaps the most drama-packed, graphic, and poetic narrative of the many pieces that would be published, and it was immediately beloved by the Wrights. As Katharine Wright described it in her first letter to Wilbur after reading it, "Ruhl has the dandiest thing, ever published about the flying machine, I think, in Collier's of this week. We must send that to you. He is a clever writer."[13] Ruhl was also exceedingly well informed about all aspects of the contemporary world of international flight. He knew that French pilots had also begun to produce some remarkable feats in their own flying machines—especially in the immediate months and weeks prior to the Wright brothers' 1908 flights. He had, therefore, arrived at Kitty Hawk in a skeptical mood. The Wrights, in his mind, would have to perform something spectacular to arouse the kind of attention currently being bestowed on a daring cadre of French pilots who were thrilling crowds in Paris almost weekly.

In describing the saga of his own trip to Kitty Hawk and Kill Devil Hills—which seemed, to him and all other outside observers, like the end of the earth—Ruhl also imaginatively captured the historic pilgrimage of the Wrights that spring:

Just about the time that Leon Delagrange broke the European record at Issy by
flying two miles and a half without touching the ground, the Wright Brothers
made their spring trek across Albemarle Sound and hid on the beach behind Kill
Devil Hill. They built a shed out of pine boards, dug a well, set the flour and
bacon and the apple-box against the wall, and started in to work. One machinist
was with them, otherwise their existence of talking, thinking, eating, and sleeping flying machine was untroubled from one glaring day's beginning to another,
except when an occasional life-saver strolled down the beach from Nag's Head,
or a gull, circling round overhead, piped down faintly at his rivals.

It was not easy for him and the other reporters to get into a position to see what
the Wrights were doing. He recounted the dreadful daylong ordeal of 4:00 A.M.
wake-up calls, noisy boat rides from Manteo to Kill Devil Hills, trekking across in-
fested sands and swamps, roasting in the hot sun on glaring white sands, and perpetually waiting for something to happen.

Despite all these ordeals, he and the other reporters had observed the Wrights
busily working around their Spartan encampment, had watched them launch their
flyer with one or two men aboard, and had seen with their own eyes their brief but
heroic feats of flight. With the veteran Jimmy Hare in their company—witty and
wise Welshman that he was—they were also able to walk away with exposed glass
plate negatives that had every promise of resulting in solid photographic images of
the Wright flights. They had come, witnessed flight, and gathered a batch of stories and images that would stock the pages of newspapers and magazines across the
world for weeks and months to come.

Most of all, as Ruhl observed in his *Collier's* article, the uninvited "attacking
party" of reporters went away well satisfied:

Being an attacking party, however, without the happy privilege of telling two
plucky young men how much they admired them, they sat right there in the
sand, along with the flies and busy "chiggers" until there was just time to tramp
back and catch the chug-chug home. Then, bedraggled and very sunburned, they
tramped up to the little weather bureau and informed the world, waiting on the

other side of various sounds and continents and oceans, that it was all right, the rumors true, and there was no doubt that a man could fly.[14]

Hare's undeniable photographs of the distant plane in flight and of the harried reporters amidst their sufferings gave visual, slick witness to a truly great moment in human history.

Ruhl's dramatic essay was neither the first nor the last to emerge immediately following the Wrights' historic seven days in May. Among the first pieces of editorial reflection were some that appeared in faraway newspapers and in the news-oriented science journals of the day. Perhaps the first reflective essay on the Kitty Hawk flights appeared in the London *Daily Mail* just days after the notable events of May 14. An article titled "The Wright Aeroplane," written by one Captain H. J. Coningham, appeared in the May 19 issue of that paper. As Alfred Harmsworth, Lord Northcliffe, the publisher of the *Daily Mail*, was waging a battle for Britain to upgrade its defensive and offensive weaponry, it was probably logical that the first news analysis of the Wrights published by his flagship newspaper should put the Wright brothers' achievements squarely in the context of military readiness.

Making use of the daily reports from P. H. McGowan, the *Daily Mail*'s onsite reporter, Coningham wrote that what was happening in North Carolina had potential implications for the future shape of warfare:

> The eyes of the whole aeronautical world have been focused on the lonely Carolina shore where the Wright aeroplane, which has been surrounded by an almost impenetrable veil of mystery for some years past, has just undergone a series of important tests, prior to passing the official trials authorized by the United States Government.

For if the tests resulted in a plane that could do all the things required by their government contracts, the history of warfare would be set on its head:

> This is no ordinary flying machine, and if the inventors' claims are eventually justified—as I am convinced they will be—writers on military tactics will have

to add to their works a fresh chapter, dealing with the strange new factor that is destined to make its *debut* in the next great war.

Even though much more would have to be learned about the Wrights' tests in North Carolina, Captain Coningham already had enough information to conclude that a revolution in military armament was underway: "In the recent trials *The Daily Mail* correspondent states that a speed estimated at forty miles an hour was attained. The machine was under perfect control, and eventually 'stopped like a partridge returning to its nest.'" These were things that could be done by no other fliers. Thus, according to Coningham, the world should prepare for a new military arms race.[15]

Another veteran from Kitty Hawk who weighed in with some food for thought was Gilson Gardiner, whose articles had appeared in the *New York World* while he was still in North Carolina. Normally based in Washington, D.C., Gardiner published his reflections on what he saw at Kitty Hawk in a series of articles in the *Chicago Journal*, the *St. Louis Dispatch*, and other papers. In the article first published on May 28, Gardiner exhibited a sense of certainty and glee as he wrote about the Wright plane he had seen at Kitty Hawk:

> It flies; it is big enough to carry two men; it is not a balloon nor any modified form of a balloon; it is an enormous modified box kite propelled by gasoline engines; it goes up into the air, travels miles, and alights without danger or difficulty. It is the real thing. It is heavier than the air in which it flies. It may be seen, touched, handled, and described. There is no mystery about it and no doubt about it.

In his second article in the series, Gardiner tried to describe what it was like to see a Wright plane in action. Using the common streetcar—well-known to his readers—as a visual point of departure, he continued:

> It moves sideways. When it starts up it looks like a runaway street car moving side forward. When the engines are started, it stands for a moment humming like a top. Then slowly it sneaks ahead, and presently it may be seen,

about twenty feet from the earth, slipping along with a noise like a stationary automobile.

Gardiner was so impressed with the Wrights' achievements at Kitty Hawk that he proclaimed, "There is no reason . . . why the machine they have made would not soar 10,000 feet into the air and travel on a straight line for fifteen or twenty miles." So far, he conjectured, it was only because "they have never tried any such spectacular stunts."[16]

In addition to these sober but enthusiastic assessments, the developments in North Carolina had also been followed closely by the editors of the most objective science news publication of the day—*Scientific American*. This prestigious weekly magazine added its authoritative voice and judgment to the debate on the Wright flights in its issue of May 30. Bearing on its cover a dramatic full-page image of the two-person flights accomplished on May 14, the magazine published a second full-page article accompanied by James Hare's photographs. Whatever skeptics might feel about the news stories emanating from a stampeding herd of journalists from the daily press, they could not dismiss the trustworthy praise of the formidable and authoritative *Scientific American*.[17]

The historical record of the *Scientific American* in accurately recording and reporting innovations in flight was impressive. From the earliest rumblings about balloonings, airships, and power-driven airplanes, the old and respected magazine, published in New York, was the most reliable source of information about new advancements in flight. Wilbur and Orville Wright swore by the stories in *Scientific American* from the first moment they took an interest in flight. There had been numerous earlier stories in the publication about their trips to North Carolina between 1900 and 1903 and their subsequent flights at Dayton—usually written by the Wrights themselves.

Indeed, as recently as the February 29 issue of *Scientific American*, published just as the brothers were preparing for their return to Kitty Hawk, Wilbur Wright had provided the weekly journal with one of the most playful, yet speculative, articles he wrote in his brief but productive life. Titled "Flying as a Sport—Its Possibilities," this 600-word article grew out of the Wrights' somewhat flailing interim period in 1907 while they were furtively seeking to sell their invention for any potential source of income. Wilbur was eager to plant the idea that some adventurous beings might take up flying as a chosen, albeit expensive, form of sport, just to experience the thrill of speed. His view was that "considered as a sport, flying possesses attractions which will appeal to many persons with a force beyond that exercised by any of the similar sports, such as boating, cycling, or automobiling." This innate attraction to flying, he continued, grew out of man's perpetual bird envy:

> There is a sense of exhilaration in flying through the free air, an intensity of enjoyment, which possibly may be due to the satisfaction of an inborn longing transmitted to us from the days when our early ancestors gazed wonderingly at the free flight of birds and contrasted it with their own slow and toilsome progress through the unbroken wilderness.

Flying above trees and hills brings a perspective and sensation that humans cannot imagine, Wilbur wrote, since all except a dozen or so human beings in recent years had been permanently glued to the earth: "The earth is spread out before the eye [while flying] with a richness of color and beauty of a pattern never imagined by those who have gazed at the landscape edgewise only." While there were some dangers associated with airplane flying, he admitted, those dangers would be diminished with time. As compared with balloon flying—a familiar pursuit at the time, which carried passengers wherever the wind took them—airplane sportsmen could start and stop from the same spot without the tedium of begging passage back from some fugitive location.[18]

While *Scientific American* often published "what if" articles such as this one by Wilbur, it was better known for its serious reporting on new developments in science and technology—especially, at the time, in aeronautics. Throughout the year 1908, the combination newspaper and magazine of science contained news reports and dramatic photographs on the crescendo in airplane development, beginning with the miniflights of Henri Farman and Leon Delagrange in France at the end of 1907. In its first issue of 1908, the editors surveyed the major realms of science and

technology and for the first time included "aeronautics" as one of them. They announced that the year 1907 had been "one of great activity in aeronautics." Indeed, "in no previous year has so much been either attempted or accomplished."
However, as an American-based and biased publication, they lamented that "the
Parisians, as usual, are foremost in this movement." Moreover, the editors observed, an aerial balloon distance contest had been held out of St. Louis in October, but it was won by a German aviator who came down three miles beyond a
French aeronaut, a total of 876¾ miles away at Asbury, New Jersey.[19]

To encourage Americans to do more in the realm of flight, the *Scientific American* had offered a prize early in 1907 for flights in heavier-than-air flying machines,
but there had been no takers in the United States. The only flights in airplanes remained in France. There Henri Farman had made "a flight in a closed circuit of
nearly half a mile, coming successfully back to the starting point." There Louis
Bleriot had also demonstrated considerable success. Although the editors knew
that the Wrights had claimed much more dramatic flights in 1905, the *Scientific
American* prize had not been able to budge them into the public competition. Somewhat cynically, the editors commented, "The Wright brothers seem to have been
too busy endeavoring to sell their invention to foreign governments [than] to find
time for any practical work with their aeroplane." The magazine's combination in-
ducement trophy and prize thus went unclaimed in 1907.[20]

In the early months of 1908 the pages of *Scientific American* were filled regularly with stories of new advancements by French pilots, complete with numerous
photographs. In its January 25 issue, the magazine reported that Henri Farman
had continued his 1907 successes by performing a closed-circle flight before judges
and without letting his wheels touch the ground during the flight. This won him
the most famous aerial prize of his time—the Deutsch-Archdeacon prize of 50,000
francs, or $10,000. In reporting Farman's achievement, the editors again ac-
knowledged that the successes of the Wright brothers, though as yet unseen, exceeded the Frenchman's feat. Drawing comparisons between the Farman machine
and what little was known of the Wright machine, the editors believed that Farman
used a much more powerful engine "to accomplish what the Wright brothers maintain by skill or by some secret method." While the world was according great credit

to Farman, the editors said, "we nevertheless wish to recall to the aeronautical world the fact that to America belongs the credit of producing the first successful motor-driven aeroplane." The editors speculated that three Americans had likely preceded Farman—the Wright brothers, Augustus M. Herring, and Gustave Whitehead.[21]

Over the following months, *Scientific American* gave weekly updates on the progress of flights in Europe and the contracts that had been awarded by the U.S. Army to three Americans to build a heavier-than-air flying machine that met its strict requirements. In addition to further demonstrations by Henri Farman, the editors greeted with pleasure the emergence of the Aerial Experiment Association (A.E.A.) under the tutelage of Alexander Graham Bell. The first successfully flown airplane designed by this new group of aeronauts was pictured in the magazine on March 21. The magazine noted on April 18 that the French innovator Paul Cornu had successfully tested a full-scale helicopter. On April 25 and again on May 9, it covered the ever longer flights of the French aviator Leon Delagrange, up to a distance of four miles, among other reports on earlier flights in France.[22]

Still, given the claims of the Wright brothers dating back to 1905—which *Scientific American* had already acknowledged—careful attention was also given to the brothers' every move in a much changed world of aeronautics, after their two-year absence from flying. In its issue of May 9, the magazine mentioned newspaper reports of astonishing Wright flights "in the presence of some army officers on April 30 at Nag Head, N.C.," but also indicated that these stories had "not been authenticated up to the time of our going to press." A week later the editors still had not confirmed the story, but wrote that "nevertheless these two secretive gentlemen are apparently experimenting with success at their camping ground near Kitty Hawk, on the coast of North Carolina." After yet another week, in its issue of May 23—nine days after the important flights of May 14—the editors were still lamenting that their only source of information was "a considerable number of newspaper correspondents [who] visited the scene of the trials." Although reluctant to base their judgment on the stories of journalists ravenous for splashy headlines, the editors finally gave their firm opinion: "In view of these semi-public demonstrations, there can be no further doubt of the claims made by the brothers as to their ability to fly."[23]

And so *Scientific American* joined its more popular rivals—the *New York Herald*, *Collier's Weekly*, and other major newspapers—in recognizing the just-completed flights of the Wrights at Kitty Hawk. Although the front page of the issue had a copy of the doctored sketch illustration originally published by the *New York Herald* on May 20, the two authentic photographs taken by James Hare on May 14, published simultaneously in *Collier's*, were also in the magazine.

Based on these photographs, the editors were now ready to proclaim the validity of the brothers' obvious triumphs. Although still discouraged with the questionable believability of the reporters who witnessed the Wright flights ("not one of these men is a qualified technical observer"), the editors based their conclusions entirely upon the stupendous Hare photographs provided for their use "courtesy of P. F. Collier & Son." Although the pictures were "taken at long range of the aeroplane in flight around Kill Devil Hill," the photographic evidence was decisive. "When magnified [they] give some idea of the actual appearance of the machine in flight," the editors continued; "but their greatest value lies in dispelling all doubt as to the ability of the Wright machine to fly and to make good its designers' claims." Given the combined proof of the newspapermen and the photographs, *Scientific American* declared that the Wright brothers' achievements proved "the pre-eminence of America in aviation."[24]

Although Wilbur Wright was an avid reader of *Collier's Weekly* and of *Scientific American*, he did not make written mention of enjoying these beautifully written renditions of the historic events he and Orville had pulled off at Kitty Hawk. It is doubtful that he was able to savor these delicious judgments of history with anything like the spine-tingling immediacy experienced by his brother Orville. Wilbur was otherwise occupied and had to wait a while before he could enjoy the fruits of their most recent success and growing worldwide fame. Besides, he was in Paris not merely to read newspapers and to talk with reporters. He was there on the serious business of selling and flying the recently fabricated 1908 versions of the Wright airplanes, which is where he focused his attention, seemingly putting other pleasures aside.

Before he laid his head to rest for a second night in Paris, Wilbur was already off by train to the city of Nantes on the Atlantic coast of France. He was in search of a flying field that he hoped would replicate the conditions he and Orville enjoyed at Kitty Hawk—wind, sand, open spaces, and remoteness from the prying press. While Orville, Katharine, and Milton were reading stirring accounts about triumphs at Kitty Hawk that fine Saturday, Wilbur spent his second night in France in the tiny village of Blain in Brittany—hoping to discover the next morning what might be his new flying field. If he had known that Orville was reading one account after another about their North Carolina exploits at precisely that same moment, he would have been green with envy. But he also would have chided his younger brother for wasting his time when there was so much to be done.

It did not take very long on Sunday morning, May 31, for Wilbur to determine that Blain was no Kitty Hawk. The field that had been reserved for the first Wright test flights in Europe was only 200 by 250 meters (2 football fields by 2.5 footballs in length). Disappointed, Wilbur—who was being guided by friends of his French business sponsors—set out to investigate other fields in the area. The only place nearby that might work was a race track for horses. Although this was a remote location, Wilbur found neither winds nor sand, either there or anywhere else he looked in the area around Blain. Tired of seeking out fields, Wilbur, by the end of the day, took up his other favorite pursuit while traveling in Europe—climbing through and inspecting churches, chateaus, and castles—especially examining how they were built, flying buttresses and all.

Orville, meanwhile, spent the Sabbath in Dayton brooding on how he would be able to deal with a growing mountain of requests coming his way—from the press, friends, family, business associates, and—most of all—from Wilbur. In a letter to Wilbur written at the end of what turned out to be a very busy afternoon for both Orville and his sister, Katharine described the hustle and bustle of dealing with the press:

> Brother and I have been laboring a good part of the day, writing things to send to the Aero Club, Scientific American, Aerophile and Mitteilungen. We have

one thing done—for the Scientific American, I think. The other things will be easy, now.

These were not the daily newspapers. These were not popular magazines. These were the publications of record in the United States, France, and Germany concerning flight. These were the venues where the Wright brothers wanted and expected an accurate record of their flights published, along with a clear explanation of the purposes of their flights at Kitty Hawk.[25]

Off in remote Blain, Wilbur was feeling pretty useless. This was probably how he would have felt if he had ever been stranded at Kitty Hawk without a plane to fly or a motor to tinker with. There had been no newspapers for the brothers to read while they were at Kill Devil Hills, and there were none in Blain either—at least none with international news in English. Besides, it rained all day in Brittany on this first day of June—not a good day to be a sightseer. So Wilbur did the third best thing for a Wright brother away from home on an unoccupied day—he wrote letters. He sent messages to both Orville and Katharine, describing his activities as a tourist and underscoring to Orville his growing concern that the brothers must immediately get their planes in the air and in front of public audiences. He used, as he frequently did, the stationery of the hotel where he was staying, the Hotel de la Gerbe de Blé of the Touring-Club de France. For Katharine he described the place as "a quaint hotel in the heart of Brittany I think about midway between Nantes, Rennes, Vannes." Also for her benefit, he described the local architecture, the local town culture, and, of course, the softness of the beds and the delicious food at his hotels. There was no particular evidence in his letters of anxiety about the immediate or distant future.[26]

His letter to Orville, written at the same sitting and on the same type of stationery as the note to Katharine, expressed something else entirely. He essentially provided his brother and business partner with a litany of complaints. The proposed flying field at Blain was no good. He could not find an English-speaking mechanic in France. The French company hired to build a new set of engines for the Wright planes in Europe seemed incapable of even starting the Wright engine that had been forwarded to them from Dayton as a model. But he was also concerned about the increasing activities of the French flyers:

> You have learned from the newspapers that Farman and De Lagrange are visiting the big cities of Europe and giving exhibitions with some success. They will prob-ably make fifty kilometers before I am ready for the demonstrations . . . How-ever the first thing is to get some practice & make some demonstrations let the future be what it may.

Wilbur could not begin his demonstrations in France until he had gathered some vital information and several needed parts from Dayton. He concluded his letter with a show of impatience: "I have no word from you since leaving Kitty Hawk, but hope to have something soon."[27]

He must have written these letters on the morning of June 1 while he awaited a telegraph message from the brothers' business agent, Hart O. Berg in Paris, on what to do about a flying field. In the evening, he finally retired to Nantes and checked into the Hotel de France for the night. Since the hotel was on the salu-brious waterfront, he could at least enjoy the smell of the salty sea breezes on the opposite side of the Atlantic Ocean from Kitty Hawk.

Orville was still in the line of fire back home in Dayton, attempting to deal with the long list of tasks Wilbur had left him while facing a host of new challenges al-most every day. It would be fair to say that during these weeks of Wilbur's ab-sence, Orville handled more responsibilities and was forced to make more crucial unilateral decisions than at any time in the history of the brothers' partnership—from the time they set up a printing press in the 1880s until Wilbur's untimely death in 1912. He was dealing with a mountain of correspondence arriving in Day-ton from all quarters. He was shipping flying machines and replacement parts to Wilbur in France. He was putting the final touches on the entirely new plane he would be flying at Fort Myer in Virginia in just two months. He was filing additional patent applications for new features included on the brothers' latest planes. He was responding to demands for information from the press. He was writing releases to be distributed to those journals and magazines where the brothers wanted information on their accomplishments to appear. And, last but hardly least, Orville was running the brothers' growing international aviation enterprise.

Business considerations for Orville increased markedly around the first of June, when several wealthy observers began inquiring about the possibility of buy-ing custom-made airplanes from the Wrights. When Orville got back to Dayton, there was a letter waiting from Charles S. Rolls, one of the founders of Rolls-Royce Ltd., who was eager to represent the Wrights in the United Kingdom. Already a veteran of various balloon and airship stunts and exploits, Rolls also wanted to own and fly the first Wright airplane in England. He would not take no for an an-swer and was determined to acquire his own Wright flyer. In a letter to Rolls from Dayton on May 27, Orville tried to placate the impatient Briton by saying that Wilbur was on his way to France and providing him with his brother's address in Paris. Rolls proceeded to chase Wilbur around France until he had a commitment from both of the brothers to sell him his own private plane.[28]

A much more immediate demand for the private purchase of a Wright plane was the Collier order. Arthur Ruhl, whose fine article on Kitty Hawk had just ap-peared in *Collier's Weekly*, transmitted the request for a plane on behalf of his im-perturbable boss Robert J. Collier on Monday, June 1. Orville had already told Ruhl that he and Wilbur were not interested in Collier's proposed Wright-Farman chal-lenge match, but Ruhl now floated another of Collier's ideas "as an obedient mem-ber of the staff." Although he had private concerns about the publisher's erratic impulses and drinking habits, Ruhl told Orville that Collier was "greatly interested in this subject [flight] and soon as it is possible for the 'layman' to fly experimen-tally, he wants to do so." He explained:

> He has no special experience in aerial navigation further than having gone up in
> a balloon, but has automobiles and motor boats and plenty of sporting spirit. In
> other words, he would like to know when you could supply him with an aero-
> plane and how much it would cost.

As the partner in charge of the Wright business in America at the moment and rec-ognizing that Collier was a publisher and business tycoon far too important to be disregarded, Orville assured Ruhl that the Wright brothers' firm would take up the matter of producing a plane for Collier as soon as they completed their current contracts to produce and fly planes in both Europe and the United States.[29]

On Tuesday, June 2, Orville was besieged with a new avalanche of demands. In addition to other matters, he was handling the brothers' intense negotiations with the U.S. government. When his request for clarification of the terms of the U.S. contract was answered, Orville issued that day a promise to General James Allen of the Army Signal Corps that he and Wilbur would begin the promised American flight trials at Fort Myer in Virginia prior to the first of September.[30]

Meanwhile, Wilbur, still frustrated and disappointed with the dearth of suitable flying fields on the coast of France, had little choice but to play the part of tourist. He visited a château in Brittany and a local cathedral. He departed Nantes at noon and headed back to Paris, where he expected that some kind of communication from Orville would be waiting. But there was neither letter nor telegram nor any form of news from Dayton. Wilbur checked into the Palais d'Orsay, a posh hotel connected to the most ornate and modern train station in Paris, for the night. But he was furious. What was going on with Orville? Obviously his younger brother was being irresponsible—or else he would have written. Or, at least, so Wilbur thought.[31]

On the morning of June 3, Wilbur—eagerly awaiting mail, but knowing that it would not arrive until later in the day—headed out from Paris to investigate another batch of potential flying fields. Practically everyone formally involved in aeronautical pursuits in France had offered his or her favorite places to Wilbur for his inspection as possible practice grounds. Wilbur was taken to see quite a few of them, one adjacent to the old royal palace grounds at Versailles, another near the grand royal retreat at Fontainebleau, and several others. Nothing at all looked promising. Nor did Wilbur care for his plush quarters at the Palais d'Orsay. He preferred to be across the Seine near Berg's offices on the Champs-Élysées, close to the headquarters of the Automobile-Club and Aero-Club de France on the Place de la Concorde. So he moved across the river to Hotel Meyerbeer in the shadow of the Louvre, almost adjacent to the two clubs, and a short walk from Berg's office.

When he and Berg returned to Paris from their day of inspections that after-noon, there was still no letter from Orville. Wilbur thus sat down and wrote one of the most scathing letters he ever sent his younger brother and business partner. "I am a little surprised," he wrote, downplaying his irritation, "that I have no let-ter from you yet. Anything mailed at Eliz[abeth] City, Norfolk, Washington, or even Dayton, should be here." Then he dived into a long list of his complaints. There was, first, no communication at all from Orville. Second, he awaited Orville's "survey of the grounds at Kitty Hawk, and the estimate of distance and speed in both the last days' trials." Then he needed Orville's analysis of the problematic en-gine used at Kitty Hawk. He also needed a copy of their English patent. He needed copies of Orville's letters to Rolls, and he needed to know what Orville had been saying to the press. The *Herald* and the *Daily Mail* published articles indicating that they had "interviewed" Orville. Was that true or false? As for things in France, they were not looking good. Their agents, Berg and his associate Lazarre Weiller, were practically in a state of panic "on account of the excitement over recent flights of Farman & Delagrange." But that would change, he thought, "when we get to doing something." Meanwhile, just for good measure, he added, "I hope you have an application for American patent on our front rudder already under way, and that it will be filed before we start here."[32]

As Wilbur was penning his grumpy epistle on June 3, Orville was also writ-ing a letter in which he tried to bring the complaining party up to date on the zoo-like atmosphere in which he was operating in Dayton. Given that only a little more than two weeks had passed since the brothers had bid each other goodbye on the sands of Kill Devil Hills, Orville had made some pretty amazing advances: he had closed down the camp at Kitty Hawk and packed up the machine and all their goods for shipment back to Dayton—though the machine itself had been carried to Elizabeth City by Captain Midgett on May 22 and, unfortunately, had not yet arrived. Before leaving camp, he and Charlie Furnas had drawn up a map and meas-ured the course and distance of the flights they had made on May 14—the day of their most important flights and of Wilbur's crash—and a copy of the map was en-closed with the letter. Despite inclement weather when he got to Norfolk, Orville had traveled on to Washington amid raging storms and had inspected the test grounds at Fort Myer, finding them cramped and far from ideal. He had also got-ten the army to revise its requirements on calculating distances traveled—distance would be based on speed of flight rather than elapsed time, thus taking wind speed into consideration. The new machines, engines, and parts had been completed and were now ready for shipment to France or wherever required. Moreover, he was set-ting up a room in which to assemble the plane he would be using at Fort Myer in just two months, thinking it would be more efficient to do this in Dayton than under peering eyes in Washington, D.C.

These were just matters relating to preparation, production, and the shipment of goods. Orville had also been overwhelmed by increasing demands pulling him in every direction. All the locals wanted to chat: "It has been a hard job to get work done since I came back[,] on account of everyone wanting to talk. The people here are immensely interested." Although Orville was the shy member of the pair, he was much more affable and outgoing around family and friends. So, in a sense, he was better suited to handle this responsibility back home in Dayton.

But that was just the beginning. "Our mail has increased about tenfold," he told Wilbur. There were letters from the reporters who had been at Kitty Hawk, including Ruhl's most recent communications on Collier's behalf. Additionally, "all the steel, aluminum, and metal works of the country are now wanting us to try their products." Dozens of other inventors had offered devices to improve their planes. Letters had also come in from *Scientific American, Aeronautics,* the Aero Club of America, *Aerophile,* and *Illustrierte Aeronautische Mitteilungen* requesting a formal statement from the brothers about their flights and future plans. The proposal from *Century Magazine,* with whom Wilbur had negotiated a $500 deal for an ar-ticle with photographs, had also arrived.

Despite the fact that all of these matters fell more directly into Wilbur's usual realm—Orville was a lifelong procrastinator in answering letters and proclaimed chronic writer's block in the matter of writing anything for publication—the younger brother commandeered the typewriter they had adopted and poured out words in every direction required. While he would have been more comfortable re-pairing the inner mechanisms of the typewriter, he instead used it to answer dozens of letters, sublime and ridiculous, to deal with the queries of Ruhl, Newton, Jones, and other members of the press as well as those of manufacturers and inventors, to prepare a credible press statement for the most important technical publications, and to outline a draft article for *Century Magazine* that exhibited a writing and storytelling skill that actually surpassed the classic technical articles Wilbur had previously written for Chicago's engineers in 1901 and 1903.

Beyond his written words—in which he always had the editorial assistance of Katharine, the only college graduate of the trio and a devoted high school classics teacher—Orville did a pretty good dance with the press in Wilbur's absence. Actually, during this period of time when their father, Milton, was in semiretirement as an elder bishop of the Church of the Brethren, when Katharine was out of school for summer vacation, and Orville was oscillating between office and shop, these three Wrights formed a troika that proved very effective in dealing with the press. Each of the three was authorized to answer questions, parry with quibbling journalists, or slam the door on reporters intruding after hours. Their patience and capabilities were put on trial with every passing day. They were especially challenged by ever more sensational articles appearing in both morning and evening papers, in magazines, and in telegraphic wire stories. The *New York Herald*'s advertising campaign on publishing "the secrets of the Wright invention" had been the toughest challenge facing this homegrown public relations office. The Ruhl article in *Collier's Weekly* had been the most gratifying. According to Orville in his June 3 letter summarizing all that had happened since their flights at Kitty Hawk, "His [Ruhl's] account . . . of the movements of the newspaper reporters in the woods is the best thing I have ever read about our experiments."[33]

Orville had probably been struggling with this letter to Wilbur for several days—wanting to make it as comprehensive, informational, and timely as possible. Katharine, knowing that Wilbur would be upset not to be getting letters from home, had written him one of her typical chatty letters two days earlier, explaining how busy they had been just keeping up with the raging train of events. As was typical of her in most letters, she shifted almost stream-of-consciousness fashion from topic to topic. She concluded the letter with one of her special playful requests: "Don't come home without getting me several pairs of gloves—number six—black and white, short and long." That note was a jesting preface to what she knew Wilbur most wanted to know: "P.S. Orv will write soon." On the same day that Orville finished his long epistle, Katharine was still not sure whether he would actually get it completed and mailed—so she wrote another whimsical letter to Wilbur just in case. Addressing it with the family nickname "Jullam," she opened the letter with a quick defense of the family: "No one else seems to be writing to you so I am bound to have a letter off tonight although the mail will go in half an hour." Signing it with her own beloved nickname, "Sterchens," made it impossible for Wilbur to take offense at his family's silence.[34]

Still lacking the information he so desperately wanted from home, Wilbur began and ended another day on June 4 as a virtual tourist in France. He took another trip "out toward Fontainebleau to look for grounds," but found no flying field. Although he walked in the shadows of Fontainebleau going out and the castle of Philip Augustus on the return—two of the most precious landmarks in all of France—he paid them little attention, being almost inconsolable at the fact that he had neither a flying field nor any word from the folks back home.[35]

Meanwhile, the Wright house was in a state of moderate madness. Orville, with Katharine's assistance, was breathlessly pushing ahead on all fronts, serving—in Wilbur's absence—as sole executive officer of the Wright brothers' enterprises in America.

On June 5 Wilbur was still ostensibly continuing his active search for a flying field in France, but in actuality, he spent the day waiting to hear from Berg, the business agent, about additional places he should inspect. Convinced that Berg was too preoccupied with other things to promote the Wrights' business interests, Wilbur again resorted to being a frustrated tourist at Chalons-en-Champagne and Sermaize-les-Bains, without recording descriptions of what he saw.[36]

Orville's responsibilities grew larger on this first Friday in June 1908. Bishop Wright, in a chatty letter to Wilbur on family and church matters, commented matter-of-factly, "Orville just mentioned that the material from Carolina had returned." This meant that the broken engine and parts of the plane that crashed at Kitty Hawk were back in the Wright workshop in Dayton at last. In addition to keeping track of business matters, Orville—to satisfy both Wilbur's demands and his own curiosity—would now have to turn his attention to the engine. He quite happily reverted from the head of Wright business operations to his old role of Wright chief diagnostic mechanic to see if he could figure out what had caused the crash of Wilbur's last flight on May 14.[37]

On the following day, June 6, Wilbur *did* look at another potential flying field near Vitry-le-Francois in France. "The grounds were of fair size and the surroundings such that we could have made flight for many miles," he recorded in his diary. But he was unimpressed with other features of the area and returned to Paris dissatisfied, arriving at the Meyerbeer Hotel at midnight.

Orville, meanwhile, spent the day setting up and testing the broken engine from Kitty Hawk. Reporting to Wilbur in a letter composed the following day, Orville said "we fooled with it all day." He worked with both Charles Furnas and Charles Taylor, the brothers' master mechanic who had remained in Dayton, building new planes, during the Kitty Hawk tests. They started the engine over and over from morning until late into the evening and every time got essentially the same results. When cold, the engine would produce its maximum number of revolutions per minute. As it got warmer, no matter what they did, the engine speed would slow down. After a long and disappointing day, Orville sighed, "I can't see where the trouble is, but at the best we are a couple of H[orse] P[ower] short." In fact, although this was a new engine, it "gives just the same power we had with the old engine in our tests just before I left for the South."[38] Exhausted and frustrated, he tumbled into bed late Saturday night, resolved to work further on the mysterious lack of power in the engine first thing on Monday morning.

While the Wright family always observed Sunday as a day of rest, that did not always mean an absence of important mental and emotional activity for Wilbur, Orville, and Katharine Wright. Although they abstained from work with the tools of carpenters, mechanics, house cleaners, or repairmen when Sunday came, they continued to work with books, paper, and pens. Writing letters from dawn to dusk was not considered a violation of the Wright family's rest rule for the Sabbath. Besides, on this particular Sunday, Bishop Wright decided to take a long walk, visiting family and friends along the way. So on Sunday, June 7, the critical eagle eye of the senior Sabbath patrol was conveniently away from home.[39]

Both Wilbur and Orville spent their day of rest writing letters, and both did some visiting as well. Wilbur spent several hours with Frank Lahm, a distinguished Ohioan who had lived in Paris for many years and who also was vitally interested in flight—especially the pioneering efforts of the youthful Wrights. Lahm was a devoted member of the Aero-Club de France and had been one of the Wrights' early links to aeronautical circles in France. Wilbur also poked around the luxuriant gardens along the Champs-Élysées. Orville, at home in Dayton, was, of course, in the constant mix of family and the many visitors who dropped by later in the day to see Bishop Wright.

Wilbur wrote two letters to Orville that day on the elegant stationery of the Hotel Meyerbeer at Rond-Point des Champs-Élysées. "I am very comfortably situated here overlooking the Champs-Élysées gardens," he wrote, knowing that Orville would probably share his letter with both their father and Katharine. Writing in a leisurely style that morning, he summarized in detail his searches for a place to fly in France. Blain, he said, would not work because the proposed flying field was too small and the location was probably too far from Paris. The field that he had just seen on Saturday near Vitry was three hours from Paris on a main train line and "would make a very suitable place for practice, demonstrations & training of operators." From the perspective of the increasingly urbane older brother it was still unsuitable, however, because "we would have to live in our camp as at Kitty Hawk."[40]

This letter was, on the whole, a pretty chatty piece of writing. Wilbur noted that he had that day just received his first communication from Dayton since leaving New York almost three weeks earlier—Katharine's letter of May 26 mentioning Orville's return from Kitty Hawk and other family and local chatter. Still, he uttered no complaint about Orville's failure to write, so he was obviously in a good mood that particular Sunday morning.

After spending the next three hours talking with Lahm about the brothers' business affairs in France, however, Wilbur's mood went from chatty to combative. He told Orville that he had shared with the kindly Lahm his frustrations with their business agents in France. He had also told Lahm of his communication with Charles Rolls about opening up a business operation in England. Whatever Lahm might have advised, Wilbur came back to the Hotel Meyerbeer that evening determined to tighten the reins on their agent Hart O. Berg, to take personal control of any Wright business in England, and to deal directly with Rolls himself. Angry that Berg had urged him not to talk to Rolls alone, Wilbur ended his second letter of the day on a far different note: "I am tired of their everlasting interference in matters outside of their proper field."[41]

Orville, still tired from tinkering with the engine from Kitty Hawk all day Saturday, patiently summarized in his own letter to Wilbur the many tests he and Charles Taylor had run on it. He also reviewed preparations he was making to launch the upcoming tests at Fort Myer and asked Wilbur to let him know as soon as possible what price he should quote for building a private plane for Robert Collier. This letter from Orville was all business, racing as he was to catch up on endless pieces of the Wright brothers' business operations.[42]

However, Orville was not without humor on that Sunday. He was renowned for teasing and playing pranks on members of the Wright family. He must have been in a playful mood at some point that day, for he composed a letter to one of the reporters who had been at Kitty Hawk a few weeks earlier filled with his own special brand of winking joviality. Byron Newton's letter of May 26 describing his disagreements with his editors at the *New York Herald*, in which he acknowledged that he had been one of the "ambushing" reporters at Kitty Hawk, had been waiting on Orville's desk when he got back from Kitty Hawk. Orville responded to that bit of old news with his tongue buried deep in his cheek. With the advantage of distance, Orville described the circumstances in North Carolina a bit differently:

> We were aware of the presence of newspaper men in the woods at Kill Devil Hills, at least we had often been told that they were there. Their presence, however, did not bother us in the least, and I am only sorry that you did not come over to see us at our camp. The display of a white flag would have disposed of the rifles and shot guns with which the machine is reported to have been guarded!

In addition to acknowledging Newton's frank and somewhat confessional letter, Orville then paused briefly to congratulate the journalist on the quality of his reporting in the *Herald*: "The reports which we have read in the Herald were in general pretty accurate." Given the standard of reporting at the time and the steady stream of misinformation about their activities and achievements, Orville's compliment at this juncture had to be considered high praise.[43]

On Monday, June 8, just twenty-five days after their historic flights of May 14, both of the Wright brothers moved symbolically and functionally beyond the trials, tribulations, and triumphs of Kitty Hawk, to the business of showing the world how they had conquered the problem of flight. They eagerly anticipated their rendezvous with destiny—the epochal moment when they would show the world how it could harness the power of flight. This was to be the last day on which they would privately ponder what had actually happened at Kitty Hawk during those memorable seven days.

Wilbur broke his impasse on June 8, finding a proper stage for the first Wright flights in Europe. He accompanied Hart O. Berg to the city of Le Mans, a hundred miles west of Paris, and found there not only a good place to fly, but also a group of people who offered to give him every possible assistance in preparing his machine for dozens of public flights. He also found there a brilliant and daring sponsor in the person of inventor and industrialist Léon Bollée. Among the most important French leaders in a worldwide transportation revolution of both automobiles and airplanes, Bollée virtually adopted Wilbur as a fellow inventor. Jealous of the stranglehold Paris bankers and politicians held on technological advancements in France, Bollée helped prepare the way for the Wrights to prevail both symbolically and financially in the heady and complicated climate of French aeronautics and politics.

It was also on Monday, June 8 that Orville came to two important reckonings: the persisting mechanical conundrum of the failed engine at Kitty Hawk and his most pressing current problem of how he would deal with the machinations of the American press. The mystery of the engine was solved first. Almost immediately after he and Charles Taylor took another look at the Kitty Hawk engine that morning, they figured out precisely why Wilbur's last flight on May 14 had ended so

abruptly. Orville relayed the finding somewhat triumphantly to his constantly carp-
ing big brother:

> We found this morning that the trouble with the engine was in the feed pipe be-
> tween the bend and the nozzle. I think when you bent it to make it more central
> in the pipe you squeezed something between the sides of the tube at the bend . . .
> When we blew backwards through the tube with the compressed air something
> flew out of the tube.

With the kink Wilbur had put in the tube relaxed, the engine's performance increased dramatically. By Orville's calculations they never achieved more than 27
horsepower at Kitty Hawk when they should have had up to 40. With the fuel
line restricted through Wilbur's inadvertent pinch, the engine had thus operated
at only a fraction of its capacity. Orville took smug pleasure in transferring the guilt
to Wilbur, but both brothers were happy to learn that the failure at Kitty Hawk
was "pilot's" (actually mechanic's) error and not a defect in the engine itself.[44]

On this same Monday, Orville finished his ruminations on how badly the
press had reported their recent flights at Kitty Hawk. He then settled on a strategy for how he would deal with the print media thereafter. In a candid letter to
Arthur Ruhl, he gave his assessment of the ongoing newspaper frenzy:

> I have never been able to discover exactly what is the "secret" of which the news-
> papers so often talk. The great mystery surrounding our work has been mostly
> created by the newspapers. They have told so many contradictory stories, that
> people are inclined to doubt all of them.

By this time he had done everything within his power to set the record of Kitty
Hawk straight. He had responded as best he could to queries from the press. He
had written concise accounts that would momentarily appear in those magazines
and journals that counted—at least in the Wright brothers' estimation. Indeed,
by this date his articles had already been received in the offices of the Aero Club
of America, *Aeronautics*, and *Scientific American* and were in the process of being

typeset. The publication of these stories, in Orville's mind, would shortly establish the permanent record of what transpired that May in Kitty Hawk. In them, Orville tried to explain the brothers' long-postponed emergence from strictly private to public flights, from virtual secrecy to constant availability for public scrutiny, from the business of innovating to publicly demonstrating their unique ability to fly at will.

There was a great irony in the separate "eureka" moments of the Wright brothers that day. It had been the shy and receding and quiet member of the pair, the brother who was convinced that he lacked confidence and the ability either to write clearly or to speak in public, who had been left alone to deal with the most stressful ten-day period in the brothers' shared career. In those ten days since departing Kitty Hawk, Orville had handled the most complex set of challenges ever faced by the Wrights, and he was able to deliver on every one of them.[45]

Orville's monumental achievements in realms where he was never totally comfortable were quietly revealed in an exchange of letters between the brothers begun on June 9—still barely three weeks after Wilbur had departed Kitty Hawk. The gulf of separation brought on by three thousand miles of ocean and three weeks of intense activities was revealed in a letter Wilbur wrote that day from Hotel Meyerbeer on the Champs-Élysées in Paris. Addressed to Katharine—but clearly meant for both her and Orville—Wilbur wryly complained,

> I have no word from Orville since leaving Kitty Hawk. Does he not intend to be partners any more? It is ridiculous to leave me without information of his doings and intentions. I have written almost every day since leaving Kitty Hawk to some of you.

Although he poked fun at the abiding and unquestionable firm footing of their partnership, he proceeded to toss out another pile of tasks for Orville to handle. File some additional patent documents, he barked. Be sure to include a list of all items enclosed in each box shipped to France. And, by all means, do more work in managing the press. Sensing that soon there would be many photographs made of their planes in flight, Wilbur suggested that Orville set about trying to sell some of their

1904 and 1905 photographs to *Collier's Weekly* or to other illustrated magazines—
"provided they are willing to pay a reasonable price."[46]

Even as Wilbur was scribbling a new set of assignments for his brother, Orville
had opened another of Wilbur's dictatorial letters that morning. This was the mis-
sive in which he had instructed Orville on what should be in the article soon to be
published in the highly illustrated *Century Magazine*. Wilbur had promised the editors that this would be the first place where the Wright brothers would publish a
secret stash of photographs showing prior flights—including a never-before-seen
photograph of their historic first powered flight of December 17, 1903.

Still, he left the entire responsibility of writing and illustrating the most important article of their careers for Orville to handle. In his letter of June 9, Wilbur
had told Orville

> to get the main [airplane design] features originated by us identified in the pub-
> lic mind with our machines before they are described in connection with some
> other machine.[47]

Noting the rapid progress of French pilots and the sudden proliferation of new flying machines in America, Wilbur now also urged Orville to include a sharp warning in this article to other would-be pilots. Orville, he argued, should use the
Century article as a place to inform aeronauts in both Europe and America that
every time they flew, they were infringing the Wright brothers' patent on the flying machine.

In this instance, and on the subject of firing a warning shot across the bow of
other aviators, Orville's cooler head prevailed. Since they had no Drinkwater available to click out their messages in real time, Orville informed Wilbur that the article had already been completed and sent to *Century*: "It is now too late to
incorporate any part of it [Wilbur's suggestions] in the article." Further, he continued, "I had some thing similar to it in the first draft, but dropped it out" on the
advice of their father. Bishop Wright, a veteran of many religious wars with rival
prelates, thought that an illustrated article on the progress of the brothers in flight
was no place to declare a war.[48]

Chapter Seven

THE WORLD ALOFT

The Watery Town of Manteo on Roanoke Island, NC, May 1908
Photojournalist James Hare could not resist taking other pictures while on assignment to make the first
photograph of a Wright brothers' flight. On arriving at Manteo on May 11, 1908, he captured a
magnificent image of the sleepy county seat of Dare County—accessible at the time only by boat.

The exchange of letters between Wilbur in Paris and Orville in Dayton on June 9 actually brought the sequence of their 1908 Kitty Hawk experiences full circle. On this date, they symbolically turned their attention from what had happened on the sands at Big Kill Devil Hill to what they would be doing separately in a few short weeks. Wilbur's letter disclosed that he had settled upon Le Mans as the place where he would make his first flights in France and thereby the first of the many flights one of the brothers would make in Europe. He would remain at Le Mans until the end of 1908, and there he would perform feats of flight never before seen nor comprehended anywhere in the world. Orville's letter concluded his last bit of work on Kitty Hawk for 1908 and also closed the books on their long-awaited coming-out story that would soon appear in *Century Magazine*. Even the postscript of Orville's letter signified his imminent change of course: "I expect to be ready at Fort Myer the early part of August."[1]

A few weeks later, for the first time ever, Wilbur and Orville Wright would be attempting new flights on totally new and untested machines, on fields where no one had ever flown, and on separate continents three thousand miles apart. With lucrative contracts requiring them to make their first public flights almost simultaneously in both Europe and America, they could no longer postpone their emergence from privacy and secrecy. But fortunately, by dint of their years of thinking, tinkering, and dedicated trial and error practice flights, they were as ready as they ever would be to show the world the fine art and science of powered flight. Wilbur began his historic flights on August 8 at a horse racing track called Les Hunaudiérès at Le Mans, France. Orville followed suit less than a month later on September 3 on the open grounds of the U.S. Army camp at Fort Myer, Virginia.

Both of them would soon astound the world, and they did so almost simultaneously on both sides of the Atlantic Ocean. Quickly and with what seemed to be the greatest of ease, they proved that the wild, zany, and often contradictory stories that came out of Kitty Hawk during their secretive seven days in May were but muddled harbingers of what the world would see only two months later.

Wilbur's initial flight at Les Hunaudiéres lasted less than two minutes. Yet in the process, he made two great circles of the race track before a small but astonished French audience of a few dozen people. This particular group included influential members of the Aero Club de France, several Paris reporters, and two Russian military officers. The news of what he had done spread like wildfire across France and to awaiting correspondents in Moscow, London, and the United States. Although Wilbur attempted to control photography on the scene, that was about as hopeless as containing the word of what had just happened.

Two days later he flew twice again—but this time in front of 2,000 spectators. On August 11 he circled the field three times before a gasping crowd of 3,000 people. On the twelfth he circled the race course six times, and on the thirteenth, seven times. Each day the crowds grew almost exponentially. By that time it was clear to Wilbur that the horse track was too confining for the distance and duration of the flights he needed to perform. Besides, the growing audiences vastly overcrowded both the seating and the standing room capacity of the track. Wilbur very wisely demanded a change of venue.

On August 21, he resumed his astonishing flights at a French military camp eight miles outside Le Mans. The new site, Camp d'Auvours, contained a vast and historic artillery range that extended to three or four miles in length and featured a number of steel towers where both judges and dignitaries could observe Wilbur's longer and longer flights. Best of all, the camp could accommodate the crowds of 10,000 spectators who immediately began appearing to witness new flights.

Not only did he attract popular attention and press from all over the country and the world, his flights were observed by a steady stream of dignitaries from all levels of French society. Military delegates flocked into the camp, not only from France, but also from Germany, the United Kingdom, Italy, Spain, Austria, and, of course, Russia. For many years military leaders across the world had imagined that a real airplane capable of controlled flight could revolutionize the nature of warfare—and suddenly, such a plane seemed to have arrived from the backwaters of the United States. No nation interested in military preparedness could afford to miss Wilbur Wright's dramatic demonstrations of what such a plane could do.

Orville's exploits at Fort Myer, meanwhile, were no less spectacular. In fact, although he was a little later getting his flights underway, he quickly matched and surpassed the distance and duration of Wilbur's flights at Camp d'Auvours. When Orville made his first flight on September 3, he too enunciated this new beginning with a giant circle around the spacious military camp. Within days, he was also flying before cabinet secretaries, members of Congress, ambassadors, and military attaches from a host of other nations. The American press was enthralled with his ability to catapult into the air and to make smooth circles around this place on the outskirts of Washington, D.C. Fort Myer was so convenient that any officer of the U.S. government or a minister of the dozens of nations with embassies in Washington could trundle out to the place by streetcar to watch the cavalcade of flights.

Both at Fort Myer in the United States and at Camp d'Auvours in France, the brothers also flew in the presence of many aspiring aeronauts with either military credentials or sporting interests. These other would-be flyers, both men and women—some converted to flight on the spot—were perhaps the keenest of all the observers. Just watching the brothers fly, they were being schooled in the most advanced methods of flying anywhere in the world. And as the Wright brothers feared, these experienced witnesses quickly grasped the nature and operation of the special machines devised by the Wright brothers for this purpose. Many of them begged for opportunities to fly as passengers—and the brothers obliged as many of them as possible, even if for brief hops of one or two minutes into what was until that moment nether air for most human beings. Virtually everyone who would be flying in Europe and America over the next two or three years watched as the brothers soared seemingly effortlessly into the air thousands of miles apart. The chills that ran down the spines of observers at either Camp d'Auvours or at Fort Myer during those hot August and September days were indistinguishable as the brothers thrilled their audiences with feats never before seen anywhere in the world.

Once Orville flew in public for the first time at Fort Myer on September 3, the confused headlines and conflicting stories that had so recently emanated from Kitty

Hawk simply melted from human memory. The seven days in May that had brought journalists from so many points of the globe to the Outer Banks for the first glimpse of a Wright airplane in the sky were immediately forgotten. The two or three fuzzy, distant photographs that came from Kitty Hawk were soon supplanted with hundreds of clear and distinct images issued from both Le Mans and Washington. From previous flights that were mainly rumors and hearsay, there were now suddenly daily demonstrations of flight on both sides of the Atlantic. The new spate of photographs were splashed into newspapers and made into full-page spreads showing both dramatic flights and every detail of the Wrights' amazing aircraft as they were cajoled into position to fly and then catapulted into the sky, making swoops and grand circles in the air.

Daily dispatches sent via telegraph crisscrossed the Atlantic and emanated outward to the corners of the earth, telling the story of the miraculous flights in both France and the United States. For two weeks in September 1908, the world was serenaded in morning and evening newspapers with daily refrains of the almost simultaneous achievements of the brothers. On the morning of September 3 at Camp d'Auvours, Wilbur flew through a gracious figure eight in a flight that lasted ten minutes; Orville responded with his own circular flight at Fort Myer six or eight hours later. On September 5, Wilbur charted his longest flight yet in France—19 minutes and 48 seconds. Four days later Orville astonished everyone—including Wilbur—with the two longest flights yet in human history. The first of these lasted 57 minutes and the second one went on for 62 minutes. Before the day was done, Orville also carried his first passenger, Army Lieutenant Frank P. Lahm, at Fort Myer on a flight of 6 minutes and 24 seconds.

Over the next three days, September 10–12, both brothers flew every day. Wilbur performed eight separate flights during that time. In the same three days Orville continued to amaze a steady stream of U.S. dignitaries and military brass with five separate flights—three of which exceeded one hour in duration. Wilbur, of course, read the daily headlines describing Orville's steady stream of new world records and set out on September 16 and 17 to do likewise. His longest efforts, however, were considerably shorter flights of 39 minutes on the sixteenth and 32 minutes on the seventeenth.

It all seemed so very easy for both of the brothers, and especially for Orville—that is, until September 17. On that day, Orville set out to see if he could establish yet another new record for flight—this time with another person onboard. His passenger that day was Lieutenant Thomas E. Selfridge—an army officer who had observed many attempted flights in both the United States and Canada. The flight went very well for almost 4 minutes and covered 4½ long loops around the flying field at Fort Myer.

Suddenly, all hell broke loose. One of the plane's rear propellers split and in the process, the machine's rear tail assembly was completely disabled. The plane immediately plunged from a height of 125 feet into the ground. Selfridge was killed almost instantly, and Orville broke enough bones and damaged sufficient spinal cartilage to disable him for months and leave him in severely recurring pain for the rest of his life.

Wilbur was dismayed at Orville's crash and surely felt empathy for the mental and physical pain his younger brother had suffered. However, as in so many of the brothers' communications over the years, Wilbur was merciless in his letters to Orville, criticizing both his carelessness in preparing his plane for flight and the reckless manner in which he surely flew the machine. Wilbur thought that Orville had not sufficiently studied the field at Fort Myer before undertaking his flights. He was sorry to read in newspaper reports that Orville had been flying at heights of 150 to 200 feet. And he also thought Orville had spent too much time patronizing the press and fraternizing with well-wishers. On the topic of the interfering press he wrote to Orville, "I have been refusing all invitations, and all but a few visitors for six weeks nearly. I found it was necessary to take the bull by the horns or break down."[2] Not even in Orville's time of suffering and his extended period of rehabilitation could Wilbur resist lording it over his brother and reminding him that he would always be the junior partner in their flying operations.

Whether it was Orville's sufferings or failures, the tragic crash at Fort Myer on September 17 seemed to drive Wilbur into even greater frenzies of flight. Just four days after the accident, still mindful of and probably stinging from Orville's accident—or perhaps to show that the crash was merely a fluke—Wilbur launched himself into a flight that lasted longer than an hour and a half—surpassing Orville's nine-day-old world record. It was both a grim memorial to Orville's failed flight and a declaration that the Wright brothers' enterprise was alive and well.

Convinced thereafter that he could fly practically whenever he wanted as long as he had fuel to stay in the air, Wilbur changed his tactics slightly after this long solo flight. He turned his attention to carrying passengers—especially potential promoters and customers. This meant carrying aeronauts from a number of nations who might persuade their own governments to buy Wright airplanes. He also had a steady stream of dignitaries who revved up their daring enough to take a flight with Wilbur. Men, women, ambassadors, generals, daredevils, and business executives took their turns to sit beside Wilbur and proceed into the air. The names of his passengers would punctuate the twentieth century: Charles S. Rolls, cofounder of Rolls-Royce Limited; Dr. Giovanni B. Pirelli, founder of an Italian tire manufacturing monopoly; Count Charles de Lambert, a renowned French nobleman; Major B. F. S. Baden-Powell of the Aeronautical Society of Great Britain; and Jose Quinones de Leon, diplomat in the Spanish mission to France were a few of Wilbur's earliest passengers. Others who merely watched for the time being included: Anne Pierpont Morgan, American banking heiress; Mario Calderara, Italy's first renowned pilot; Baron and Baroness de Sennevoy, avid French proponents of flight; Count Georges Castillon de Saint-Victor, another pro-flight French nobleman; Baron Paul d'Estournelles de Constant, the principal French actor in the creation of the League of Nations; Georges Clemenceau, sporting son of the sitting French premier; Baron Henri de Rothschild, international financier; Dowager Queen Margherita of the royal family of Italy and an early promoter of flight in Italy; and Prince Singh of the royal family of India. Whether flying or watching, all of these people from stations high and low participated in the awe-inspiring ceremonies that saw the world plunge into the age of human flight.

But even though the Wright brothers soared into the air to the astonishment of thousands, almost as if performing feats of magic, the mysteries of flight had already been widely dispelled by the time they decided to go public in 1908. Indeed, even before the Wrights launched their public flights at Le Mans and Fort Myer, other aeronauts were demonstrating their own quite separate abilities to make sustained flights. On June 23, 1908, the French pilot Léon Delagrange put his modified Voisin airplane in the air for 18 minutes and 30 seconds at Milan, Italy. Two weeks later on July 6, on the same grounds at Issy near Paris, two other French pilots showed comparable skills: Louis Bleriot flew his own modified plane for 8 minutes and 25 seconds, while Henri Farman kept his modified Voisin plane in the air for 20 minutes and 20 seconds. And after the Wrights opened their flights to public audiences, these and other flyers quickly ascended to the air or achieved records nearly comparable to those of the Wrights. Delagrange increased his longest duration for a single flight to over 30 minutes on September 17, the same day of Orville's great crash, and Farman increased his best to 44 minutes and 31 seconds on October 2.

In addition to their sustained flights, these other aeronauts also achieved some feats not yet attempted by the Wrights. Louis Bleriot, for example, introduced the use of ailerons during June 1908 and the first monoplane on July 4, 1908. He flew the novel single-winged plane that day for five minutes. Four days later, Léon De-lagrange took up the world's first female passenger—Thérèse Peltier—at Turin. New native pilots emerged around the world, such as Hans Grade in Germany, J. T. C. Moore-Brabazon in the United Kingdom, and Glenn Curtiss in the United States. On October 30, 1908, Henri Farman broke loose from the relatively safe practice of flying circuits in a confined practice field and performed the world's first cross-country flight of sixteen miles from Bouy to Reims in France.

Wilbur Wright waited until the last day of 1908 to perform his longest flight—a herculean feat that lasted 2 hours and 20 minutes, a new world record. Although this achievement won him the Michelin Cup in 1908 and he intended it to be a feat that could not be equaled in the foreseeable future, the admirable milestone would be lost in history. A simultaneous volcanic eruption in Italy, caus-ing an untold number of deaths, became the world's principal news story for weeks thereafter. Moreover, the sudden emergence of flight as a mania across the world meant that Wilbur's effort to leave an indelible mark on December 31, 1908 did not succeed.

In January 1909 Wilbur opened a flight school at Pau, a town lying in the shadow of the Pyrenees Mountains in southern France. He was joined there by the recuperating Orville, hobbling along with a cane and the assistance of Katharine, to watch Wilbur fly—and to share some of the acclaim accorded to the brothers. Wilbur's students were a platoon of fledgling French pilots—mainly drawn from the ranks of nobility. While he would soon fly before more crowned heads of Europe—Edward VII of the United Kingdom and Alfonso XIII of Spain—and in the presence of mighty crowds of spectators, the magic cast by the brothers' flights at Le Mans and Fort Myer was already waning.

In April 1909 Wilbur organized another flying school at Rome, this one for Italian military pilots. Orville and Katharine followed as eager witnesses and wide-eyed tourists in the magical city. One of the most enthusiastic witnesses of Wilbur's flights was King Victor Emmanuel III, who hoped the Wright influence would help make Italy one of the world's leaders in flight—and his plan succeeded. But while the people at Pau, including many from the British upper crust who vacationed in the area, and in Rome gloried with the presence of the famous Wrights in their own towns, the whereabouts and activities of the Wrights was no longer front-page news. The moment of special glory for the Wrights had already peaked in the eyes of the world and was already on the decline.

By the time Wilbur conducted his last flights in Rome on April 27, 1909, there were other aeronauts flying not only in France, Germany, Italy, the United Kingdom, and the United States; there were still more plunging skyward in Austria, Sweden, Rumania, Russia, Turkey, Portugal, and Canada. Tractor-style flying machines, with propellers in front of the wings, had already emerged as a good option to the Wrights' pusher-style crafts; monoplanes were in the air with wing-warping capabilities; ailerons were beginning to replace wing-warping techniques. The world was abuzz with speculation as to who would be the first flier to take up a challenge prize of £1,000 promised by the London *Daily Mail* for the first pilot who could cross the English Channel. The longish flight performed by Wilbur around a closed circuit on December 31, 1908, was quickly being replaced by popular stunt flights and symbolic competitions.

In the space of less than a year, from the moment Wilbur and Orville Wright made their last attempts to fly secretly at Kitty Hawk in May 1908, the world of flight had changed immensely. Just as suddenly as the brothers had rushed into public acclaim, they were already in the process of being ushered out. While there was no feat yet accomplished a year later that they could not easily have done themselves, the technology of flight had advanced so much in just one year that the Wrights were on the verge of being surpassed. And if they were to be outdone in terms of the technology and design of the airplane, they would not be able to reap the handsome profits they had been hoping for since they first realized they had discovered how to fly back in October 1902 at Kitty Hawk. Even though they had almost immediately thereafter applied for a U.S. patent on the flying machine, as of May 1909 they still had not achieved the wealth they hoped would come tumbling in. Seven years later, they were still trying to prove to the world that their flying machine was a bargain at almost any price.

While it might have been fun for the Wrights to hang around Europe in May 1909 for Wilbur to provide additional proofs of their abilities, they made a very practical decision to return to the United States, where they still had not met the requirements of the U.S. Army for a viable flying machine. Following Orville's crash on September 17, 1908, the army had kindly extended the deadline for delivery almost a year to permit Orville's full recovery. But the army had extended the date for the other competitors as well, leaving open the question as to whether the other bidders might be able deliver—one year later—a better plane than the Wrights. New demonstration flights were scheduled for Fort Myer for June and July 1909, and this time, the Wrights would take no chances. Wilbur would be there to assist, but not to replace, Orville.

When the brothers—with Katharine by their sides—made their way from Rome back to the United States in May 1909, they had already achieved great heights of fame. But the arrival of their wealth was still pending. They were feted in Rome for their contributions to the world and, more recently, to the advancement of flight in Italy. From there they returned to Le Mans where, on May 1, Léon Bollée gave them a large bronze sculpture symbolizing the Muse of Aviation and the city bestowed upon them a gold plaque bearing a municipal coat of arms. They next made a stop in London, where they were still trying to sell planes, and received the gold medal of the Aeronautical Society of Great Britain on May 3. Toasts and a feast were also held by the Aero Club of the United Kingdom at the Ritz Hotel.

More symbols of fame came to them when their ocean liner *Kronprinzessin Cecilie* arrived in New York on May 11. The next day they were celebrated at the Aero Club of America in New York. On May 13, the brothers and Katharine arrived home in Dayton, where they received a not unexpected heroic welcome from the city. At the railroad station they were greeted by a throng of thousands. Speeches, certificates, plaudits, and platitudes followed. An ornate carriage, drawn by a team of four white horses, awaited them and conveyed them to their home. This most memorable day in the history of Dayton was concluded with a fireworks display worthy of the best July 4 ceremonies.

The brothers, hankering to get back to work on planes that they needed to put in operation if they were going to make a profit, could not escape from the steady stream of honors and ceremonies. They won certificates and medals everywhere they went. The biggest honor came from America's most respected public figure at the time. President William Howard Taft presented both brothers with gold medals in the East Room of the White House on June 10 in a crowded space filled with a thousand people. Like everyone else, Taft focused on the brothers' discoveries and not on the cash they hoped to collect when he proclaimed: "You made this discovery by a course that we of America like to feel is distinctly American—by keeping your nose right at the job until you had accomplished what you had determined to do."

The brothers probably would have preferred to go directly from the White House to Fort Myer, where their crucial demonstration flights were to begin before the end of June. But the folks back home, not satisfied that four white horses and some speeches should stand as the final symbols of Dayton's pride, had other ideas. The most prominent figures in town—politicians and corporate heads—staged a two-day celebration of the Wright brothers on June 17 and 18. On the first day there was a parade of every local person with a uniform or a horn or a drum, which the brothers dutifully watched. The parade was followed by a reception and another fireworks display, in which 80-foot portraits of the brothers were unveiled. On the second day there were more speeches and gold medals. Bishop Wright glowed with pride as he made a speech about his boys, and various dignitaries presented the brothers with Congressional medals, the Ohio Medal, and the City of

Dayton medal. A second parade followed, with floats presenting the history of locomotion up to the invention of the airplane.

Little more than a week later, the brothers were put on the spot to prove that they were in fact worthy of all this glory. They headed to Fort Myer on June 19 and had their new plane assembled by the twenty-fourth. Following two days of engine tests, they were ready to fly on the twenty-sixth. The U.S. Senate even adjourned in order to witness the first Wright flights in the United States since Orville's disastrous crash the year before. Members of Congress, diplomats, engineers, military brass, and a full press corps showed up. Unfortunately, the winds that day proved too strong for the launching of an entirely new machine, and the anxious throng of dignitaries disbursed in disappointment.

Finally, on June 29, atmospheric conditions, machine, and pilot were all in readiness and the brothers commenced with short flights. It was not until the third week in July that the new machine operated completely as the Wrights wished. On July 17, Orville kept the machine in the air for 16 minutes; on the nineteenth he made separate flights of 25 and 29 minutes. On the twentieth and twenty-seventh Orville completed duration flights in excess of one hour each day. The flight on the twenty-seventh was with a passenger, thus meeting that requirement. On the thirtieth Orville completed the last test—a speed trial in excess of 40 miles per hour with a passenger onboard. On this flight, Orville flew to Alexandria and back. Upon his return, President Taft was there to greet him and to congratulate both brothers for delivering the plane they had promised more than a year before.[3]

On August 2, the brothers met in the offices of General James Allen, Chief of the U.S. Army Signal Corps, where their airplane was formally accepted by the U.S. Army as meeting all of its requirements for performance. By approving the plane and officially putting it into service on this date, the U.S. government became the first nation on earth to incorporate flight into its military fleet.

Finally, it seemed possible that the Wright brothers—just nine years after their first trip to Kitty Hawk—might be on the verge of adding a little bit of wealth to their great fame. When the brothers left Europe in May 1909, they made a business decision—just as they had done upon learning to fly in 1902, developing a practical flying machine in 1905, and deciding to keep their photographs, their plane, and their flying techniques secret from the world. Just as quietly and secretively as they had decided to get a patent of the flying machine in 1902, they now decided, in 1909, that they would devote their energies to whatever legal proceedings might be required to protect their patent. While they started out as idealists and quite innocent campers on their way to Kitty Hawk in 1900, they had gradually been transformed into entrepreneurs for whom every decision had to be controlled by their business interests. Fame was only good—in the end—if it helped to sell the product.

The brothers could easily have accepted the *Daily Mail* challenge to be the first pilots to cross the English Channel. They could have been the darlings of the first international aviation meet at Reims, France, in August 1909. Wilbur could easily have extended his two-hour flight at the end of 1908 to three or four or five hours in 1909—but they already had all the fame they wanted or needed. Louis Bleriot thus became the first pilot to cross the English Channel on July 25, 1909—giving him a mighty and lasting parcel of fame. A dozen European and American pilots dazzled an international audience at Reims in August. Those pilots—including the person who would become the Wrights' greatest American nemesis, Glenn Curtiss, achieved worldwide fame at Reims. That August, Henri Farman also easily broke Wilbur's short-lived endurance record by flying over three hours and covering more than a hundred miles. This added to his already considerable renown.

The Wrights, meanwhile, still secretive to the core, quietly sought business deals wherever they could get them and began filing lawsuits either to stop the flights or collect royalties from anyone they thought had infringed their patent rights. After all, they had solved the problem of flight before anyone else—just as Morse had invented the telegraph, Bell the telephone, and Edison the electric light. Those men wallowed in riches. The brothers Wright, by the same token, believed they had every right to reap the financial rewards of their own success in being the human innovators who literally conquered the sky.

Epilogue

THE VERDICT
ON SECRETIVENESS

The Spying Reporters Got Stories and Chiggers Too
Big city reporters on the trail of the Wright brothers at Kitty Hawk and Kill Devil Hills were ill-prepared to deal with either swaggering locals or with mosquitoes and chiggers perennially infesting the wooded realms of the Outer Banks of North Carolina as here captured in painful lament by photojournalist James Hare.

There is much in the papers about the Wright brothers. They have fame, but not wealth, yet. Both these things aspired after by so many, are vain.

—Bishop Milton Wright in his diary, November 30, 1906

Bishop Wright's advice to Orville that he should not declare a patent war in a popular article such as the Wright brothers' much-awaited *Century Magazine* spread was wise not only at the moment, but also for the sake of history. None of the Wrights involved in this stressful and historic juncture—Wilbur, Orville, Katharine, or Bishop Wright himself—could divine the future. The article that had just been compiled around May 20, 1908, and written and illustrated by Orville—under the most extreme of circumstances—turned out to be the most complete account of their long process of inventing flight that would ever be written by either brother. Both of the brothers had lifelong intentions of writing a more comprehensive history of their years of innovation and experimentation that would detail their many milestones in perfecting the world's first controlled flying machine.

Sadly, Wilbur died at the age of forty-five in 1912 before he could undertake the task. Or, it might be appropriate to ask—given the driven, peripatetic, and almost self-destructive character of his life and his very being—would he ever actually have been able to focus long enough to complete the task?

With regard to Orville, on the other hand, one might similarly ask—would he ever have been capable of writing a full account of the brothers' shared history? In contrast to Wilbur, he lived to a ripe old age of seventy-seven years, dying in 1948—thirty-six of those years following Wilbur's death. This should have been plenty of time to recount past glories, and to set forth an official history—indeed, several histories.

However, Orville was shattered by the loss of Wilbur. It was not that he never recovered from Wilbur's early death. It was rather that he lost his right hand with the departure of his partner in conquering flight. When all was said and done, the brothers worked in perfect symmetry; one of the brothers was the right hand and the other was the left. While individual beings might recover from the loss of a limb and go on to adapt to perfectly comfortable and productive lives, this was not possible in the case of the Wright brothers.

Ultimately, neither of the Wrights operated very well without the presence and support, the urging and cajoling, and the filial rivalry of the other. Theirs was one of the most creative partnerships of brothers in human history. The severance of their bond by the death of one of its vital members led to the burial of the partnership itself, and in some ways, the fruit of its labors. The evaporation of the partnership resulted in Orville's abandonment of the will to rehearse its history and the vibrancy and creativity it had contained. There was no Wilbur to bark out orders or to force him to rise above the perennial quiescence in which he felt most comfortable for the rest of his life.

But it was also good that Bishop Wright had counseled Orville to leave out momentary pique and anger in this historical statement for another reason. The Wrights were not only on the verge of losing control of their great invention; they were also about to lose historical credit for being the very first humans to completely solve the problem of flight. They had dallied for almost five years before going public after their great first flights at Kitty Hawk in 1903; they stopped flying completely after they devised an even more practical airplane in October 1905; and they had been so secretive about almost all of their activities and achievements from 1900 until 1908 that they were in serious danger of losing even the judgment of history. It was at an earlier juncture in the Wright brothers' history that Bishop Wright had made another wise observation on the evolution of his two extraordinary sons. On November 30, 1906, when the brothers were deeply embroiled in secret negotiations for the sale of their invention and were provoking sporadic public notice of their activities, Bishop Wright penned perhaps his most sage evaluation of his sons when he observed in his diary that "they have fame, but not wealth, yet." That tiny word "yet" here loomed as a colossal commentary and judgment on the trajectory of their careers in the pursuit of flight. If they did not watch out, he thought, they were going to be sucked into the most ancient sin of all, the worship of Mammon over God. Both as a father and as a stern judge of the secret motives in men's souls, Bishop Wright saw his boys teetering on a narrow path between virtue and destruction.[1] Although he had been somewhat on the periphery as his sons secretively went about inventing and developing the world's first true flying machine, he could see the transforming force of their eventual pursuits of fame and wealth. He hoped and prayed that his gifted boys would not ultimately be destroyed by these venal and destructive sins.

Bishop Wright lived on for another decade after making this prophetic utterance. He lived through the years when his sons transformed themselves from innovators into litigators as they vigorously sought to protect their 1906 patent on the flying machine. He watched as Wilbur raced from courtroom to courtroom, attempting to beat back a new generation of aviators who flew at will and paid little attention to the legal rights and maneuvers of the Wright brothers. He lamented Wilbur's gnawing obsession to strike down rival flyers. He witnessed Wilbur's flagging energy, declining health, virtual self-destruction, and eventual death in May 1912. Beyond his own profound grief at the loss of this most amazing son, he was also around to watch the muffled voice and withering powers of his youngest. Without his partner, Orville suffered a complete loss of will to pursue any further wealth or fame. Orville would focus for the next thirty years on what he and Wilbur had done, not on what was left for him to accomplish.

Moreover, Bishop Wright observed the emergence of what seemed to be a jealous conspiracy in the United States and abroad of those who sought to deny the Wright brothers a major place in history, who thought it would not be proper to give a place of unique honor to the Wrights' great 1903 flyer in America's national museum, and who fought tooth and nail to annul or circumvent the lock that the Wright brothers' patent exercised on the development of new flying machines in the United States. Bishop Wright supported Orville's efforts to carry on after 1912, but he noted that Orville pursued the chase each year with less and less energy and focus. Orville kept his office in Dayton isolated from the rest of the sprawling Wright Company operations. In 1915, he retired from the airplane business entirely by selling all of his interests in the Wright Company. He even gave up the patents he and Wilbur had worked so hard to win and that Wilbur had spent his last moments on earth attempting to protect. He retired, in part, to remove himself from the fray and, also in part, to focus on salvaging the Wright brothers' name in the history of flight. Although this would be his primary focus for more than thirty years, he never wrote a history to supplant the one he threw together in haste in the summer of 1908.

Bishop Wright died at the age of eighty-eight on April 3, 1917. His witness to history ended just as America was about to enter combat in the First World War. As a part of its entry into the war, the U.S. government unilaterally modified a stranglehold of the Wright patent on aviation in the United States. At that moment, history's judgment of the legacy of the Wright brothers had not yet been rendered. Bishop Wright would thus never know for sure whether or not his sons' secretive pursuit of fame and wealth for so many years had gained them a proper place in history.

The verdict on their secretiveness was thus complicated, with many interconnecting parts. Yes, other aeronauts would have immediately absconded with their innovations if they had flown publicly prior to the summer of 1908. This was, in fact, what happened as soon as they went fully public both in the United States and France.

Yes, their efforts to protect the patent on their flying machine prevented widespread recognition of their pioneering achievements in flight for many years. It was not that they were alone in fighting to protect proprietary knowledge—so did such luminaries as Alexander Graham Bell, Thomas Alva Edison, and Henry Ford. But there was a substantial difference. Those great innovators formed giant companies that continued to produce their inventions, which evolved along with newer innovations in their fields.

The Wrights desperately wanted to spend their time innovating, not creating a company, and experimenting, not fighting patent infringements. Yet, innovations in flight came so quickly in the fall of 1908 and the spring of 1909 that the Wright brothers were almost instantaneously left behind. Having spent so many years finding a solution to the problem of flight, they were not able to move forward at the pace of those daring young men and women who watched them fly in the summer and fall of 1908. As a consequence, when they followed the example of their contemporaries—the Bells, Edisons, and Fords—in establishing an airplane company, the chief business of the firm was to protect their patents, not to develop new machines.

The secretiveness of the Wrights up through May 1908 was a double-edged sword. It served to protect their discoveries, but it also insulated them against a vibrant world marketplace where ideas could quickly be converted into ever more efficient machines. While the Wrights thus laid the groundwork for a worldwide revolution in flight and presented their innovation to the world in 1908, they almost immediately became casualties of their own achievement.

This revolution came so quickly and so decisively that the Wrights' secretiveness up until its opening phases nearly served to extinguish their place in history. Without Wilbur by his side, unable to vie for a place in the revolution, Orville was consigned to spend the rest of his years attempting to prove that the brothers, in all of their secretiveness, had actually been the brilliant innovators we now know they were.

Appendix

EYEWITNESS TESTIMONIALS

First Graphic Photo of a Wright Plane in Flight, Scientific American, August 29, 1908
Since the Wright brothers had not yet published the famous
photograph of their first powered flight at Kitty Hawk on December
17, 1903, this starkly detailed image of Wilbur's plane, when it
appeared on the cover of Scientific American on August 29, 1908,
was the world's first exposure to the operating systems of a Wright
plane in flight.

This book is, among other things, a chronicle of those people who observed, in one way or another, the historic activities and flights of Wilbur and Orville Wright in North Carolina during April and May 1908. There were many observers of these remarkable events: ferryboat pilots, operators of powered launches, passing fishermen, lifesavers, rumormongers, reporters, photographers, and everyday people who dragged their children out to witness history in the making.

Most of these observers either did not write, could not write, or chose not to write about what they witnessed. However, that does not mean that their voices and testimonials cannot be heard. We are fortunate that many of the articulate writers who were present in May 1908 recorded not only what they themselves saw, but also what others—particularly the outspoken Outer Bankers—said they saw. Indeed, there are elements of wonder, discovery, and anthropological observation contained in many of the accounts written by the journalists who made their first visit to what they quaintly viewed as the ends of the earth.

So that readers can get a true flavor for the period, the people, and the events covered in this book—through the eyes of several of the most articulate witnesses—three eyewitness accounts written by journalists are reproduced below. The final entry here is the story told by the most subjective of all the witnesses—Orville Wright—as he set forth his "official" interpretation of what happened at Kitty Hawk in April and May 1908.

For more information on the three journalists and some of the people they mention, consult brief biographies included elsewhere in this book.

COLUMBIA STATE (COLUMBIA, SOUTH CAROLINA)

Filed May 17; published May 20, 1908

Although Zachary (Zach) McGhee did not appear at Manteo until after the last great flight, he visited the scene soon enough to talk with the other reporters and to interview the lifesavers who had been present for the flights and who had conveyed information to reporters. Since he left Manteo on the same ferry as Wilbur Wright, he was also able to get some perspective from the, for once, somewhat talkative brother. His description of the people and personalities he found is perceptive and nicely told.

THE FLYING MACHINE THAT REALLY FLIES[1]

The Wright Brothers' Aeroplane, Which They Are Trying at Kill Devil Hill
Some of the Stories About It
By Zach McGhee

Manteo, N. C., May 17.—Kill Devil Hill—that's the place where the flying machine is, and where the day before I started out to look for it, it got smashed up . . . far out towards the stormy dangerous eastern shore of North Carolina, some 10 or 12 miles the other side of the end of the world, which is at Manteo. It is the hill upon which some several hundred years ago—the historians and the story books know when—the Indian chief Manteo, or some other "heap big Injun," killed the White Doe, in which the spirit of Virginia Dare had taken refuge. He killed this White Doe with a silver arrow presented to him by Queen Elizabeth. And when he did it, there was great rejoicing in Injun land, because they thought the White Doe, which had been wandering for years up and down the shore, was the devil. And now this flying machine has taken its first flight from this same Kill Devil Hill, the first time in the history of the world that man has really flown successfully in a heavier than air machine, soaring back and forth up and down the bleak shore among the sand dunes, sand crabs and pebble-filled winds of the shore. Is it the soul of Virginia Dare, the first white child born in America, or is it the devil?

Chartering a fisherman's boat, propelled by a greasy chu-chuing, throbbing gasoline engine, I gathered a small party at Manteo and hied me away across Albemarle Sound for Kill Devil Hill. Nag's Head was our first stop. Once there was an old pirate by the name of Edward R. Teach, who had his office on the narrow strip of land which encloses Albemarle Sound, just a few miles below Kill Devil Hill. He had an old nag upon whose head he used to tie a lantern at night and drive her up and down the beach. It was a particularly dangerous shoaly shore there and sailors out at sea going past would see the light moving and think it was a boat. Since the sailors were having a pretty hard time of it themselves and seeing the other boat moving smoothly along, they would steer their vessels toward the supposed boat to get into a better channel, when low, they would strike the shoals. This was what the old pirate was wanting, and he would go out, stick knives through the sailors and take their gold and jewels. He was a sharp old pirate, and if he lived at the present day he would have his office in Wall Street instead of on that desolate place, which was named after his horse.

After the usual experiences with the motor boat's engine, somewhat automobilious, you understand, and after climbing over a few sand dunes, marshes, quick-sands and things, we reached Kill Devil Hill, and there, sure enough, was the flying machine—nailed up in boxes, they say: I know only that it was not flying, and if it existed anywhere, it was in the big barn like house they called the "camp."

The only "natives" anywhere in the sight of the whole neighborhood were some six or eight life savers—technically or professionally so-called—at the United States life saving station beside the roaring sea, a short distance from the camp. These life savers have been at this station since 1878, during all of which time they have never been known to handle a wreck or to save a life. Their specialty seems to be, not to save life, but to kill time. This may be another reason for calling the place Kill Devil Hill, Old Father Time being the devil, as many folks are quite willing to attest.

The flying machine was a boon to these poor fellows away there on the desolate uninhabited shore, who had nothing to do all the live long but to sit and look at one another, stare at the ocean or make toad frog houses in the sand. They watched the wonderful performances of the flying men from the top of the sand dune. Each one of the life savers could tell wondrous things about it, and they each had a theory about the puzzling Wright brothers and the problem of flying. Ever since I had struck the North Carolina line I had found the air full of the flying machine and the Wright brothers, not anywhere visible, but everywhere in the air audible. At Elizabeth City, on the boat going to Manteo, and, of course, in Manteo, nobody could talk of anything else. The monstrous performances over at Kill Devil Hill seemed to occupy the minds of all, men, women and children. Very few had seen it, though everybody claimed to be on intimate personal terms with the inventors. Accordingly I was entertained with the most wonderful tales.

At last I had reached folks who had actually seen it. And these life savers or time killers told me about it, what was, what had been and what was going to be, not going it particularly strong, however, on the last, for they had little imagination, in spite of their intimate association with the mystic and majestic sea. One of these fellows showed me a picture of the machine in flight in a New York paper, which, by some wonderful, inexplicable process, had been blown across the wide expanse of water, shifting sand dunes and a still wider expanse of ignorance.

"That's the picture," said he. "The fellow sho' got a good un."

It was an excellent picture indeed, and, as I was admiring it and envying the luck of the man who had managed to take such a perfect photograph, I asked, "When was this picture taken?"

"Thursday," he replied.

"Why, the paper's dated Thursday," I said.

"That don't make no diffrunce," he said. "That ar' picture wuz tuk Thursday, 'cause Thursday's the only time thar wuz two men in the machine, and the picture has two in it."

So he had figured it out. And I quickly figured out that the magnificent picture marked as a "Photograph of the Wright Brothers' Aeroplane In Flight" was a pure fake. It would have taken two whole days to get a picture from there to New York, and two more days to get the paper back.

At the hotel in Manteo I met a whole bunch of newspaper men from Norfolk, Washington, New York, London. On the day of the flight the woods were full of them—the woods far away from the camp and from the big sand dune. Not one of those newspaper men saw the machine fall, though they all saw it fly. Some of the wildest accounts had been printed in some of the papers about this flying performance. A Norfolk paper printed a story that the Wrights had taken a flight of 10 miles and over the sea. The same paper after the accident said that the Wrights had cut their machine into unrecognizable splints to preserve their secret. The newspaper men who saw it were at least a quarter of a mile away. It is but just to those who did see it, and to the profession generally, to say that Norfolk paper did not have a man on the scene at all and the absurd stories were evidently written by some expert think artist in the home office. Other wild stories were printed in other papers.

The Wright brothers would not operate their machine when any newspaper men were present. In order to see it, they had to stand afar off, and many humorous accounts of their experiences were related. Some of these experiences were not quite so humorous, though, at the time, such as getting blistered in the sun, skinning their shins climbing trees, making a close acquaintance with the enterprising and distinguished Mr. Chigoe [i.e., chigger], who inhabits the little patches of woods all through this country. They saw the long eight-mile flight, though, and they learned from a reliable source through a man who was there at the time that one of the Wrights pressed the wrong lever of the steering apparatus, causing the machine to shoot down instead of up. It shot into the sand, and as the speed was something like a mile a minute, great was the fall thereof.

The flying machine consists of two horizontal oblong discs, or planes, 40 feet long, six and a half feet wide. A propeller is in the rear, run by a gasoline engine set between the discs or plane. There is an arrangement to steer by raising or lowering the edges of the planes, and by shifting the direction of the propeller. The engine is 25 horsepower, and weighs 160 pounds. The whole machine when it took its long flight the other day weighed, including the two men, 1,100 pounds. There is no balloon or gas bag attachment, nothing about the whole thing which is lighter than air. It is maintained in the air on the same principle exactly as a disc sailed by throwing it laterally into the air. The disc you throw is held up by the motion imparted in the throwing. If this motion did not spend itself against the resistance of the air and gravity it would go on forever. Now, what the Wright brothers have been trying to do is to put some motion-generator on the disc itself so that instead of the one impulse given to it at the start it shall have a continuous force operating upon it.

Before putting a motor on their machine, the Wrights practiced for years riding on it as it was projected into the air with one impulse given it in starting. They have been coming down to Kill Devil Hill for seven years getting upon one of these sand dunes and gliding off on a simple little track made of two parallel planes. By climbing upon the top of the hill and sliding down part the way they would generate enough motion to sail out into the air, and they would practice steering it in this way. When they had become skillful in doing this and had contrived a steering apparatus they made a gasoline engine and continued the motion. For a long time and until this year they would lie down between the planes, but they thought it would be better to sit up. And that was the principal thing they went to camp for this year, to practice with the new steering apparatus which had to be changed so they could handle it sitting up. And it was likewise the reason of the accident the other day. The steering arrangement being changed, the positions of the levers were new to them and by mistake one of them grabbed hold of the wrong lever and shot down instead of it.

When they fly they keep very close to earth, from 15 to 20 feet all the time. The longest flight they have yet made was made three years ago at Dayton, Ohio, which was 24 miles. This distance they made in 38 minutes. They flew eight miles the other day in about nine minutes.

Now, this disc sailing principle with the engine to impart a continuous force is all right, so far as it goes. But suppose the engine should go wrong or something should happen to the propeller or other part of the apparatus, what would happen? Would the machine, men and all, like a bird shot in the wing, come tumbling down? There is where the danger would seem to be, for it must be remembered that there is no danger in going up into the air, unless you go pretty high up where the air is very rare and you might take cold or run out of oxygen. The real danger in all aeronautic performances is in coming down. But a disc thrown into the air after the manner so well known does not come suddenly to the ground when the original force imparted in the throwing is exhausted; it sails slowly to the ground. This is what the planes would do. If the engine is shut off it would have a certain amount of momentum which is [it] must expend, and this it would do gradually, and thus if the steering arrangement is properly manipulated the thing would slowly glide down and light like a disc thrown or like a bird. The momentum would be expended gradually against the resistance of the air and gravity, like a child in a swing "letting the old cat die."

Very simple: Isn't it?

Then, why don't you fly? It beats waling all to holler—especially over hot sand dunes in the blistering sun.

COLLIER'S WEEKLY (NEW YORK, NEW YORK)

Filed and published May 30, 1908

This very fine article with photographs was prepared by Arthur Ruhl, reporter/writer, and James H. Hare, photographer, for Collier's Weekly. They were dispatched to Kitty Hawk as soon as reports began to appear that the Wrights were testing again at Kill Devil Hills. Since Ruhl worked for an illustrated weekly news magazine rather than a daily newspaper, as did the other reporters at Kitty Hawk in 1908, he could not compete in producing searing headline stories. But he did write an informed and reflective article complete with Hare's photographs to deliver the first photo news story on the Wright brothers.

HISTORY AT KILL DEVIL HILL[2]

A Description of the First Flight of the Wright Brothers' Aeroplane Witnessed by an Uninvited and Impartial Jury Representing the World at Large
By Arthur Ruhl
Illustrated with photographs by James H. Hare

From their ambush in the scrub timber the attacking party gazed out across a mile of level beach tufted with marsh grass to a long shed which, at that distance looked like a pine box set on the sand. There were dazzling white sand-dunes and a glimpse of the sea, and the Carolina sun, pouring down out of a clear sky, immersed everything in shimmer and glare.

To the left of the shed, two black dots, which were men, moved about something set on the sand. It was a rectangle of hazy gray lines, with a white streak at the top, which might have been taken for the white line receding wave trails along the beach. To the attacking party, who had used railroads, steamboats, gasoline chug-chugs, had waded, climbed sand-mountains, and tramped miles over slippery pine needles to gain that particular spot of sun-baked, tick-infested sand, this white streak and the skeleton lines beneath it was, in a way, the centre of the world.

It was the centre of the world because it was the touchable embodiment of an Idea, which, presently, is to make the world something different than it has ever been before. The two little dots working out there in the sun knew more about this idea and had carried it farther than anybody else. The five bedraggled men crouching behind the trees were the first uninvited, as it were "official," jury of the world at large to see the thing in action and judge its success. Really it was not four or five newspaper reporters, it was the world's curiosity which had ridden, climbed, waded, and tramped all those miles and now lay hiding there, hungry and insatiate, peering across the intervening sands.

It had come, as it always does come, after the planning and risking and working are over, and the dream is just about to become something simple and real. It had hunted out this buried, sun-glorified workshop. Quaintly embodied in the shapes of five weary young men, who wiped sweat from their foreheads, and now and then irritably discouraged ambitious "ticks" from crawling up their legs, it passed there at the edge of the woods as though embarrassed to go farther—as though the passive interest scarcely had the right to intrude upon those too busy little dots, who, while it had been amusing itself all these years with its futile distractions, had captured a real Idea, eaten, slept, worked with it and not deserted it for a day.

Suppose you ran a dingy little bicycle shop in a town like Dayton, Ohio, and a secret like that came to you—at least the partial answer to a riddle which men have been trying to solve—have even killed themselves for not infrequently—ever since they began to move about on the earth at all. Possibly it would oppress you somewhat, drive you off into the desert, where you might look at it calmly and unhurried and work at making it exactly clear until an attacking party would be sent out to find out what you were doing.

Well, that was what happened to these Wright Brothers, Orville and Wilbur, six or seven years ago. One of them, shut in with a long illness, amused himself by reading all he could find about aerial navigation. When he was well, he and his brother set to work. They found that many accepted theories were not practicable in the field, and they made laws for themselves. They built a gliding apparatus—two planes set one above the other, with the operator lying on a sort of cradle across the centre of the lower one—with which they soared downward from hilltops.

They brought this gliding machine down to Kill Devil Beach, out beyond Albemarle Sound, off the coast of North Carolina, partly because of its convenient hills and wide sands and the helpful wind currents which always blow here, and partly to get away from humans. Close beside the pine shed in which they worked this spring is another, now tumbling to decay, where these shy, silent, indefatigable young men—"cranks" they would have been if they hadn't succeeded—were working long before Farman and Delegrange and Deutsch-Archdeacon prizes were heard of, and the crowd were reading new-world romances and wondering if people would ever really fly.

They learned a great many things. They saw that hawks and buzzards, which soar for miles without flapping a wing, are merely balancing on rising currents of air; that gulls, following a steamer for hundreds of miles, are merely sliding downhill of rising currents from her smoke-stacks or her wake. They learned what rate would sustain their aeroplane and its operator. They mastered the trick of balancing, so that even without any motive power they could remain motionless in one position in the air for a much as half a minute.

Finally, after three years' experiment, they fitted a gasoline engine to their machine. It weighed 240 pounds, developed twelve or thirteen horse-power, and the aeroplane itself, with its operator, weighed about 745 pounds. On December 17, 1903, this machine made four flights on the Kitty Hawk Beach, in the longest of which it sustained itself in the air fifty-nine seconds and moved 852 feet against a twenty-mile wind.

The 1904 machine weighed, with operator and ballast, 925 pounds and had a sixteen-horse-power engine. With this they made some 150 flights, averaging, it is said, a mile apiece. The great difficulty was that of equilibrium; to turn and keep the machine on an even keel in the continuously changing air currents. After many experiments in a swampy meadow near Dayton, they caught the knack of this. Six flights made in the autumn of 1905 averaged over fifteen miles each, and once, they say, in a curved course, they flew twenty-four miles, at the rate of forty miles an hour.

Nothing that the cleverest of the Europeans has yet done compares with this, and naturally people began to talk. Newspaper correspondents and other pilgrims journeyed to Dayton, even penetrated to the upstairs of the little bicycle shop. The brothers were very pleasant and very embarrassed and shy. Orville, a winning, studious-looking man of perhaps thirty-five, did the talking; Wilbur, taller and older, with the high bald head, long nose, and deeply lined face of one who would apparently say something rather dry and droll if he said anything at all, sat by. It was about as difficult to get anything out of them as out of a couple of furtive wood animals. They wanted no publicity. All they asked was to be left alone.

The 1908 machine, which an unlucky accident smashed the other day, was similar to the others in recent years, the most noticeable change being that the operator sits upright, instead of lying down flat, as in the original gliding machine. I have seen it fly and seen it on the ground close enough to touch it, and I believe that in issuing a personal challenge to the Wrights for a race, Mr. Henri Farman has shown a sporting spirit almost heroically admirable. As it must be described with technical accuracy so soon, however—its flights for the Government taking place in August—I shall not attempt to describe it in detail here.

Roughly speaking, it is very similar in appearance to the bi-plane machine with which Farman won the Deutsch-Archdeacon prize, except that the box-kite rudder, which projects rather ponderously some distance behind Farman's machine, is replaced here by a small, vertical fin rudder, set directly behind the machine like a fish's tail. In front is a bi-plane rudder similar to the main bi-plane in miniature, with which the machine is steered up and down. The two main planes are each constructed in three sections, the centre one rigid, the two outside "wings" so jointed that when the big bird tips laterally, a pull on a lever causes one wing to lift slightly and the other to be depressed. The angle of resistance is thus increased in the latter wing uniformly with its decrease in the other and the machine returns to an even keel. The engine is of thirty horse-power, and the two men are carried with as much apparent ease as one.

Just about the time that Leon Delagrange broke the European record at Issy by flying two miles and a half without touching the ground, the Wright Brothers made their spring trek across Albemarle Sound and hid on the beach behind Kill Devil Hill. They built a shed out of pine boards, dug a well, set the flour and bacon and the apple-box against the wall, and started in to work. One machinist was with them, otherwise their existence of talking, thinking, eating, and sleeping flying machine was untroubled from one glaring day's beginning to another, except when an occasional life-saver strolled down the beach from Nag's Head, or a gull, circling round overhead, piped down faintly at his rivals.

Kill Devil Hill and Kitty Hawk Beach are, you might say, at the end of the world. You go to Norfolk, then down into Carolina and across a corner of the Dismal Swamp country to Elizabeth City. Then, if you arrive before the early afternoon, you embark on a sort of converter oyster-boat for a six hour chug down the Pasquotank River and across the Albemarle Sound. At nightfall you reach Roanoke Island and the ancient town of Manteo. It was on Roanoke Island that Raleigh's lost colony landed, and from here they disappeared, leaving behind only the word "Croatan" carved in a tree.

You can still see the ruins of their little star-shaped fort a few miles out into the pines and sand from Manteo, and in the front yard of the Hotel Tranquil is a mound of barnacle-covered stones, part of the ballast of Raleigh's ship, which the colonists cast overboard so that they could cross the bar. You sit on the porch of the Tranquil House, then, looking at those stones, and breathing that velvety Carolina air, sweet with the odor of the pine-needles and bay-leaves it has blown across, and listen to the story of the Lost Colony and Virginia Dare. It is a nice little town, with that air of individuality and pleasant isolation which island towns have, and as one strolls to the post-office, at one end of it, or to the weather bureau at the other, where the young telegraph operator, in his shirt-sleeves, sits ticking rumors about the flying machine out to the great world, the little girls one meets step aside from the path and say: "Good evening!" very kindly and respectfully.

At five the next morning you catch the launch that chug-chugs out to Nag's Head and Kitty Hawk with the mail. It seems like going out to sea, but, as a matter of fact, it is going to the mainland, because the strip of beach that encircles the whole North Carolina coast, like a sort of front-porch rail, sometimes a mile or two out, sometimes, as at Cape Hatteras, far out of sight at sea, here extends unbroken clear up into Virginia and Cape Henry. Out of the chug-chug half a mile from shore and into a skiff, across the gunwales of which, as it is poled miraculously shoreward with one oar, the rollers sleepily climb and deposit themselves in your lap. If you stand, the skiff will sink, and to sit requires fortitude and repose of manner almost superhuman. At the precise moment of swamping, the boat conveniently touches bottom and you wade ashore.

Then comes the tramp through the woods to the Kill Devil sand-hills. Geographically, this may be only four or five miles, but measured by the sand into which your shoes sink and which sinks into your shoes, the pine-needles you slip back on, the heat, and the "ticks" and "chiggers" that swarm up out of the earth and burrow into every part of you, it seems about thirty-five. After a couple of hours the woods give way at last, the squirrels and the razor-backs are left behind, and you come into the glare of the sand-hills.

This, when our attacking party arrived there, was the enemy's country. The shortest way, of course, would have been to climb up one side and down the other, and thus descend directly on the beach and the aeroplane camp. And then there would have been no flights that day. We must needs, therefore, act exactly as if a platoon of sharpshooters were intrenched on the other side, with their fire raking the summit of the slope, turn to the left and make a wide detour to gain the timber on the farther side. A swamp came up close to the skirts of the sand-hills. We waded midway up the slope, the sand over our shoe-tops, and blowing off the summit, in the continuous ocean breeze, like faint smoke from a chimney. At last we debouched on solid ground and an open space, and the long, loose-jointed correspondent of the Norfolk "Landmark," who was leading the attack with the experience drawn from getting up at four o'clock every morning for ten days and tramping through these same woods, motioned casually off toward the right. "There they are!"

Obviously, a gross tactical blunder. The pine box and the little busy dots were no more than a mile away and nothing between us but open ground and heat shimmer. He should have been court-martialed, undoubtedly, but there was no time then to reason why, nothing for it but to drop below the line of vision and crawl for the nearest cover.

All went well enough until a swampy inlet intervened, to skirt which would be to expose ourselves fatally. Several priceless minutes were wasted in carrying dead limbs to the bog and throwing them in, in the hope of bridging it—abandoned as impractical. The Japanese war veteran, recalling tactics at the Yalu, thought that a screen of bamboo branches should be erected to mask an advance. A careful search was made, but no bamboo could be found. An argument then ensued as to whether greater risk would be run by crossing the zone of fire in a body, in one quick rush, or by dribbling over one by one. There was, obviously, much to be said on both sides, but as every one continued advancing *while* he talked, and was presently across, it can scarcely be held that either tactical theory was properly tested or substantiated. A quick rush in open skirmish order, through the underbrush, a junction at the farthest sheltered point, and there lay the "enemy" in unobstructed view, scarcely a mile [a]way.

Suddenly, just behind the rectangle, there was a quick flicker. Two whirling circles appeared, and across the quiet distance came a sound like that of a reaper working in a distant field. The circles flashed and whirled, faster and faster, then, the white streak above tilted, moved forward, and rose. Across the flat, straight for the ambush, it swept, as fast as an express train. It grew into shape as it approached, the planes, rudders, the operator, amidships—swerved and tilted slightly, righted itself, dipped and rose, now close to the ground, now thirty or forty feet above it. It had come perhaps half a mile when the operator saw, for the first time apparently, a dead tree-trunk directly in his path. He swerved, but had to alight, coming down easily with a slight splutter of sand.

Some more little dots—men from the life-saving station, who had remained behind, hurrying out with a couple of low wheels. These were put under the machine, the propellers started, and away the quaint bird rattled to the starting-point again, the men trotting alongside like little boys. Again it was put on the starting-rail. Two climbed in this time. Again the propellers started, the white streak tilted and rose, and the hazy rectangle, with the two dots amidships, bore down across the field.

The Japanese veteran, reckless with excitement, ventured out from under cover, pointing his camera skyward. "Don't shoot till you see the whites of their eyes!" came a stern command from the London "Daily Mail" man, whose six years' experience as correspondent amid the bombs and emotions of St. Petersburg had taught him absolute self-control. A hundred yards away, the great bird swung to the right and swept grandly by, broadside on. Some cows grazing on the beach grass threw their heads upward, and whirling about, galloped away in terror ahead of the approaching machine. It swept on far above them indifferently, approached the sand-hills three quarters of a mile to the left, rose to them, soared over and down the other side.

Again it swung to the right and again passed broadside on. It had covered perhaps a third of the last leg of the journey back to the shed, when the flash of the propellers could be seen to stop and the aeroplane soared down and alighted lightly as a bird. Something had gone wrong in the engine, it was explained afterward. The attacking party, examining their watches, decided that the flight had lasted two minutes and fifty seconds. The machine had flown about two miles.

"If they had gone back to the house," declared one of the invaders suddenly, with the solemn emphasis of one whose personal enthusiasm over the achievement of two of his countrymen was violently struggling with his professional duty not to show himself and thus stop the flights of another day—"If they'd gone back to the house—by thunder, I'd have gone right over there and congratulated them!" Everybody nodded tensely, the same emotional struggle having worked itself out similarly in each mind.

Being an attacking party, however, without the happy privilege of telling two plucky young men how much they admired them, they sat right there in the sand, along with the flies and busy "chiggers" until there was just time to tramp back and catch the chug-chug home. Then, bedraggled and very sunburned, they tramped up to the little weather bureau and informed the world, waiting on the other side of various sounds and continents and oceans, that it was all right, the rumors true, and there was no doubt that a man could fly. The next day that same machine was smashed because the man running it happened to pull the wrong lever—it doesn't take long to strike bottom when one starts, at the rate of forty miles an hour, from thirty feet above the earth—but it had flown eight miles before this happened, and there was no other reason why it might not have traveled fifty. After all, it was a kind of history.

AERONAUTICS (NEW YORK, NEW YORK)

Filed May 30; published June 1908

The culminating and perhaps the most reflective of the on-site reporters' commentaries on the events at Kitty Hawk in 1908 was this piece published in the June issue of Aeronautics. *It was writ-*

ten by the New York Herald's gifted writer Byron R. Newton, perhaps the most knowledgeable observer of the world of flight who was sent to Kitty Hawk. This was the story that would have been in the New York Herald had he and the editors of that international paper not come to a misunderstanding about how to represent what the Wright brothers had accomplished at Kitty Hawk. Embarrassed with the circus antics of his newspaper, Newton severed his ties with the Herald (or perhaps was set adrift) before he could submit his considered evaluation of what had been accomplished in those seven days of semipublic flights. Not wanting to waste an opportunity to describe for the press what he had seen, he took his story to the magazine Aeronautics, also in New York, which published the piece in its June issue under the title "Watching the Wright Brothers Fly." Unlike articles written by some of the other reporters, Newton's shows his acute awareness that what he had seen was an earthshaking and epochal demonstration of flight that would permanently change the world.

WATCHING THE WRIGHT BROTHERS FLY[3]

By Byron R. Newton.

(Editor's Note.—As correspondent of the New York Herald Mr. Newton witnessed the important flights made recently by the Wright Brothers in North Carolina and besides giving to the world exceptionally interesting and accurate accounts of their achievements, took the first photograph ever published of their motor aeroplane in flight.)

The month of May, 1908, will doubtless be known to future generations as the most important period in the development of aerial navigation. There may have been other months when more was accomplished in a rudimentary way, but during the middle week of May civilization learned that mechanical flight was at last a reality and not a mere human aspiration. The world received its first news that this dream of the ages had been realized—that Wilbur and Orville Wright of Dayton, Ohio, had surely mastered the mighty problem, and, with the sea gulls and the buzzards, were soaring about over a desolate strip of beach on the coast of North Carolina.

And, singularly, too, of the world's millions eagerly interested in the matter, there were exactly five persons there as witnesses of these magical performances—five newspaper correspondents, each of whom had regarded the Wright Brothers as little more than theorists, dreamers or fakirs, until they saw the big aeroplane mount into the air, and, clacking like a great sea bird, come circling over their heads. I went down to North Carolina a pronounced skeptic. I had no doubt that the Wrights had been very successful in experimenting with their motor driven machine, but I did not believe they had made conspicuous progress in sustained flight and I did not believe they had made a record of twenty-four miles as claimed by them.

I believe all of these things now and much more. About a year ago Frank S. Lahm, the veteran aeronaut, told me he was certain the Wrights could make sixty miles an hour with favoring conditions and that the duration of their flight was measured only by the amount of fuel they carried for the motor. I was sorry to hear the old gentleman utter this statement because I felt sure he did not believe what he said. I am convinced now that he knew perfectly well what he was talking about. On the afternoon of May 14, there is not the slightest doubt in my mind that their machine was making nearly, if not quite, that speed when it disappeared from our view and was hurled to the ground behind one of the big sand hills.

There is a vast difference between the aeroplane on paper and the aeroplane in the air. We study the drawings and photographs of these wonderful machines and imagination fashions an outline of the thing in action, but imagination cannot anticipate the sensations that come when, for the first time, one beholds this huge mechanical creature leap into the air and glide away with the grace of a swallow and the speed of a racing automobile. Thinking men and women of our generation have in store a great treat when they shall have the good fortune first to witness this marvel of creation.

I suppose most of us have dreamed of flying or of seeing others soaring comfortably about above familiar places and have awakened with feelings of regret that it was only a dream. When one first looks up at an aeroplane sailing in mid air, it is like waking from such a dream to find that the vision is a thrilling reality. It brings a singular exhilaration. It is different from the contemplation of any other marvel human eyes may behold in a lifetime. It awakens new emotions. It brings to one the imperfectly defined consciousness that another world has been opened to us. The thought comes: "Is not this great ocean of air above us to become as useful for our pleasure and our activities as the sea or the land?" We get our first real conception of the new element in which we are to perform our human functions. It is not until then that we appreciate the limitless possibilities of air navigation, for, no matter how skeptical we may have been about the practical phase of flying machines, those doubts are largely dispelled when we behold a perfectly balanced craft carrying two men and its own weight of half a ton through the air just as easily as a motor boat skims the water of a placid lake. Looking at this thing, one forgets theory, forgets doubt, forgets past ages of painful effort and ridicule and turns with intense thought to the wonders of the near future.

Weather worn and decaying, the old gliding machine used ten years ago by the Wrights is gradually disappearing under the drifting sands at Kitty Hawk Hill. It lies near their abandoned aerodrome, built for the first experiments there, so far removed from human paths that vandals and relic hunters have never disturbed it.

Some day, when the world has had time to understand the great achievements of these modest men, scientists and historians will dig up the fragments of this old gliding machine and civilization will erect a great monument there. And why not? Glance backward over the list of human achievements and see if you can find a man or group of men who have made so great a discovery as have these humble bicycle makers of Dayton. What other achievement compares with theirs! Men learned to navigate the water by slow degrees. It was a process of gradual evolution. Rapid transportation over the earth came naturally with the discovery of steam power. The telegraph and telephone and the many benefits that have accrued to civilization through the utilization of electricity were the result of years of investigation by thousands of scientists; but the discovery of mechanical flight was in reality the work of two men, wrought, miracle-like, within a brief decade, here among the sand dunes of the Atlantic coast.

This is not an unfair claim for the Wrights, because, no matter what may now be accomplished by other inventors, it is undisputed that rudimentally and progressively they worked out the great secret, perfected the gliding machine, made the first successful use of the motor, as applied to aviation, and performed hundreds of sustained flights of a mile or more long before any other airplane in the world had made a considerable start in the work already completed by the Ohio men.

This article, however, is not designed to deal with the technical or historical aspects of the Wrights' performances. It is intended only to relate briefly what they did between May 10 and May 15 on the Carolina beach. Scientists will soon begin to analyze their work and historians will presently delve deeply into their lives and the story of their antecedents. If there is anything in heredity doubtless we shall discover, somewhere among the Wrights' progenitors, men of great mechanical and inventive genius, because much of the success attained by Wilbur and Orville Wright may be credited to their extraordinary knowledge and skill as mechanics.

It is often asked why the Wrights selected a corner of the earth so remote from human activities and comforts, for their testing grounds. Look at a map of North Carolina and you will understand, in part. The map will indicate the inaccessibility of the place, and that was the principal thing they were after. But the map will not show the weird isolation, the primitive wildness and the oppressive solitude and loneliness of a spot so far removed from the zone of civilization. The map will show the narrow strip of beach extending for hundreds of miles between the ocean and Albemarle, Pamlico and Roanoke sounds, but it does not show the noisome swamps and jungle, the thousands of moccasins, rattlers and blacksnakes, the blinding swarms of mosquitoes, the myriads of ground ticks and jiggers, the flocks of wild turkeys and other fowl, the herds of wild hogs and cattle and the gleaming white sand mountains which have played so important a part in the Wright's famous achievements. The nearest human habitation is the little hamlet of Manteo, on Roanoke Island, ten or twelve miles distant, with Roanoke Sound lying between that spot and the sand hills.

It is a singular coincidence that on Roanoke Island another great event in the world's history took place. There, in 1585, was made the beginning of Anglo-Saxon civilization in the Western Hemisphere by the settlement of a colony of Englishmen sent across the ocean by Sir Walter Raleigh. The colony was lost and the world has never known what became of it. The forest grew up over the old fort and the greater part of the island is as silent and wild today as on the July morning that Raleigh's ships sailed into the sound. The present dwellers on the island are as ignorant of the modern world as if they lived in the depths of Africa. The sound of a steam locomotive is as unknown to them as the music of Mars. An automobile is as much a myth as Noah's ark and the flying machine across the sound they regarded as a sea serpent yarn invented by Yankee reporters, the first strangers since the Civil War to invade their island domain. With this environment it may be understood how these secretive Ohio men were able for more than ten years to keep their secret from the world.

When the little band of correspondents arrived in Manteo they decided to feel out the ground by sending one of their number to ascertain if there was any change in the Wrights' policy of secrecy. It was a day's journey and a fruitless one. When the scout reached the aerodrome, nestled between Kitty Hawk and Kill Devil Hills, the Wrights were about to make a flight, but at the approach of the stranger they wheeled the aeroplane back into the building, closed the doors and advanced to meet their visitor. They were civil but very firm. "We appreciate your good intentions," they said, "but you can only do us harm. We do not want publicity of any sort. We want to go on with our experiments, but so long as there is a stranger in sight we shall not make a move. Come back a month from now and we will show you something worth telling to the world. At present, we are simply experimenting with new features of our machine."

Then one of the brothers and their assistant mechanic walked with the correspondent back to his boat and watched it far out on the sound toward Manteo.

The next morning at 4 o'clock, equipped with a guide, water and provisions we set out determined to ambush the wily inventors and observe their performance from a hiding place in the jungle. After a tedious journey over sand hills, through long vistas of pine forest and through miles of swamp and marsh land in which two of the men narrowly escaped the poisonous fangs of moccasins, we found a spot opposite the aerodrome commanding a clear view of the beach and sand hills for a distance of five miles in either direction. There for four days we lay in hiding, devoured by ticks and mosquitoes, startled occasionally by the beady eyes of a snake and at times drenched by heavy rains. But it paid. We saw what few human eyes ever before had witnessed and had the satisfaction of telling the world about it.

Often we wondered if these men ever slept. They were at work before the sun came up, they frequently made flights in the early twilight and lamps were flickering about the aerodrome until late into the night.

The first flight we all witnessed was made early in the morning. As we crept into our hiding place we could see the doors of the aerodrome were open and the machine standing on its mono rail track outside. Three men were working about it and making frequent hurried trips to the aerodrome. Presently a man climbed into the seat while the others continued to tinker about the mechanism. Then we saw the two propellers begin to revolve and flash in the sunlight. Their sound came to us across the sand plain something like the noise of a dirigible balloon's propellers, but the clacking was more staccato and louder. The noise has been described as like that of a reaping machine and the comparison is a very good one. We were told by a mechanic who assisted the Wrights that the motor made 1,700 revolutions a minute but was geared down so that the propeller made but 700 revolutions.

For several seconds the propeller blades continued to flash in the sun, and then the machine rose obliquely into the air. At first it came directly toward us, so that we could not tell how fast it was going except that it appeared to increase rapidly in size as it approached. In the excitement of this first flight, men trained to observe details under all sorts of distractions forgot their cameras, forgot their watches, forgot everything other than this aerial monster chattering over our heads. As it neared us we could plainly see the operator in his seat working at the upright levers close by his side. When it was almost squarely over us there was a movement of the forward and rear guiding planes, a slight curving of the larger planes at one end and the machine wheeled about at an angle every bit as gracefully as an eagle flying close to the ground could have done.

It appeared to be twenty-five or thirty feet from the ground and so far as we could judge by watching its shadow sweeping along the sand, was going about forty miles an hour. Certainly it was making the average speed of a railroad train.

After the first turn it drove straight toward one of the sand hills as if it were the intention of the operator to land there, but instead of coming down, there was another slight movement of the planes and the machine soared upward, skimmed over the crest of the mountain, 250 feet high, and disappeared on the opposite side. For perhaps ten seconds, we heard indistinctly the clatter of the propellers, when the machine flashed into view again, sailed along over the surf, made another easy turn and dropped into the sand about one hundred yards from the point of departure. No sooner had it touched the sand than men started from the shed with two wide-tired trucks. These were placed under the machine, the motor started and the aeroplane at once became a wind wagon rolling itself back to the starting track with the power of its own propellers. After each flight all the mechanism was examined in most painstaking manner, and the operator always came down when the slightest thing about the machinery was found to be working imperfectly.

When the machine was near us, in the air, we could see enough of its mechanism to indicate the recently published mechanical drawings purporting to give all details of the perfected machine, fall far short of disclosing all of its important features. There are several vital features of control by the new system of levers that the published drawings do not show. These improvements were added very recently and used for the first time last month.

As a matter of truth, these recently published mechanical drawings have been an old story in the technical magazines for some time. Everything which is alleged to have been disclosed has been known to those interested in aerial science for several weeks. On May 1st the "Aerophile," the official organ of the Aero Club of France, printed all of the drawings recently produced in a New York newspaper, together with the specifications and descriptive matter presented by the newspaper as startling news. Even the "La France Automobile," subsequent to the publication by the "Aerophile," printed the same technical information.

During the first few flights we could not make out the meaning or function of a series of flat pipes resembling somewhat the segments of a steam radiator, set vertically and very close together near the motor. Later we learned these were the water cooling apparatus for the motor. It was discovered also by the remark of one of the Wrights that they depend very largely upon the gyroscopic principle for their equilibrium. A visitor was expressing surprise that the machine could carry two persons, when Wilbur Wright remarked that once in the air he had no doubt that a weight of two hundred pounds could be placed on the other end of the main planes without affecting the equilibrium of the craft.

After the first flight, we saw many others more remarkable. In the very next flight we were astonished to discover that two men were in the machine. At first we thought we were deceived by some optical or shadow effect, but when the aeroplane came down after making a flight of more than two miles, we plainly saw two men get out and examine the mechanism.

One thing that surprised us was its performance in the wind. With nearly every flight a fresh breeze was sweeping along the coast, usually about twenty miles an hour. It appeared to be the purpose of the operators to start against the wind, but from our point we could not discover that the air currents had any appreciable effect upon the craft, either in its speed or steadiness. If anything, it moved steadier when driving against the wind. On several occasions we saw the machine sail straight away up the beach, until it was a mere speck, scarcely distinguishable from birds and other indistinct objects near the line of the horizon. During these flights the sound of the propellers would be lost altogether until the machine turned about and came back, frequently landing within a few feet of the starting point. These long flights must have covered a distance of four to six miles.

On the afternoon of May 14 when the machine was wrecked after making two circular flights of about eight miles, we learned that the Wrights had started with the purpose of making an endurance run of more than an hour, in which they expected to cover from fifty to eighty miles.

From the layman's viewpoint this last trip was the most interesting. They had just finished a very pretty short circuit of about two miles, with two men in the machine, and we expected the next one would be of similar character. The aeroplane started off in a very wide detour around three hills instead of two, and seemed to be flying a little higher than usual. It started near the aerodrome and in completing the first circuit, came back squarely over the same spot. We expected it to come down then, but when we saw the men on the ground swing their hats and heard them shout to the aviator, we realized that a performance of unusual moment was in progress. As the machine started on its second lap, it appeared to be increasing in velocity, gradually, and at the moment it disappeared behind the sand hill its shadow was racing across the sand plain with the rapidity of the fastest express train. The motor was making more of a buzzing sound and the machine appeared to be travelling much faster than we had ever noticed before. We did not learn of the accident until several hours later.

But there was a weird, almost uncanny side to the whole thing. Those present at the international balloon races at St. Louis last October will recall the feeling that swept over the thousands of men and women when they saw dirigible balloons go spinning away over the housetops like horses in a trotting race.

There was something an hundred fold more romantic, or ultra human, just as you please to express it, abut these wonderful flights there on the lonely beach, with no spectators and no applause, save that of the booming surf and the startled cries of the sea birds. Often as the machine buzzed along above the sand plains, herds of wild hogs and cattle were frightened from their grazing grounds and scurried away for jungle, where they would remain for hours looking timidly out from their hiding places. Flocks of gulls and crows, screaming and chattering, darted and circled about the machine as if resentful of this unwelcome trespasser in their own and exclusive realm. There was something about the scene that appealed to one's poetic instincts,—the desolation, the solitude, the dreary expanse of sand and ocean and in the centre of this melancholy picture two solitary men performing one of the world's greatest wonders.

We were talking along these lines one afternoon when one of the correspondents reflectively asked: "I wonder if the Wrights ever feel this thing as we do?"

"No," answered another, "you may be very sure they do not. If they were addicted to poetry, rum and other common vices, the world might never have had a flying machine."

SCIENTIFIC AMERICAN (NEW YORK, NEW YORK)

Written ca. May 31; published June 13, 1908

What follows is Orville Wright's official version of what happened at Kitty Hawk in April and May 1908—written specifically for the consumption of technical and scientific observers in the world of flight. This piece was written solely by Orville without the assistance of his brother Wilbur, who was already in France at the time.

OUR AEROPLANE TESTS AT KITTY HAWK⁺

By Orville and Wilbur Wright

The spring of 1908 found us with contracts on hand, the conditions of which required performance not entirely met by our flights in 1905. The best flight of that year, on October 5, covered a distance of a little over 24 miles, at a speed of 38 miles an hour, with only one person on board. The contracts call for a machine with a speed of 40 miles an hour, and capable of carrying two men and fuel supplies sufficient for a flight of 125 miles. Our recent experiments were undertaken with a view of testing our flyer in these particulars, and to enable us to become familiar with the use of the controlling levers as arranged in our latest machines.

After tedious delays in repairing our old camp at Kill Devil Hills, near Kitty Hawk, N.C., we were ready for experiments early in May. We used the same machine with which we made flights near Dayton, Ohio, in 1905; but several modifications were instituted to allow the operator to assume a sitting position, and to provide a seat for a passenger. These changes necessitated an entirely new arrangement of the controlling levers. Two of them were given motions so different from those used in 1905 that their operation had to be completely relearned.

We preferred to make the first flights, with the new arrangement of controlling levers, in calm air; but our few weeks' stay had convinced us that in the spring time we could not expect any practice at that place in winds of less than 8 to 10 miles an hour, and that the greater part of our experiments must be made in winds of 15 to 20 miles.

The engine used in 1905 was replaced by a motor of a later model, one of which was exhibited at the New York Aero Club show in 1906. The cylinders are four in number, water cooled, of 4¼-inch bore and 4-inch stroke. An erroneous statement, that the motor was of French manufacture, has appeared in some papers. This is, no doubt, due to the fact that we are having duplicates of this motor built by a well-known Paris firm, for use in European countries.

The longer flights this year were measured by a Richard anemometer attached to the machine in the same manner as in 1905. Except in the first few flights, made over regular courses, it was found impracticable to secure accurate measurements in any other way. These records show the distances traveled through the air. The measurements of the velocity of the wind were made at a height of six feet from the ground at the starting point, and were usually taken during the time the machine was in flight.

The first flight was made on the 6th of May, in a wind varying from 8 to 12 miles an hour. After covering a distance of 1,008 feet measure over the ground, the operator brought the machine down to avoid passing over a patch of ground covered with ragged stumps of trees.

In the morning of May 8 several short flights were made in winds of 9 to 18 miles an hour. In the afternoon the machine flew 956 feet in 31 seconds, against a wind of a little over 20 miles an hour; and later, a distance of 2,186 feet in 59½ seconds, against a wind of 16 miles. These distances were measured over the ground.

On May 11 the Richard anemometer was attached to the machine. From this time on the flights were not over definite courses, and the distances traveled were measured by this instrument. Three flights were made on this day in winds varying from 6 to 9 miles. The distances were: 0.78 mile, 1.80 miles, and 1.55 miles.

On May 13 four flights were made. The anemometer on the machine registered a distance of 0.60 mile in the first; 1.85 miles in the second; no distance measured in the third— time, 2 minutes and 40 seconds; and 2.40 miles in the fourth. The velocity of the wind was 16 to 18 miles an hour.

On May 14 Mr. C. W. Furnas, of Dayton, Ohio, who was assisting in the experiments, was taken as a passenger. In the first trial, a turn was not commenced soon enough, and to avoid a sand hill, toward which the start was made, the power was shut off. The second flight, with passenger on board, was in a wind of 18 to 19 miles an hour. The anemometer recorded a distance traveled through the air of a little over 4 kilometers (2.50 miles) in 3 minutes and 40 seconds.

The last flight was made with the operator only on board. After a flight of 7 minutes and 29 seconds, while busied in making a turn, the operator inadvertently moved the fore-and-aft controlling lever. The machine plunged into the ground while traveling with the wind, at a speed of approximately 55 miles an hour. The anemometer showed a distance of a little over 8 kilometers (5 miles).

The frame supporting the front rudder was broken; the central section of the upper main bearing surface was broken and torn; but beyond this, the main surfaces and rudders received but slight damage. The motor, radiators, and machinery came through uninjured. Repairs could have been made in a week's time, but the time allowed for these experiments having elapsed, we were compelled to close experiments for the present.

These flights were witnessed by the men of the Kill Devil life-saving station, to whom we were indebted for much assistance, by a number of newspaper men, and by some other persons who were hunting and fishing in the vicinity.

The machine showed a speed of nearly 41 miles an hour with two men on board, and a little over 44 miles with one man. The control was very satisfactory in winds of 15 to 20 miles an hour, and there was no distinguishable difference in control when traveling with, against, or across the wind.

NOTES

ABBREVIATIONS

KW   Katharine Wright, younger sister of Wilbur and Orville Wright
MW   Bishop Milton Wright, father of Wilbur and Orville Wright
OW   Orville Wright
WW   Wilbur Wright
W&OW   Wilbur and Orville Wright

CHAPTER ONE: RETURN TO THE SOARING PLACE

1. WW memorabilia fragment, September 13, 1900, Papers of Wilbur and Orville Wright, Library of Congress, Washington, D.C. Hereafter LC Wright Papers.
2. Arthur G. Renstrom, *Wilbur & Orville Wright: A Chronology* (Washington, D.C.: Library of Congress, 1975), 26.

CHAPTER TWO: OF SWAGGERERS AND SCRIBES

1. WW to OW, April 8, 1908, Papers of Wilbur and Orville Wright, Library of Congress, Washington, D.C. Hereafter LC Wright Papers.
2. WW to MW, letter, April 16, 1908, LC Wright Papers.
3. WW diary, April 24, 1908, LC Wright Papers.
4. WW diary, April 20, 1908, LC Wright Papers. Kill Devil Hills Life Saving Station Daily Log, April 18, 1908. The original copies of these reports are in the National Archives Regional Office at Atlanta, Georgia. Copies of these reports for the days the Wright brothers were on the Outer Banks are on deposit at the North Carolina Collection, Joyner Library, East Carolina University. Hereafter Kill Devil Hills LSS daily log, Joyner Library, ECU.
5. Information on Kill Devil l Hill Lifesavers compiled from Wright letters and diaries and from information on birth, residence, and death from research data supplied by William Harris, Kitty Hawk, North Carolina, to the author over several years. The day-to-day operations of the Kill Devil Hills Life Saving Station is also documented in the daily reports prepared by Jesse E. Ward, Keeper. Kill Devil Hills LSS daily log, Joyner Library, ECU.
6. WW diary, April 13, 1908, LC Wright Papers.
7. WW diary, April 24, 26, 30, 1908, LC Wright Papers.

8.   *Charlotte* [North Carolina] *Observer*, April 30, 1908.
9.   WW diary, April 30, May 1–2, 1908, LC Wright Papers.
10.   *New York Herald*, May 1, 1908.
11.   Norfolk *Virginian-Pilot*, May 2, 1908.
12.   Norfolk *Virginian-Pilot*, May 2, 1908.
13.   Norfolk *Virginian-Pilot*, May 2, 1908.
14.   Kill Devil Hills LSS daily log, April 27, 1908, Joyner Library, ECU.
15.   Kill Devil Hills LSS daily log, April 27, 1908, Joyner Library, ECU. WW diary, April 27, 1908, LC Wright Papers.
16.   *Charlotte* [North Carolina] *Observer*, April 30, 1908. Norfolk *Virginian-Pilot*, May 2, 1908.
17.   Norfolk *Virginian-Pilot*, May 3, 1908.
18.   Arthur G. Renstrom, *Wilbur and Orville Wright: A Chronology* (Washington, D.C.: Library of Congress, 1975), 26–27.
19.   WW diary, May 2, 1908, LC Wright Papers.
20.   Kill Devil Hills LSS daily log, May 1, 1908, Joyner Library, ECU.
21.   These observations are based on a careful analysis of the daily logs of the Kill Devil Hills Life Saving Station across all of the periods the Wright brothers were encamped at Kill Devil Hills, including logs from 1900, 1901, 1902, 1903, 1908, and 1911. Kill Devil Hills LSS daily logs, Joyner Library, ECU.
22.   Kill Devil Hills LSS daily logs, May 1–5, 1908, Joyner Library, ECU.
23.   *New York Herald*, May 3, 1908.
24.   London *Daily Mail*, May 4, 1908.
25.   The full list of known reporters who traveled to Kitty Hawk to cover the 1908 flights of the Wrights included the following: *Chicago Journal*—Gilson Gardiner, correspondent; *Collier's Weekly*—Arthur Ruhl, writer, and James H. Hare, photographer; *Columbia* [South Carolina] *State*—Zachary McGhee, Washington, D.C., correspondent; London *Daily Mail*—P. H. McGowan, correspondent; *New York American*—William Hoster, correspondent; *New York Herald*—Byron Newton, correspondent; Norfolk *Virginian-Pilot*—D. Bruce Salley, freelance reporter.
26.   The story of hunters and hunt clubs in this area of the Outer Banks is nicely described in Archie Johnson & Bud Coppedge, *Gun Clubs & Decoys of Back Bay & Currituck Sound* (Virginia Beach, Va.: CurBac Press, 1991).
27.   WW diary, May 2, 1908, LC Wright Papers.
28.   WW diary, May 3–4, 1908, LC Wright Papers.
29.   WW diary, May 5, 1908, LC Wright Papers.
30.   WW diary, May 5, 1908, LC Wright Papers. Norfolk *Virginian-Pilot*, May 6, 1908.
31.   WW diary, May 6, 1908, LC Wright Papers.
32.   Norfolk *Virginian-Pilot*, May 7, 1908. *New York Herald*, May 7, 1908. London *Daily Mail*, May 8, 1908.
33.   Norfolk *Virginian-Pilot*, May 7, 1908.
34.   Kill Devil Hills LSS daily logs, May 5–8, 1908, Joyner Library, ECU.
35.   WW diary, May 7, 1908, LC Wright Papers.

CHAPTER THREE: MIXED MESSAGES FROM MANTEO

1.   WW diary, May 8, 1908, Papers of Wilbur and Orville Wright, Library of Congress, Washington, D.C. Hereafter LC Wright Papers.

2.   WW diary, May 8, 1908, LC Wright Papers.

3.   WW diary, May 8, 1908, LC Wright Papers. *New York Herald*, 9 May 1908.

4.   Bulluck to Wright Brothers, transcript of telegram, May 8, 1908, LC Wright Papers.

5.   Editor, London *Daily Mail* to Wright Brothers, [n.d., but May 8, 1908], LC Wright Papers.

6.   *New York Herald*, May 9, 1908.

7.   *New York Herald*, May 9, 1908.

8.   London *Daily Mail*, May 9, 1908.

9.   Norfolk *Virginian-Pilot*, May 9, 1908.

10. All of the foregoing are from the article in Norfolk *Virginian-Pilot*, May 9, 1908.

11. The lifesaver from Kill Devil Hills Station who had this particular day off was Robert L. Wescott (1869–1925), who was known in later years to expand upon his role in aiding the Wright brothers. He was also the "inventor" of the perpetual motion machine discussed with Wilbur Wright. Kill Devil Hills LSS daily log, May 8, 1908, Joyner Library, ECU.

12. MW diary, May 9, 1908, in Bishop Milton Wright, *Diaries, 1857–1917* (Dayton, Ohio: Wright State University, 1999), 676. Hereafter Bishop Wright *Diaries*.

13. OW to KW, May 10, 1908, LC Wright Papers.

14. WW diary, May 10, 1908; OW to KW, May 10, 1908, LC Wright Papers.

15. WW diary, May 11, 1908, LC Wright Papers.

16. WW diary, May 11, 1908, LC Wright Papers.

17. London *Daily Mail*, May 12, 1908.

18. *New York Herald*, May 12, 1908.

19. *New York Herald*, May 12, 1908.

20. WW dairy, May 12, 1908, LC Wright Papers.

21. WW diary, May 17, 1908, LC Wright Papers. James H, Hare, *A Photographic Record of the Russo-Japanese War* (New York: P. F. Collier & Son, 1905).

22. *New York Herald*, May 13, 1908.

23. *New York Herald*, May 13, 1908.

24. WW diary, May 13, 1908, LC Wright Papers.

25. WW diary, May 13, 1908; OW to KW, May 13, 1908, LC Wright Papers.

26. OW to KW, May 13, 1908, LC Wright Papers.

27. OW to KW, May 13, 1908, LC Wright Papers.

28. WW diary, May 13, 1908, LC Wright Papers.

29. *New York Herald*, May 14, 1908.

30. *New York American*, May 14, 1908.

31. London *Daily Mail*, May 14, 1908.

32. *New York Herald*, May 14, 1908.

33. London *Daily Mail*, May 14, 1908.

34. *New York American*, May 14, 1908.

35. All quotes from May 14, 1908 issues of *New York Herald*, *New York American*, and London *Daily Mail*.

36. All quotes from May 14, 1908 issues of *New York Herald*, *New York American*, and London *Daily Mail*.

37. London *Daily Mail*, May 14, 1908.

38. *New York American*, May 14, 1908.

39. London *Daily Mail*, May 14, 1908.

40. *New York Herald*, May 14, 1908.

41. These words are my own and are intended to illustrate my interpretation of what happened on May 13, 1908. Twiford's leave on the 13th is indicated in the Kill Devil Hills LSS daily log, May 13, 1908, Joyner Library, ECU.

42. The files of the Manteo Weather Station housed at the U.S. Weather Information Center, U.S. Department of Commerce, Asheville, N.C., contain copies of many of these madly reorganized stories. On numerous anniversary occasions, beginning with the 25th anniversary of the Wright's first powered flight of December 17, 1903, Drinkwater took special joy in telling the story of how he was able to manage these contending reporters. In the process, Drinkwater suggested by vague innuendoes that he had controlled information about virtually all of the Wrights' flights and doings in North Carolina from 1903 forward.

43. *New York Herald*, May 14, 1908.

CHAPTER FOUR: THE SEVENTH DAY IN MAY

1. WW diary, May 14, 1908, Papers of Wilbur and Orville Wright, Library of Congress, Washington, D.C. Hereafter LC Wright Papers.

2. OW to MW, May 15, 1908, LC Wright Papers.

3. *New York Herald*, May 15, 1908.

4. London *Daily Mail*, May 15, 1908.

5. *New York American*, May 15, 1908.

6. *New York American*, May 14, 1908.

7. WW diary, May 14, 1908, LC Wright Papers.

8. OW to MW, May 15, 1908, LC Wright Papers.

9. London *Daily Mail*, May 15, 1908.

10. *New York American*, May 15, 1908.

11. *New York World*, May 15, 1908.

12. My description of the probable scene in Manteo that evening. Captain Jesse Ward probably helped form the words Midgett would use. In the station log for the day Ward wrote, "Wright Brothers made a flight with their air ship of Eight miles and completely wrecked their machine." Kill Devil Hills LSS daily log, May 14, 1908, Joyner Library, ECU.

13. The interpretation here presented is informed by two sources: WW diary, May 18, 1908, LC Wright Papers, where Wilbur wrote after investigating information on the reporters in Manteo, "The reporters did not know anything of the accident till informed by the life savers after their return to Manteo." This view is also corroborated by the article written by Zach McGhee of the *Columbia State* on May 17 and published on May 20, 1908. His description of the situation was as follows: "Not one of those newspaper men saw the machine fall, though they all saw it fly. Some of the wildest accounts had been printed in some of the papers about this flying performance. A Norfolk paper . . . after the accident said that the Wrights had cut their machine into unrecognizable splints to preserve their secret. The newspaper men who saw it were at least a quarter of a mile away."

14. All of these headlines appeared in the May 15 issues of the respective newspapers.

15. Norfolk *Virginian-Pilot*, May 16, 1908.

16. MW diary, May 15, 1908, in Bishop Milton Wright, *Diaries, 1857–1917*. (Dayton, Ohio: Wright State University, 1999), 676. KW telegram to WW, May 15, 1908, LC Wright Papers.

17. KW to WW, May 17, 1908, LC Wright Papers.

18. McGhee's story appeared in the *Columbia Star*, May 20, 1908.

19. All of the foregoing from McGhee's article in the *Columbia State*, May 20, 1908.

CHAPTER FIVE: AFTERMATH

1. WW diary, May 14, 1908, Papers of Wilbur and Orville Wright, Library of Congress, Washington, D.C. Hereafter LC Wright Papers.

2. WW diary, May 15, 1908, LC Wright Papers.

3. OW to MW, May 15, 1908, LC Wright Papers. If pictures of the tattered flyer or of the Wrights in action recovering their plane were actually taken, they either have not survived or have not yet surfaced.

4. London *Daily Mail*, May 16, 1908.

5. London *Daily Mail*, June 16, 1908.

6. *New York World*, May 18, 1908.

7. WW diary, May 16, 1908, LC Wright Papers.

8. MW diary, May 14 & 16, 1908, in Bishop Milton Wright *Diaries, 1857–1917*. (Dayton, Ohio: Wright State University, 1999), 676. Hereafter Bishop Wright *Diaries*.

9. London *Daily Mail*, May 16, 1908.

10. London *Daily Mail*, May 16, 1908.

11. *New York Herald*, May 17, 1908.

12. Norfolk *Virginian-Pilot*, May 17, 1908; *Charlotte Observer*, May 18, 1908.

13. WW diary, May 17, 1908, LC Wright Papers.

14. WW diary, May 17, 1908, LC Wright Papers.

15. WW to KW, May 17, 1908, LC Wright Papers.

16. WW to OW, May 17, 1908, LC Wright Papers.

17. London *Daily Mail*, May 19, 1908.

18. Charlotte *Observer*, May 18, 1908.

19. KW to WW, May 18, 1908, LC Wright Papers.

20. WW diary, May 18, 1908, LC Wright Papers.

21. WW to OW, May 20, 1908, LC Wright Papers.

22. MW diary, May 18, 1908, Bishop Wright *Diaries*, p. 677.

23. MW to OW, May 18, 1908, LC Wright Papers.

24. WW diary, May 18, 1908; WW to OW, May 20, 1908, LC Wright Papers.

25. *New York Herald*, May 19, 1908.

26. *New York World*, May 20, 1908.

27. WW diary, May 19, 1908; WW to OW, May 20, 1908, LC Wright Papers.

28. WW to OW, May 20, 1908, LC Wright Papers.

29. Newton's refusal to embellish his stories on the Wrights' flights in North Carolina and his resignation over the matter are recounted in an exchange of letters between Newton and Orville Wright over the next month. Byron Newton to W&OW, May 26, 1908; OW to Byron Newton, June 7, 1908; Byron Newton to OW, June 11, 1908, LC Wright Papers.

30. *New York Herald*, May 20, 1908.

31. *New York Herald*, May 20, 1908.

32. WW diary, May 20, 1908; WW to OW, May 20, 1908 (2 letters), LC Wright Papers.

33. *New York Herald*, May 21, 1908.

34. *New York Herald*, May 22, 1908; Norfolk *Virginian-Pilot*, May 22, 1908.

35. WW to OW, May 21, 1908, WW diary, May 28, 1908, LC Wright Papers. MW diary, May 21, 1908, Bishop Wright *Diaries*, 677.

36. WW to OW, May 20, 1908 (2 letters), LC Wright Papers.

37. WW to OW, May 20, 1908 (2 letters), LC Wright Papers.

38. Arthur Ruhl to "Orville (or Wilbur) Wright," May 21, 1908; Arthur Ruhl to OW, telegram, May 21, 1908, LC Wright Papers.

39. OW to WW, June 3, 1908, LC Wright Papers.

40. OW to WW, June 3, 1908, LC Wright Papers. MW diary, May 23, 1908, Bishop Wright *Diaries*, 677.

41. Norfolk *Virginian-Pilot*, May 23, 1908. Jardin's name does not appear in the published papers of the Wright brothers and has not been elsewhere encountered in their unpublished papers.

42. KW to WW, May 26, 1908, LC Wright Papers.

43. OW to WW, June 3, 1908, LC Wright Papers.

44. *Scientific American*, May 23, 1908, 367.

45. MW diary, May 24, 1908, Bishop Wright *Diaries*, 677.

CHAPTER SIX: THE BROTHERS WRIGHT ON SEPARATE SHORES

1. OW to George Spratt, May 26, 1908, George Spratt Papers, Library of Congress.

2. KW to WW, May 26, 1908, Papers of Wilbur and Orville Wright, Library of Congress, Washington, D.C. Hereafter LC Wright Papers.

3. *New York Herald*, May 28, 1908.

4. Arthur Ruhl to OW, telegram, May 27, 1908; OW to Arthur Ruhl, May 27, 1908, LC Wright Papers.

5. *New York Herald*, May 28, 1908.

6. KW to WW, May 31, 1908; OW to WW, June 3, 1908, LC Wright Papers.

7. OW to WW, June 3, 1908; Ernest La Rue Jones to OW, May 28, 1908; Arthur Ruhl to OW, May 29, 1908, LC Wright Papers.

8. *New York Herald*, May 28, 1908.

9. WW to MW, May 28, 1908, LC Wright Papers.

10. WW to OW, May 29, 1908, LC Wright Papers.

11. WW diary, May 30, 1908. KW to WW, May 31, 1908.

12. Arthur G. Renstrom, *Wilbur & Orville Wright: A Chronology* (Washington, D.C.: Library of Congress, 1975), 158. The flight was on October 3, 1908 at Camp d'Auvours near Le Mans, France.

13. KW to WW, May 31, 1908, LC Wright Papers.

14. Arthur Ruhl, "History at Kill Devil Hill," *Collier's Weekly*, May 30, 1908, 18–19, 26.

15. London *Daily Mail*, May 19, 1908.

16. *Chicago Journal*, May 28 and 29, 1908.

17. *Scientific American*, May 30, 1908, 391, 393.

18. Wilbur Wright, "Flying as a Sport—Its Possibilities," *Scientific American*, February 29, 1908, 139.

19. *Scientific American*, January 4, 1908, 5.

20. *Scientific American*, January 4, 1908, 5.

21. "New European Aeroplanes and Airships," *Scientific American*, January 18, 1908, 40. "The Farman Aeroplane Wins the Deutsch-Archdeacon Prize," *Scientific American*, January 25, 1908, 54. As time would tell, two of these three supposed powered flyers were even more rumor than fact. Neither Herring nor Whitehead would prove to be successful innovators of powered flying machines.

22. *Scientific American*, February 22, 1908, 122; February 29, 1908, 138; March 7, 1908, 164; March 21, 1908, 200; April 18, 1908, 271; May 9, 1908, 336.

23. *Scientific American*, May 9, 1908, 336; May 16, 1908, 347; May 23, 1908, 367.

24. "The Wright Aeroplane Test in North Carolina," *Scientific American*, May 30, 1908.

25. KW to WW, May 31, 1908, LC Wright Papers.

26. WW to KW, June 1, 1908, LC Wright Papers.

27. WW to OW, June 1, 1908, LC Wright Papers.

28. Charles S. Rolls to W&OW, March 26, 1908; OW to Charles S. Rolls, May 27, 1908; Charles S. Rolls to Hart O. Berg, June 4 and 11–12, 1908; Charles S. Rolls to WW, June 16, 1908, LC Wright Papers.

29. Arthur Ruhl to OW, June 1, 1908; OW to WW, June 3, 1908, LC Wright Papers.

30. OW to General James Allen, June 2, 1908, LC Wright Papers.

31. WW diary, June 2, 1908, LC Wright Papers.

32. WW to OW, June 3, 1908, LC Wright Papers.

33. OW to WW, June 3, 1908, LC Wright Papers.

34. KW to WW, June 1 and 3, 1908, LC Wright Papers.

35. WW diary, June 4, 1908, LC Wright Papers.

36. WW diary, June 5, 1908, LC Wright Papers.

37. MW to WW, June 5, 1908, LC Wright Papers. MW diary, June 5, 1908, in Bishop Milton Wright, *Diaries, 1857–1917*. (Dayton, Ohio: Wright State University, 1999), 677. Hereafter Bishop Wright *Diaries*.

38. OW to WW, June 7, 1908, LC Wright Papers.

39. MW diary, June 7, 1908, Bishop Wright *Diaries*, 677.

40. WW to OW, June 7, 1908 (letter 1), LC Wright Papers.

41. KW to WW, May 26, 1908; WW to OW, June 7, 1908 (letter 2), LC Wright Papers.

42. OW to WW, June 7, 1908, LC Wright Papers.

43. OW to Byron Newton, June 7, 1908, LC Wright Papers.

44. OW to WW, June 8, 1908, LC Wright Papers.

45. OW to Arthur Ruhl, June 8, 1908; Ernest L. Jones to OW, June 8, 1908, LC Wright Papers.

46. WW to KW, June 9, 1908, LC Wright Papers.

47. WW to OW, May 20, 1908, LC Wright Papers.

48. OW to WW, June 9, 1908, LC Wright Papers.

CHAPTER SEVEN: THE WORLD ALOFT

1. OW to WW, June 9, 1908, Papers of Wilbur and Orville Wright, Library of Congress, Washington, D.C. Hereafter LC Wright Papers.

2. WW to OW, September 24, 1908, LC Wright Papers.

3. Most of the highlights outlined above may be found in Arthur G. Renstrom, *Wilbur & Orville Wright: A Chronology* (Washington, D.C.: Library of Congress, 1975), 32–43, and Charles H.

Gibbs-Smith, *Aviation: An Historical Survey from Its Origins to the End of World War II* (London: Her Majesty's Stationery Office, 1970), passim.

EPILOGUE

1.   MW diary, November 30, 1906, Bishop Milton Wright, *Diaries, 1857–1917* (Dayton, Ohio: Wright State University, 1999), 654.

APPENDIX

1.   A clipping of this article is preserved in Wright Brothers Scrapbooks, LC Wright Papers.
2.   Arthur Ruhl, "History at Kill Devil Hill," *Collier's Weekly*, May 30, 1908, 18–19, 26.
3.   Byron Newton, "Watching the Wright Brothers Fly," *Aeronautics*, June 1908, 6–10.
4.   Orville Wright, "Our Aeroplane Tests at Kitty Hawk," *Scientific American*, June 13, 1908, 423.

ACKNOWLEDGMENTS

Some time in my childhood near Winston-Salem, North Carolina, I learned that the Wright brothers had made their great trailblazing flights around about 1903 on tar heel soil. That happened at a place known as Kitty Hawk, which was located on something known as the Outer Banks. I had also been told that there were wild ponies roaming around those thin islands that make a chain perimeter between North Carolina and the Atlantic Ocean. From those islands, it was said, one could look across a vast and dangerous part of the ocean known as the Graveyard of the Atlantic. Here, I heard, sunken ships littered the coast line. Of course Blackbeard had also plied these waters and had somewhere around there buried his treasure, which was still waiting to be found. This was also the locale where the unfortunate "lost colony" had been lost and had never been found. Sir Walter Raleigh had something to do with the disappearance of that colony. But even though he misplaced his colony, we all knew from our school books that he had been forever memorialized by having his name attached to our state capital. Raleigh was also, you know, the guy who put his cape down so that Queen Elizabeth—who must have been something like Walt Disney's Cinderella—would not have to sully her slippers when crossing a muddy street in London. Another part of our popular folk schooling in tarheelia embedded in our minds a factoid that the first English child born in America—also in these same parts—was named Virginia Dare and that she, sorry to say, was also lost with the lost colony.

Thinking about the Outer Banks if you were a landlubber growing up in the hilly and red-clay-muddy realm of piedmont North Carolina was a little bit like imagining a world where Cinderella did indeed live and where Jack also climbed the beanstalk to the castle where he encountered the mean sleeping giant. Thanks to a surfeit of Disney images in our brains, I could see it all in my mind's eye.

At the Outer Banks one would look upon an ocean with water extending as far as one could see. But in that water there would be hundreds, even thousands, of ships with bows and masts extending into the air, perhaps with labels saying, "Here lies the *Mary Rose* sunk in 1697." Among the graves there might be a pirate ship still lurking, awaiting a moment to send peg-legged ruffians ashore to find the lost treasure. On shore, there would be fleet ponies racing to and fro, frolicking in the sandy expanses. They (the ponies) would surely be whizzing by some previously unnoticed marker at a trail-head that would lead to the lost colony. Somehow in all of these mental gymnastics I do not think I ever conjured an image of finding the remains of a Wright brothers' airplane or a flying field. I just thought the Wright boys went out, like we did, into an open field and flew their planes like we flew our kites. And when they finished they packed up their planes—as we did our kites—and went away with nothing left behind—except maybe a piece of string, a wooden rib, or a piece of cloth.

My anticipation of what one might see at the Outer Banks of North Carolina was at its most excited pitch when my parents announced that our next family vacation would be to this very spot on God's earth. As we drove the 300 or so miles from Winston-Salem to Nags Head—the only developed vacation spot on the Outer Banks at the time—my childlike imagination rose even further when my mother said that most of the people on the Outer Banks were said to be midgets. I asked her why there were so many midgets at this increasingly curious place. She responded that it had something to do with the fact that all of the Outer Bankers had been isolated from the time of Sir Walter Raleigh to the present and that they had intermarried—you know, cousins and all—and that's what happens when you marry your cousins. Marrying cousins was one of those horrible sins we had learned at church not to commit if we wanted to avoid just this kind of situation.

By the time we pulled into Nags Head, I was bursting with curiosity and excitement about the adventure that was momentarily going to transpire. I was on the alert for any and all of the strange phenomena we were getting ready to encounter. Our first stop was at Jennett's Fishing Pier, right in the middle of Nags Head. Not being ourselves fisher people, we watched the fishermen fish. Somehow that did not exactly fulfill my grandiose expectations. As we stood on what seemed to be a pretty spindly and porous flange into ocean, a fierce and cold storm threw great walls of water against the wooden structure and spanked our faces with stinging fingers of rain. Seeing that we were a bunch of landlubbers from the outback of North Carolina, a salty fellow who looked as if he were surely a permanent fixture on the pier told us that we were staring in the face of a nor'easter. It was all made worse, he said, because it was "hoi-toide."

It may have been then that we retreated from the fury of the storm. Or it may have been after we huddled for a while in our rented beach cottage. Whatever it was, we drove out of Nags Head in the direction of Virginia. Not knowing the territory, we were simply exploring, as I recall. The road signs said that we were approaching Kill Devil Hills and Kitty Hawk. It was not too long after we saw the words Kill Devil Hills that there appeared in the mists a tall structure that had all of the appearances of a gigantic ship's rudder rising from a wake that was an undulating sandy earth. It was, of course, the signature art deco column rising 160 feet above sea level (that is a 60-foot structure on top of a gigantic 100-foot sand dune) that had been built and dedicated in 1932 as a memorial to the Wright brothers. It was placed there to mark man's first successful powered flight on December 17, 1903. It was as somber as the Lincoln Memorial, the Jefferson Memorial, and the Washington Monument. It was, of course, intended to be that way, and it was built around about the same time that the memorials to Lincoln and Jefferson were also created.

Despite the cold monumentality of that soaring and quite solitary structure, I was smitten by the story of the Wright brothers as it began to unfold through the exhibits at the Wright Memorial and through the books I began to read about the brothers and their feats at Kitty Hawk and Kill Devil Hills. But almost from my first acquaintance with the Wright story—at least as it was told at the Wright Memorial—I was both confused and bothered by the fact that the entire focus seemed to be on just one day in the lives of the Wright brothers, indeed only one day in the entire history of flight. Perhaps it was the pure paucity of the story told there that provoked me to want to know a lot more about what was not told.

Indeed, the more I read about these seemingly inseparable brothers, the more I began to wonder about many other facets of their lives and careers: Who were these strange young men? How did they grow up? How did they become interested in flying? What did they do in those sheds (actually reconstructions) on the beach at Kill Devil Hills when they were not trying to fly? In fact, why did they seem to be statues cast in stone at this the memorial to them when their story was one of action, extreme motion, and daring? How did they get to Kitty Hawk? And why, really, did they come there? What did they do after their historic first powered flight in 1903? Whatever happened to them after 1903?

A part of my curiosity was answered by a little book written in stirring narrative by Fred C. Kelly (*The Wright Brothers*), which I acquired and devoured practically on the spot. But his little book provoked even more questions. Why were the Wright brothers—always portrayed as such nice Midwestern guys—so embattled against the world? Why did they seem to have so many enemies? Why did they have so much trouble with the Smithsonian Institution? Why did Orville Wright in a fit of anger send the 1903 Kitty Hawk Flyer to England, where it remained from 1928 until 1948 while he waged a war with our venerable national museum? What in the world did Orville Wright do for thirty-six years after the death of his brother Wilbur in 1912? And, most disturbingly, why did so much of the world not recognize the Wright brothers as the most important pioneers in flight? There seemed to be a pretty large pantheon of other flyers who seemed to get just about as much attention as the Wright brothers—at least away from the Wright Brothers Memorial.

So it was the accident of my birth in North Carolina and a family vacation at a very impressionable moment in my life that got me hooked on the story of the Wright brothers. Through the years I have read various books on the Wrights as they emerged, notably the excellent biographies written by Fred Howard (*Wilbur and Orville*, 1987) and Tom D. Crouch (*Bishop's Boys*, 1989). Because I happened to be the director of the North Carolina Division of Archives and History at the time of the seventy-fifth anniversary of the first powered flight at Kitty Hawk in 1978, I got deeply involved in the organizing of those celebrations. While I was the executive director of the Benjamin Franklin National Memorial in Philadelphia in the early 1990s, I was happy also to have curatorial responsibility for the large collection of Wright brothers' schematic drawings and air foils left by Orville Wright in his will to The Franklin Institute. And then, when the State of North Carolina began planning its commemoration of the centennial of the Wright brothers' 1903 flight, I happily became the consulting historian for the state's First Flight Centennial Commission.

That last responsibility led me to spend four summers as faculty fellow at the NASA Langley Research Center, which had been visited many times by Orville Wright while he served as a presidential appointee to NACA (National Advisory Committee on Aeronautics)—the predecessor agency to NASA. My association with the First Flight Centennial Commission also led to my appointment as the Wilbur and Orville Wright Distinguished Professor of History at East Carolina University.

In these capacities I have had the good fortune to be able to delve quite deeply into many of those questions that occurred to me at the time of my first encounter with the Wright Brothers' Memorial as a boy. My ultimate goal has been to produce a comprehensive collection and edition of all of the materials relating to the Wright brothers' activities from 1900 through 1911 at Kitty Hawk and also the efforts to memorialize them at Kill Devil Hills beginning in 1926 and extending to the time of Orville Wright's death in 1948. As of this time I have identified and transcribed about 4,000 pages of documents on this long and complicated story. This has led me to produce an earlier book titled *Hidden Images: Discovering Details in the Wright Brothers' Kitty Hawk Photographs, 1900–1911* (2005). The present book is another volume in a series in which I will explore different facets of the Kitty Hawk Wright story.

Many individuals and institutions have been helpful to me in my general Wright brothers' research and in the compilation and understanding of historical materials that resulted in this book. As always, I am most grateful to William Harris, supreme Kitty Hawker, and lebame houston, Manteo major domo, for their many, many conversations and good advice and counsel along the way of trying to understand both the world of the Outer Banks and the special story of the Wright brothers. A similar fireplug along these lines has been my faithful friend, Lois Pierce Smith, who has frequently explained to me the rarified world of those Outer Bankers who are descendants of the people who knew the Wright brothers. It is a special badge of honor on the Outer Banks to be one of these folk. They frequently possess family stories, artifacts, and heirlooms relating to the Wright brothers that have taken on separate lives of their own. These three folk—all three with serious Outer Banker twangs and inclinations—have been patiently generous with their time and wise counsels. Without their guidance, it would not have been possible for this landlubber to get acquainted with the mysterious folkways of the Outer Banks.

I am also grateful to my many former colleagues at the North Carolina Division (now Office) of Archives and History who have opened their doors and other doors for me as I have pursued this Wright story: William S. Price Jr., Jeffrey Crow, Elizabeth Buford, Dick Lankford, Stephen Massengill, and George Stevens are a few of the folk I hired or promoted or associated with while at Archives and History from 1973 to 1981 and on to the present. Some of the newer faces who figured in this book are the helpful folk (past and present) at the Outer Banks History Center in Manteo—KaeLi Spiers, Sarah Downing, and Kelly Grimm.

The four summers I spent at NASA Langley allowed me to immerse myself completely in the Wright-Kitty Hawk world. These summer fellowships were arranged by Dr. Samuel Massenberg, former director of the Office of Education at NASA Langley. My association with other faculty fellows, particularly the historian Anne Millbrooke, then of the University of Alaska at Fairbanks, was extremely helpful in introducing me more rigorously to the history of flight. Being primarily a social historian, this exposure to the world of flight was eye-opening.

Association with the Thomas Harriot College at East Carolina University has opened up some other new worlds as well. The two deans of Thomas Harriot College I have known, Dr. Keats Sparrow (emeritus), and his successor, Dr. Alan D. White, have been most generous in supporting my appointment as Wilbur and Orville Wright Distinguished Professor of History at ECU. They have also been unfailingly supportive of many projects—a Web site, exhibits, books, special purchases, and more so that I could continue to explore the story of the Wrights and the world of the Outer Banks. Many of my colleagues in the History Department at ECU, especially the chairs (Michael Palmer and Gerry Prokopowicz) have provided a very collegial environment in which to pursue this and a number of other areas of research. The History Department staff—especially Rebecca Futrell—have also provided inportant assistance and much entertainment.

Perhaps the greatest bump into new methods of exploring Wright materials has come through my association with the cadre of digital collections librarians at Joyner Library on the ECU campus. Diana Williams (who later moved on to other interests) introduced me to the arena of digital exhibits. The folk who worked with her or came along later have subsequently built a stellar digital resources capability at Joyner Library. They have been unfailingly great advisors and doers in introducing me to a new frontier of digital research—Michael Reece got me started; Joseph Barricella has greatly expanded my range; and Gretchen Gueguen (subsequent director of this program) has continued the support. In addition to the digital collections staff of Joyner Library, I have also gotten extensive assistance from the North Carolina Collection (Maury York at the crucial times) and from Special Collections (Ralph Scott) and from the Interlibrary Loan Office. All three of these offices have searched out or acquired books, photos, and microfilm for my use in researching the Wright story.

In addition to the good resources of Joyner Library, I have also found another haven for rich advancement into digital studies and elaborate productions in the ECU Multimedia Center. Laurie Godwin and a steady stream of talented students from ECUs School of Art and Design working in her office have enlarged my horizons even further. Laurie and her associates helped me organize both a Web site and an exhibit for the Wright Brothers' Memorial at Kill Devil Hills on the subject matter of this book, making use of many of the images relating to the story.

In researching a story like that of the Wright brothers, one becomes inevitably connected with and almost soulmates with librarians around the world. Chief among my debts is that to the Manuscript Department of the Library of Congress. Although Orville Wright also had strained relations with the Library of Congress (its librarians sometimes sided with the Smithsonian in its disputes with Orville), the aeronautical papers of Wilbur and Orville Wright were presented by Orville's executors to the library in 1949. And since that time the library has maintained an aeronautical division and a curator of aeronautical materials. The curator of aeronautics throughout my research on the Wrights has been Leonard Bruno. Dr. Bruno has been with the division for many years and has been able to share with me many stories surrounding the personalities who have had responsibility for the Wright papers from 1949 to the present. The library has been a very responsible custodian of this trust and has done much to make the Wright papers available in an intelligent manner.

I have also received courteous, professional, and informed assistance when I have made use of the vast Wright Family Collection of papers and photo materials at the Paul Dunbar Library at Wright State University. Dawne Dewey and the special collections staff there have been very responsive to numerous requests for information and have given me the privilege of looking at original photographs and other precious materials.

The largest collections of original Wright materials are at the Library of Congress, Wright State University, and The Franklin Institute in Philadelphia. But there are other collections of related materials which I have been fortunate to see at other institutions: Museum of the Albemarle, Elizabeth City, North Carolina; North Carolina State Archives, Raleigh; North Carolina Collection at the University of North Carolina at Chapel Hill; Norfolk Public Library; NASA Langley Research Laboratory, Hampton, Virginia; National Park Service Regional Curatorial Office at Fort Raleigh, Manteo, North Carolina. In each of these institutions I have been received graciously and have been given very professional assistance.

One repository, in particular, stands out in this litany. When I first began to study the 1908 Wright brothers Kitty Hawk story, I suspected that the much-revered photojournalist James Hare surely must have taken a passel of pictures while he was at Kitty Hawk that year. Knowing that one of the most incurable diseases known to man is that which compels the owner of a camera to snap photographs, I reasoned that Hare—despite the nuisance and clutter of glass plates—had to have taken more than just one or two photographs of the Wright brothers' airplane in flight. Several years ago I learned that Hare's photo collection had ended up at the Harry Ransom Humanities Research Center at the University of Texas at Austin. I contacted the curators of that collection only to find that the large Hare Collection had never been organized for research.

I accepted that answer for a while, until I began planning to write this book. Then, in the summer of 2007, I contacted the curators again and pretty much announced that I was going to go to Austin to see what was there. Rather than having my threats repelled, I entered into one of the most enjoyable sleuthing correspondences of my researching career. Two of the curators at the Ransom Center, Linda Briscoe Myers and Kristin Ware, took up my challenge with tremendous verve and good humor. Following months of the most joyful correspondence and comparing of notes, I made my visit to Austin. And, sure enough, there they were. A batch of glass lantern slides made by Hare from his original glass plate negatives (which no longer seem to exist), which he created for his use in giving talks about his adventures "On the Trail of the Wright Brothers." I will be forever grateful to both Ms. Myers and Ms. Ware for their numerous informative and colorful notes as we solved this mystery together.

In March 2008 I received a phone call out of the blue from a young man named Ron A. Ciarmello of Kill Devil Hills, North Carolina. Mr. Ciarmello thought that he might have just purchased the original kitchen table made and used by the Wright brothers in their camp at Kill Devil Hills. He had seen a photograph of what he thought to be the table in my book of *Hidden Images*. This contact led to another detective adventure. After much study and scrutiny of the table both personally and in my documentary editing class at ECU, we all came to the conclusion that Mr. Ciarmello undoubtedly had come into the possession of the original table.

It was a case of serendipity. I was teaching a class on documentary editing focusing on the historical documents of the Wright brothers. And here, like magic, surfaced one of the most extraordinary documents possible directly from the Wright brothers. It was and is a table. But the table is itself a document filled with information and a very interesting story. For allowing me the pleasure of unfolding that original Wright story I have to express my appreciation to Mr. Ciarmello, but I am also grateful to the seven students with whom I shared that story on the centennial of the Wright brothers' historic 1908 flights. The students of that class were Michael Kegerreis, Thomas J. Long, Nancy B. Muller, Kiana Pritchard, Ralph Scott, Mindy Spain, and Ashley B. Wingate.

All of which is to say that although the flights described in this book occurred a century ago, the documentary, photographic, and oral residues of the Wright brothers' visits to Kitty Hawk are still around us, just waiting to be discovered and identified. Thanks to all of the hands—professional, amateur, and student alike—who have joined with me and happily helped advance this ongoing process of research and recovery.

ILLUSTRATIONS

Appendix   *First Graphic Photo of a Wright Plane in Flight*, Scientific American, *August 29, 1908*
Courtesy of University Multimedia Center, East Carolina University, Greenville, NC, USA, from
an illustration published on the cover of *Scientific American*, August 29, 1908

INDEX